IRREVERENT ACTING

ERIC MORRIS

A Spelling Publication

A Perigee Book

Perigee Books
are published by
The Putnam Publishing Group
200 Madison Avenue
New York, NY 10016

Library of Congress Cataloging-in-Publication Data

Morris, Eric, date.
  Irreverent acting.

  1. Acting.   I. Title.
PN2061.M59   1985   792'.028   85-3378
ISBN 0-399-51139-3

Printed in the United States of America
1   2   3   4   5   6   7   8   9   10

DEDICATION

This book is dedicated to the memory of Dr. Lawrence Schwab, a true friend who was always supportive. At this very moment Larry must be conducting a seminar in heaven.

ACKNOWLEDGMENTS

My thanks to Tony Lani, a student and friend, for all his efforts and support; to Dan Spelling for his tireless work in the publishing of the first edition of this, my third book; to Stephen Schubert for his many fine pictures, some of which appear in this book; and to all the actors who constantly keep me on my toes.

To Scarlett Gani for her tireless dedication to the editing and revising of this book. Her contribution was enormous.

And to my wife, Jessie "Joy," who was at my side through every page I wrote, reading and rereading. Her help and contribution to my work were immeasurable.

CONTENTS

CONTENTS

CONTENTS

CONTENTS

CONTENTS

CONTENTS

CONTENTS

Mark Levine doing a vulnerability craft preparation for a scene.

INTRODUCTION

Over a period of thirty-four years I have been searching for answers and a specific way to work. I spent many desperate years as an actor being confused by terminology and concepts that did nothing for my work. Out of desperation and the need for clarity, I asked questions, experimented, worked with people and ideas, and, finally, arrived at a system which I feel is a complete approach to acting that really works and can be depended on.

After I started teaching, I really began to experiment with different techniques and exercises. I made some very important discoveries: I found that the emotional obstacles and blocks that people bring with them to the study of acting are the very things that keep them from being able to use acting techniques. I went to work to find exercises and approaches that were specifically designed to eliminate and strip away the inhibitions and fears that actors have. I devised a system of work I call BEING which is the necessary prerequisite to the use of artistic craft. There were hundreds of exercises I explored to help actors experience and express their emotions.

As a result of this kind of emphasis in my work, I drew a lot of criticism from the theatrical community. I was accused of playing therapist and departing from the more conventional way of training actors. I was considered too "psychological." Nevertheless, I stayed with what I truly believed, and continued to help people to open up their internal realities. The proof of any theory is in the results, and we were getting spectacular results. Actors who at first couldn't express their true feelings were able to eliminate their blocks and to stimulate a variety of unpredictable emotional impulses. Through the use of craft techniques they were able to expose many more facets of their personality than ever before.

This book is about craft, a process of work. Craft is a method of creating realities on the stage and in front of the camera. It is the means by which one actually builds a performance, fulfills characterization, identifies the obligations and responsibilities of the material, and makes choices

1

to accomplish the author's intent. Craft is *your* process, and that is specifically what this book is dedicated to: process. Many actors talk about craft without really having one, or they practice techniques that are abstract and intellectual and do not stimulate organic behavior. Quite often these actors create an overwhelming liability to their work by burdening themselves with useless intellectual concepts. This not only doesn't help them to stimulate real organic impulses, but actually prevents it. In other words, they would probably be far better off to simply trust their own instincts.

The key word here is *how*. If you know what to do but not *how* to do it, well, then you can't. The word *how* has only three letters in it, but it is the longest word in the English language in terms of meaning and content. If, on the word "Action," or as the curtain rises, you don't have a *how*, you are in trouble. You are dependent on the will of the gods, accident, imposition, or the hope that your intuitive talent will come to your rescue. The antidote to all of this is to solidly know your process of work and to use it.

In my first two books, *No Acting Please* and *Being & Doing*, the major emphasis was on the exploration of instrumental preparation. I dealt almost exclusively with the instrument and only secondarily explored the craft. This book deals exclusively with the craft process. I have taken a voluminous amount of craft material and organized it into four major categories. Hopefully, this focus makes the work pragmatic and easy to understand.

The concept and philosophy of irreverence in acting are a very strong thrust of the material. It is long overdue that the actor take his rightful place as a contributor, along with the writer and the director.

Byron Teegarden and Tony Lani in a scene from "Mass Appeal," directed by Eric.

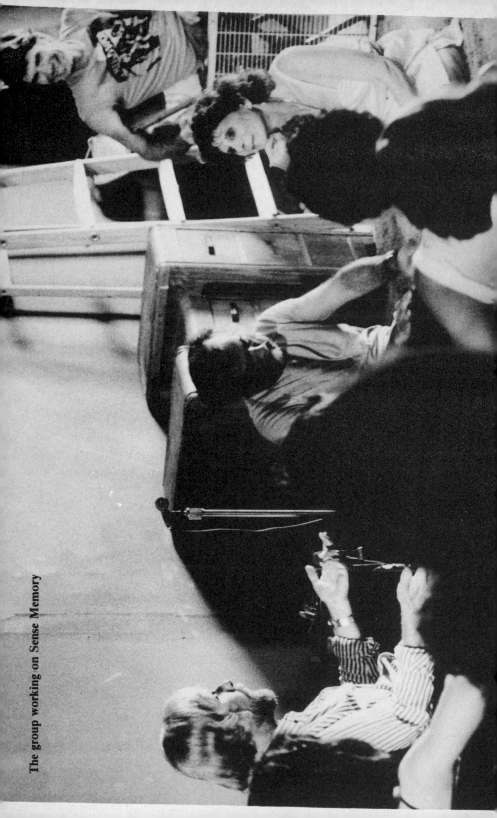

The group working on Sense Memory

Chapter 1

A REPRISE ON BEING

I gave a lot of thought to whether or not to say anything more about BEING, since I have already explored it in both my other books. I decided that any book on acting must have in it the very foundation from which art evolves—the nucleus of one's talent. Talking about a craft process and not starting with a word or two about BEING would be like starting the alphabet at letter D.

BEING is a state of experience and behavior wherein one is affected by internal and external stimuli, and responds by expressing one's feelings on an organic moment-to-moment basis. BEING is a state of life where the greatest number of personality facets are available to one as a creative artist.

In the last decade, or even longer, there has been a giant shift toward self-realization, sensitivity training, consciousness movements, etc. Almost all of these approaches talk about getting the most from yourself—BEING who you are. As a result of a greater consciousness in the world, we have experienced more truth in the theater and in films. The audience will no longer accept the stylized level of acting they did in the 1940s, nor will they respond to actors singing in front of a rippling backdrop; they demand realism and truth. As a result of this maturation, acting has become more natural, but not necessarily more real. There are, to be sure, a lot of fine actors doing very good work. However, there are a lot more actors being "natural," which is not truth but the imitation of truth. There is sometimes a very high degree of emulation taking place. You see an actor you like, and often without even knowing it, you pick up some of his mannerisms. That is the danger of not BEING. In a BEING state the actor is truly an individual, unique and unlike any other living person. If someone establishes that connection with the inner self and can allow himself to function from total honesty, he then makes a very pure and individual statement on the stage or the screen.

THE DEVELOPMENT
OF THE BEING CONCEPT

You either believe an actor or you don't. I have watched actors all my life and have either been affected by them or not. After I was teaching for a while, I could see the obvious separation between what an actor was expressing in a scene and what I sensed he was feeling *under* that behavior. That experience not only undermines an audience's belief in the reality, it is also very uncomfortable to watch. The split between the actor's real impulse and the life he chooses to express is the basis for my search for BEING. If there is such a separation between experience and expression, then the more colorful and exciting life is really taking place deep within and essentially lost to the actor's work. I stopped scenes almost at the beginning and asked the actor what he or she was feeling at that very moment. What was going on right now? I started to work almost exclusively with the instrument, leading actors to search for the truth in the moment. I developed hundreds of exercises in this search for reality and called them instrumental exercises. From this emphasis, students began to experience more and more honesty and dimension in their scene work. Actors were evolving with greater individuality and unpredictability.

The entire concept of BEING developed as a philosophy related to living and acting and as a very necessary preparation for acting. The first step in approaching a scene is to get in touch with everything you are feeling, including all the obstacles and distractions standing in the way of the real life. When an actor identifies a specific block of fear, it is essential to delve into the area of fear and find a technique to eliminate it. What was behind the block is then allowed to flow freely into the actor's work.

If a character in a play is in a "BEING state" (in touch with himself) and, as the play progresses, moves from one BEING state to another, then it is simply the actor's responsibility to start with how he's really feeling. Through the process of creative choices, he stimulates the emotions of the character, thereby making acting a kind of BEING journey from the beginning of the play to the end. If you look at it in those terms, it underscores the reality emphasis. The BEING state of the character is the emotional life that the character is experiencing in the scene. If you identify all the aspects of the character's BEING state, then you relate to the hypothetical reality of the play in very real, behavioral terms.

Truth can be created only from a place of TRUTH. You can get into quite an argument about what truth is; one person's definition of truth will vary considerably from another's. This is very relevant to the authenticity of the emotional life and expression of the actor getting ready to approach a piece of material. The base truth is whatever the actor really feels and however he is expressing that on an impulsive level. When that kind of emotional freedom is achieved, then the actor is ready to deal with the first obligation of the material, which is to stimulate the *true* emotional life of the character in that scene. If the actor maintains that truth in the exploration of his creative choices, he has begun to achieve the truth of the play.

THE MISSING LINK IN THE METHOD

The Method, as the system devised by Konstantin Stanislavsky is commonly called, has become so widely known that one would think it was used extensively by actors around the world. Isn't it? The fact is that it has had limited use, even in Russia, where it originated. It was brought to America in the thirties by Lee Strasberg, Stella Adler, and others, who had gone to Moscow to learn from Stanislavsky and who later, in New York, founded the Group Theatre, which was the basis of the Method in this country. The Group Theatre flourished for many years and did many productions, developing and using the Stanislavsky system. As time went on, the Group Theatre dissolved and gave way to other groups like the Actors Studio, the Actors Lab, etc. Teachers of the system began to surface, and the Method was part of our theater and motion pictures. The number of "Method actors" was quite small in comparison to actors of other persuasions, and it became a kind of in thing to ridicule these "mumblers." Of course, the people who were the most critical were people with the greatest ignorance of the system. The Method derived a great deal of its bad reputation from so-called "Method practitioners" with little or no valid Method training. These were groupies who wanted the recipe for instant success. Nonetheless, the Method has not been what one would call a raging success in the world, and not because of any of the aforementioned reasons. No, the reason for its lack of universal use is a much more practical one: the Stanislavsky system does not recognize the need for *instrumental preparation!* By "instrumental" I mean the actor himself—his personal instrument. Actors with a high level of availability and easy access to their emotions have had success with the techniques of the Method, and actors with impressive or expressive obstacles found the techniques quite difficult, if not impossible, to apply. So does this mean that those who, by gift or accident, are emotionally free are able to use the system and those with difficulties are just out of luck and sentenced to a career of fakery? Well, obviously, that doesn't have to be the case. Stanislavsky himself admitted that his approach was incomplete and needed development. The missing link in the Method is the gap between theory and application. The theory sounds logical, for the most part, and easy to understand, but a lot of the techniques have not worked. This breach is what makes most actors abandon the use of the Method.

For whatever reason, Stanislavsky himself and many of the master teachers did not address themselves to the need for in-depth instrumental preparation. Many teachers felt that if they did they would be crossing the line from acting training into the province of the psychotherapist. Others seemed to feel that actors should come to the study of acting already prepared to do the work.

Most actors experience tension and anxiety in their work, which blocks the creative flow. If the tension is not alleviated, they cannot function organically. Stanislavsky, Strasberg, and some of the other Method pioneers dealt with the need to eliminate tension. However, there are literally dozens of other instrumental problems and conditions that stand in the way of the creative process: fear in all its shapes, insecurity, behavioral conditioning, and social obligations, to name just a few.

It has been my conviction for the last twenty-five years that in order for an actor to be responsive to a process of work, he must first be emotionally available to the effects of the process. Preparation, then, must relate to the human instrument with the emphasis on exercises that deal very specifically with the problems standing in the way of the actor's personal truth.

If, for example, an actor makes a choice to stimulate an anger state and uses Sense Memory to reach the anger, the technique would be useless if the actor had, for a lifetime, been taught to deny impulses of that kind. Conditioning can be very subtle, but our parents and peers have an enormous impact on our growth. Without realizing it, we can develop inhibitions that cause us to redirect real feelings and impulses into more socially acceptable areas.

Therefore the bridge between theory and its application is the achievement of a state of life wherein the actor is affected by the tools of the Method, a state of life that is authentic and comfortable, a place from which the actor can feel and express anything—BEING!

HOW TO GET TO BEING

An actor's responsibility is a twenty-four-hour involvement. There is nothing that should not be of interest to you as an actor, because you never know when you might be called upon to know or use something that relates to a certain subject. If you decide to make yourself increasingly aware of all the things around you in the world, you should also become more aware of what is going on within you. One way to accomplish a greater connection with BEING is to check yourself out many times a day. Ask yourself how you feel, and express your responses to the question (Personal Inventory exercise, discussed in detail in *No Acting Please*). This technique should be used whenever you happen to think about it. If some large emotional event takes place, find out how it affected you, even if it is after the fact. By becoming familiar with how you really feel many times each day, you will also find out the things you do to avoid or redirect your true responses. If you question a variety of people about their emotional point of view in relation to a large number of objects and people, you will be surprised to find that most people really are not sure of a specific response to stimuli. There is a vague feeling about most things.

Starting right now, ask yourself how you feel about everything in the room you're in. Do you have a feeling or response to all the objects? Possibly your response is "I don't know"—that is a response! If you explore your environment like that frequently, you will come up with a lot of responses, and when you string those responses together in an unbroken chain, you are expressing your moment-to-moment impulses· you are BEING. The inventories of expressions you compile on a daily basis will help you to identify your obstacles to BEING and, indeed, stimulate a BEING state.

Reaching and maintaining a state of BEING is the prerequisite to success with the acting process. It is completely necessary to prepare the personal instrument to work, and almost always the actor must start with some kind of BEING preparation. There are a great number of exercises for BEING, and most of them are discussed in great detail in both my other books. I will, however, describe a few exercises in this section to help promote a better understanding and use of them in relation to other elements of the process.

BEING EXERCISES AND TECHNIQUES

EMOTIONAL POINT OF VIEW, WITHOUT WORDS

An Emotional-Point-of-View exercise is done by encouraging your expression on a moment-to-moment basis. Ordinarily, you might use words, verbalizing all your thoughts and impulses. In the nonverbal version of this exercise you translate all your impulses into unintelligible sounds. Starting with the immediate environment, let your eyes slowly sweep the place, and instead of responding with words, encourage yourself to make sounds. The sounds could come from your direct response to the objects in the place. While you are doing this exercise, be aware of any tendency to be arbitrary with the sounds. The trap in the exercise is to lead yourself into some kind of musical activity which may have nothing to do with your real feelings. The purpose of this exercise is to establish a connection with your real organic impulses, whether you understand them or not. By doing the exercise nonverbally, you avoid the possibility of becoming intellectual with it. Words often take on the responsibility of *describing* feelings rather than expressing them. If you do this exercise for a period of time, five minutes or longer, you will begin to notice a greater vocal variety than when you are using words. The reason for this, simply, is that words often take the place of the real expressive fabric of feelings. If you practice this exercise every day, soon you will establish a bond with your real impulses, thereby accomplishing the BEING state.

THE BEING INVENTORIES

One of the major prerequisites to BEING is the knowledge of what you are feeling—being in touch with your impulses in the first place. There are a number of good inventory exercises that will help you to find out what is going on inside. There are two kinds of Personal Inventory exercises, and you can find out all about them in either of my other books. The one I would like to discuss here is Emotional-Point-of-View Inventory.

All the inventories have one thing in common: you ask yourself questions. With Emotional Point of View you ask yourself how you feel about the things around you. This technique has a twofold purpose:

First, it helps the actor to know how he really feels about many things that he may not have had any previous awareness of. So, in essence, just as the word inventory implies, it is the gathering of awareness of how objects in the world affect you. Most people who grow up wearing blinders are only aware of the "major" stimuli in life. To achieve a wider, more open BEING, this kind of inventory puts you in touch with a far greater panorama of stimuli. Secondly, when used properly and frequently, the Emotional-Point-of-View Inventory also builds your ability to respond and express all your impulses, thereby creating a flow of organic life called BEING.

EMOTIONAL-POINT-OF-VIEW INVENTORY

Do it out loud—whenever and wherever possible. Start by asking yourself how you feel about the place you are in: "How do I feel in this room?" Answer with your real response. A response doesn't always have to be verbal. It may be physical, or it may be both at the same time. "I like this place—it makes me feel creative... How do I feel about the table I'm sitting at?... It's OK—I don't really much care about it one way or another." (The last response may take on a variety of vocal and physical intonations; you might even be impelled to stand up or move away from the table to get a better view of it, or you might just go on with the inventory.) "I really like looking out the window at the lake; it makes me feel the way I used to feel when I was a kid on vacation . . . How do I feel about the sounds coming into the room? . . . Funny, until I asked the question I didn't hear too many of them . . . Wow, there are a lot of different kinds of sounds. How do I feel about the conglomeration of the sounds? . . . They comfort me in a funny way. I can't put it into words, but I can express the feeling . . . I hear my wife moving around in the kitchen. How do I feel about those sounds? . . . A moment to reflect on what I am feeling . . . Reminds me of when I was real young after school, doing homework, and my mother made sounds like that making dinner . . . I feel rather nostalgic . . . I also feel a warmth for my wife filling me up . . . I'm aware of a smile on my face . . . How do I feel now? . . . I feel vulnerable . . . I feel cozy in this place; I feel like I never want to leave this spot . . . I hear a horn blasting from down the hill. All of a sudden, I feel a flash of irritation . . . I hate city sounds . . . I lost those other feelings I had . . . How do I feel about the fire going out in the fireplace? . . . I love to look at fire and smell the wood burning . . . I feel pleasant about that . . . I don't want to get up right at this moment and put a log on it, so I will celebrate the death of this fire and build another one later. It's getting dark now . . . How does that make me feel? . . . The shadows in the room are real interesting, but dusk depresses me a little . . . I feel just a little depressed."

All the time that this process is taking place, you should be responding and expressing the emotions that are inherent in the responses. When you establish the moment-to-moment responses to the objects around you, a very interesting and varied life evolves—a behavior filled with surprises and colorful emotions. Practicing this exercise continually promotes BEING and is the starting place for the craft process.

The Emotional-Point-of-View Inventory differs from an Emotional-Point-of-View Workout in that the Workout is a stream of consciousness leading to an unbroken flow of expressions. Earlier in this section, the Nonverbal Point-of-View exercise was discussed. The verbal type is very similar except for the use of words. When you are on the stage or in front of the camera, there is always a life going on—a life that goes on under and through the lines. That life, the inner monologue, is the thought process. It is your unverbalized reaction and responses. It is the dimension of behavior that occurs in *real life*, that dimension that is very often cut off by an actor when he acts. That cutoff, or interruption, of the normal internal process is the very thing that stops reality. The actor replaces reality with an awareness of how he is acting, what the next line is, and a complex variety of commentary and evaluation of performance. The terror most actors feel when they act stimulates the need they feel to "watch" themselves or to hang on to the moment. After years of this kind of acting, the habits are very practiced and solid. To break old habits you must create newer and better ones. What could be better than a habit that comes from nature and real life? When you make the Emotional-Point-of-View exercises a part of your daily life, and then carry that into your acting, you stimulate a large number of organic changes, all for the better. In the first place, the involvement with your own flow of reality eliminates most tension. Secondly, the internal stream of consciousness dimensionalizes the expression of life on the stage. Of course it makes your work infinitely more compelling and unpredictable.

For the audience, watching an actor who is actually experiencing this kind of inner life while "acting" is a real treat. The difference between the representation of life and the actual experience of life is the difference between glass and diamonds.

BEING is a living state; it is a behavioral reality that should exist twenty-four hours a day, not just when you are acting. Therefore, dealing with the many and varied obstacles to BEING is definitely an instrumental involvement. The scores of exercises and techniques that help you to condition life at the BEING level are explored and investigated in *No Acting Please* and *Being & Doing*. The total emphasis of this text is craft and the application of process to acting. All the BEING exercises herein are therefore craft oriented and are executed in a craft framework.

THE INCLUSION EXERCISE

Some of the BEING preparations fall into the instrumental category, and others lean more heavily into the area of craft and material. Some, of course, fall into both categories. The Inclusion technique is used mostly in relation to written material. It is a technique you can use as practice and also when you are doing a scene.

In the midst of a monologue, or in a dialogue with another actor, you often experience impulses that are not consistent with the emotional life of the play. They can be impulses that come from anywhere: distractions, commentary, self-consciousness, or whatever. These impulses are *real!* They are not to be disregarded or swept under the carpet. *They must be included* as part of the life you are experiencing on the stage. If the actor refuses to recognize and include these impulses, it seriously damages the level of organic flow. It, in fact, creates a short-circuiting process that leaves the actor split from his internal reality and stops the flow of organic impulsive life. To avoid the separation from reality, he can *turn a liability into an asset* by *including* all the impulses into the lines of the scene. In the process, a variety of interesting things happen. We, as an audience, experience more colors of life in the actor. We see no interruption in the flow of authentic life, and the awkwardness that occurs as a result of a split no longer exists. The actor goes on with the scene, *including* all the life he is experiencing. It is not only interesting but unpredictable.

To practice this technique, use a monologue that you know very well. Recite the monologue out loud and be aware of all your impulses. Allow everything that you think and feel to express itself through the words of the monologue. Don't concern yourself with fulfilling the meaning or statement of the piece, just use the material to practice the technique. Allow whatever happens to be expressed, no matter how outrageous it may seem. Do the monologue several times, and encourage every impulse to ventilate through the words. Each time you do the monologue you will experience a wide variety of different impulses, which, by the way, is a very good way to check yourself If the monologue has very different elements each time you do it, you are more than likely functioning in terms of your real impulses. If, however, you notice that certain words or sections of the monologue sound exactly the same each time, then you are not trusting the moment but servicing your concept of the meaning of the material.

After practicing this exercise for a while, you might use it in a scene or monologue while obligating yourself to attempt to fulfill the material. Identify the emotional obligation of the piece, and work for whatever will stimulate the life of the character in the scene, all the while *including* all the moment-to-moment life you are experiencing. As you learn to trust your own impulses and include them in your acting, you will get more and more in touch with the uniqueness that is you. It will infiltrate all of your expression with the individuality of your emotional point of view.

INNER–OUTER MONOLOGUE

This involvement is also dependent on inclusion; however, it is done differently from the above exercise and has other values also. Again, you approach this exercise with a well-memorized monologue. Knowing the words very well is necessary, since any distraction often derails an actor from the lines. You start the words of the monologue out loud, saying three or four lines as written, then go to your own personal words for the same length of time. You go back and forth between the written monologue and your inner stream of consciousness. All of the exercise is verbalized audibly. Repeat the exercise as often as you wish and work with the same technique, as an exercise, when dealing with the demands of the material. It might sound something like this:

WRITTEN MONOLOGUE
"Four score and seven years ago . . . "
INNER MONOLOGUE
I'm looking around the room and thinking of the next line . . .

WRITTEN MONOLOGUE
"Our fathers brought forth on this continent . . . "
INNER MONOLOGUE
I'm breathing. I feel anxious, a little preoccupied . . .
WRITTEN MONOLOGUE
"A new nation, conceived in Liberty, and dedicated to the proposition . . . "
INNER MONOLOGUE
Lincoln really was prolific. I feel boring as hell. What's the next line? . . .
WRITTEN MONOLOGUE
"That all men are created equal. Now we are engaged in a great civil war . . . "
INNER MONOLOGUE
People are looking at me. I feel a little foolish. Wonder what they think I'm doing . . .

And so goes the process of the exercise. The most important thing to remember while doing this exercise is to carry over the life that comes through the inner monologue into the written monologue. If this is not done, you defeat the entire purpose of the exercise.

This is a great technique for establishing a connection within yourself and also for expressing the inner life going on. It connects the flow of your real impulses with the material, and very soon the words that someone else wrote are coming from your inner organic life.

The Inner–Outer Monologue exercise not only is used for practice and preparation but is also a good rehearsal tool. If, in the midst of a rehearsal, you realize there is a separation between what you feel and what is being expressed, then you can employ this technique. Almost immediately, it bridges the gap. All of the exercises and techniques in this book are tools; they are means to an end.

ATTAINING THE BEING STATE WITH THE OTHER ACTOR

Since truth can be stimulated only from an environment of truth, the first step in preparing to rehearse a scene with another actor is to reach your own truth. It is very important that you both do some kind of BEING exercise or preparation together, since you both must come from an organic place.

There are a number of good techniques, and some of them are discussed in *No Acting Please*. One that has served me well over the years is the BEING Workout.

THE BEING WORKOUT

This exercise can be done sitting, standing, walking, or in any position. Facing each other can be helpful, since it allows you to deal with any obstacles that exist between the two of you. Start the Workout by acknowledging how you feel at the moment. Relate to each other on a moment-to-moment basis, conversationally expressing all the obstacles you experience as you relate to each other. Obstacles to the BEING state are distractions, fears, tension, and concerns that usually stop us from honestly expressing what we really feel. The value of including the expression of these obstacles is that when our fears and concerns are exposed and brought into the open, we no longer feel the need to hide them or function in spite of them. It makes it all right to be distracted or tense. In addition to this newfound permission, including the obstacles creates an unbroken flow of reality that becomes a part of the BEING state.

Example:

"I feel anxious about starting. How do you feel?"

"I'm OK. I see you looking at me and I wonder what you are thinking. I feel a little embarrassed and a little flushed."

"I feel like I don't know what to say at this moment . . . I like you—that puts me on the spot a little . . . I feel more comfortable now that I've said that and that I have started to express my feelings . . . I feel like looking away. I'm seeing things in the room, and I really don't care about the room. What I'm really doing is avoiding looking at you . . . I feel like you can see through my bullshit, so I'm going to look right into your eyes."

"Funny, I felt some of the same self-consciousness with you—I want you to think I'm talented, so I do things to promote that when I act. I don't want to do that!"

"I feel much more exposed and open right now. I'm more able to accept the feelings of fear and inadequacy that come and go in waves . . . I still feel very obligated to keep this thing going. I would be very uncomfortable if I didn't say anything for a few minutes."

"It's hard not to feel I should be doing something every moment. I'm looking for a direction to go in . . . I don't have to do that . . . What do I really feel? I guess I feel a little dull, and that scares me."

"You're not dull to me. I'm interested in what I see in you."

"That's true for me too—when you're expressing your problems I can identify with you."

The exercise can go on for quite some time until both actors feel very comfortable *doing no more or less than they feel!* Everything should be included as part of the whole and accepted as the true flow of the inner organic life. By starting a rehearsal in this manner, you achieve a threshold of real life—a flow of impulses that are not redirected into more socially acceptable areas. The choices that you explore from that place can stimulate true and authentic emotional responses that structure an unbroken stream of exciting reality.

One of the major obstacles to BEING is conditioning. We grow up with a lot of restrictions that we are not even aware of. Most people are very private; they do not talk about "personal" things except to the closest of friends or relatives. If, in your quest for BEING, you are encumbered with a lifetime of taboos, it will follow that achieving an impulsive state on the stage will be close to impossible. For example, if you do get a fairly comfortable BEING state and are functioning honestly with a high degree of impulsive flow in a scene, and all of a sudden you hook into one of your conditioned taboos or "private areas," you will short-circuit the flow of those impulses. Anything you feel uncomfortable about expressing will create an interruption in the flow of your impulses. When that occurs, you go into a kind of "tilt" state, and at this point most actors panic and begin to "act" and impose life that seems right for the scene. The alternative to this short-circuiting phenomenon is to *include* the feelings that occur at the short-circuit point. They then become a part of the total behavior of the character as opposed to an unwanted interruption. When the actor includes all the comments and dissatisfactions he is feeling at the moment, he becomes compelling, unpredictable, and colorful.

Including all that you feel is part of the irreverent approach to acting, and I will explore this in greater depth when we get into irreverence. Please keep in mind that there isn't any creative alternative to inclusion; if you elect to deny any reality on the stage, you interfere with the structure of *stimulus–affect–response–expression*. When you do that, you are messing with the natural living process. In an earlier exercise, Inner–Outer Monologue, you can clearly see how to practice including all the life that you experience. There are other exercises and techniques for inclusion, and they will be sprinkled very liberally throughout this book.

INTIMATE SHARING WITH ANOTHER ACTOR

A major block to BEING freedom is fear of exposure. There are all kinds of fears and a variety of ways in which a person can feel exposed. What is too personal? What is it that is really private? What kind of visibility strikes terror into the actor's heart? Whatever the answers are to the above questions, the fact is that fear of exposure, no matter how irrational, keeps actors from BEING in life and also on the stage.

To begin with, let me stress a point. There is never any time when you should, when you must, or even when it would be wise to, expose anything that you hold truly private. *Your privacy is sacred!* The trick is to determine that which is truly private and that which falls into the category of personal emotional responses. Of course it is you who must decide the difference, but you would be surprised to know how "private" some people are—they won't even discuss what they had for breakfast. When almost everything you feel and do falls into the private sector, it is hard to be impulsively expressive. But if at the start of every rehearsal you begin with Intimate Sharing, pretty soon you will climb over the obstacle to exposing your intimate and personal feelings.

Start by expressing your reluctance to say anything. Then slowly verbalize your innermost feelings, starting with here and now. If it is more comfortable to fit this into a conversational framework between the two of you, that is fine. If you want to do it as "I am going to take the time to do this exercise before I do anything else in this rehearsal!" then you can approach it that way. In either case, take emotional responsibility for everything you express:

"I feel really scared—I'm not sure of what . . . I know that I always feel anxious at the beginning of a rehearsal. I'm lonely; I feel lonely a lot . . . I would like to get more response from you . . . I feel very vulnerable right now . . . and I'm afraid to let you see it—I'm afraid to let anyone see it! . . . I don't want to be laughed at . . . Do you like me? Don't answer that. I'm afraid that I can't handle the answer either way! . . . I don't think you think I'm a good actor . . . I feel like I want a lot from everyone and I never let anyone know that. I feel more open now and that scares me, too—I really feel like I could get hurt real easily right now. Oh boy, do I feel like running for cover! . . . I'm not going to let that happen! I feel hurt a lot, and when I feel that way I pretend that everything is all right and that I can handle anything, and it isn't true! I sometimes feel that I can't handle anything, like right now for instance . . . "

The exercise or relationship might continue for as long as an hour or more. As the exercise proceeds, it should get more fluid and the impulses should begin to flow with much less restriction. The end result is a level of availability where almost anything you might work for will easily affect you. In addition to being available, you must also be free and impulsive to promote an organic state. So, as your vulnerability level climbs, so does your tendency to be impulsive, and this is a necessary ingredient to reality. The highest form of organic acting is ensemble work. Ensemble is achieved when two or more actors are functioning organically and are going with their moment-to-moment impulses. The expression of these impulses affects both actors, and they respond to the way they have been affected. In turn, this mutual response triggers a kind of emotional chain reaction that moves unpredictably with the feeling that no one, including the actors, knows where this will all lead.

When you are fortunate enough to experience watching this happen to a couple of actors on the stage, it is electrifying. It is what we as actors all aim for. At the bottom line it is why we act. Ensemble is achieved ultimately through trust: trust in yourself, trust in your impulses, trust that, no matter what happens, it can be right for the piece. What is the function, then, of BEING, and how does BEING relate to ensemble? Without achieving the state of BEING and promoting that flow of organic life, it is not possible to reach ensemble. If, logically, ensemble is a kind of chain of organic responses between actors, then it follows that they be impulsively available to each other on a second-to-second basis. If, indeed, you are fulfilling an intellectual concept of behavior and presenting emotion which promotes your concept, then that representation is not organic; therefore, real ensemble work would not be possible.

BEING is the basis of organic reality, irreverence, Ultimate Consciousness, and ensemble. It is what theatrically memorable performances are made of.

Chapter 2

IRREVERENCE

During the time when an actor is building a character and moving toward performance, an exploration must take place. He/she must identify the responsibilities and obligations to the piece, the character, and the emotional life inherent in each scene of the play and find ways to create all of those *realities* through his/her instrument. *Reality* is the key word here. If, from the very first reading of the material, concepts are formed, behavior decided upon, polishing of "line readings" and a lot of other external and result-oriented techniques practiced, then it would probably be better to read the material rather than watch someone impose his/her behavioral concepts. If, however, the actor does his job creatively and uses the rehearsal period productively, then *he must be "irreverent" to the material* in order to follow the impetus of the choices to see where they lead.

Irreverence simply means honoring your *real* feelings and impulses rather than servicing the material conceptually. If in a scene you know that the emotional obligation is to feel a certain way but at that moment in the rehearsal your choice is affecting you differently, then you *must* express that which is real rather than that which isn't, even though you know that what is real at the moment does not fulfill the requirement of the material.

There are a lot of very important reasons for irreverence and the need to honor the reality rather than the concept; the most important is that *nothing takes the place of reality!* If the actor succumbs to playing the concept and presenting behavior that does not have an organic origin, what happens is that the real impulses are "short-circuited," stopped, stifled, and the actor is left with nothing but a "split" between what is really happening internally and what the external expression is. Since it is impossible for the instrument to lie, the lack of reality connection shows up in the voice and the body. While an audience doesn't have the knowledge or the technical expertise to know what is happening, they simply do not believe the actor, nor are they really affected by his work. Therefore, there isn't any alternative to irreverence without interference with the flow of real impulses. This does not mean, however, that the actor ultimately distorts or misinterprets the material. Quite the contrary, it is the actor's responsibility to fulfill the author's intent, to reach the goals of the piece, and, in the final period, to bring to it his own unique contribution. If an actor uses his time in rehearsal to explore and discover the stimulus that creates an inner organic life, in relation to what the playwright structured, then the process is complete: the material is fulfilled and from a totally organic origin. An actor who functions from reality *exposes himself!* The moment-to-moment flow of feelings, impulses, and thoughts through the character is the way an actor "ventilates" the uniqueness of his personality and the individuality of his emotional point of view. That is why when you see two different actors play the same role, it can be a completely different experience—not just because of the interpretation of the role, but because of the fact that they are two completely different human beings. The variations in the exposure of the individual facets of each personality create a singularly unique fabric of life in the character that no one else in the world can bring to that role.

In order to encourage and permit our real life to expose itself through acting, we must first achieve a BEING state and allow our impulses to flow from that state. To recognize the responsibility to the scene, the actor must identify the emotions he is experiencing in his here-and-now BEING state and contrast them with the emotional state of the character in the scene. The next step in the process is to find a way to influence his present BEING state in order to change the emotional life to that of the character. This process is a craft process. First he identifies the emotional obligation; then he finds a choice out of his own life experience that he hopes will affect him in the way he wants to be affected. Through the use of a choice approach, he works with and for the choice, allowing his moment-to-moment reality to express itself through the lines of the scene. While all of this process is taking place, the actor must avoid imposing any behavior other than what he is really experiencing at the moment. Concept is very seductive, and an actor can slip into servicing the material from the intellect without knowing it sometimes. If the actor continues to work for the choice and irreverently expresses what he feels from one moment to the next, the choice will begin to affect him, and the life of the play will begin to germinate in his behavior and relationships. If he approaches it in this manner, the life on stage has dimension and color. It is filled with surprises and is undeniably a real experience, both for the actor and for the audience.

In addition to establishing an authentic impulsive flow by allowing yourself to be irreverent, it is of the utmost importance to be free to explore the choices you have decided on. Once an actor decides to use a choice, he must explore it, work for it, and follow the impulses produced by that choice.

The choice is made, of course, with an intention of stimulating the desired response for the material. However, until the actor actually executes the choice, he doesn't really know exactly where it will lead or how it will make him feel. During the time of pursuing the choice, the actor must be irreverent, even to his expectations of the choice. This means that if he chooses an object in hopes that it will make him feel a certain way and, to his surprise, it takes him in another direction, he must honor that and go with where it leads. By doing this, he has a lot to gain in addition to the creative and organic possibilities. He also finds out how a specific choice will affect him, and, even if it's not right for this material, he has discovered the possibility of a new choice for future use. More often than not, a choice will open up possibilities of life and behavior that he never thought of, and if indeed a choice goes in a different direction, it might be a much more imaginative direction for the material. Being irreverent to the material means being reverent to yourself!

THE THREE STATES OF IRREVERENCE

PHILOSOPHICAL IRREVERENCE

There are several steps in irreverence, and the very first step an actor must take is to accept and embrace the concept itself. Most actors are exposed to a potpourri of acting techniques and styles after just a few years in the field. There is a great deal of confusion among actors and even more among teachers of acting. Competition and intimidation are rampant, and everyone thinks he has "the answer." So when an actor begins to deal with a role, he must climb over his fear and insecurity and use whatever technique he has to approach it. If—and it is mostly the case—an actor does not have a solid craft, a way that he is secure about, he stumbles and grabs onto whatever seems to work at the moment. This usually results in a continued kind of life that he hopes will pass for truth. Usually the most remote possibility is to go within and to trust that as a beginning point in the creative process. If only everyone knew that if all the actor did was be honest and express himself organically, he would be a thousand times more interesting and compelling on the stage!

The first step in irreverent acting, then, becomes acceptance of the concept of irreverence. What is that? It isn't a complex abstraction, for sure! Accepting irreverence is accepting yourself; it is acknowledging that who you are, what you feel, how you express yourself, and the way you experience the world are the most important things you have to contribute to the planet. It means having the courage not to run scared under the pressure of the take or an entrance onto the stage. It means standing your ground and allowing, permitting, accepting, and including all that you feel, and encouraging the expression of that. It is doing the work you believe in, whether or not it is popular and acceptable in your environment.

It is human nature to be influenced by the people around you. If what you do in rehearsal or while you are building the role is unfamiliar or different from the way everyone around you is working, then you are going to meet with a lot of resistance and criticism. It is at this point that the actor must stand his ground and not be one of the "gang" and allow his process to suffer for the sake of popularity. If you believe in your approach and it promotes reality, then you are on the right track. A critical point in the process is in the early rehearsals; if you are irreverently exploring your choices and allowing them to take you wherever they may, you will certainly be taking liberties with the obligations of the material. Most directors, especially the ones who are unaware of your process, will become very insecure with the departure from the material. It is important that the actor tell the director what he or she is doing, making sure to acknowledge the ultimate responsibility to the material. Most creative directors, once they understand the actor's exploration, will go along with it if they feel secure with the outcome.

There are, of course, many actors who take liberties with the material and do not know what they are doing. Often this kind of "false irreverence" is a ploy to cover their lack of knowledge or craft, and, unfortunately, they make it harder on the real craftsman. In spite of the obstacles that are encountered along the creative path, your process is the way you work and what you believe in, so you must stand by it.

There are many traps that an actor can fall into, and most actors have had experience with those traps. One of the biggest is result consciousness. Knowing what the responsibility of a scene is, the actor naturally wants to reach it emotionally. If that responsibility becomes stronger than the impulse at any given moment, the actor tends to lead or "manipulate" the emotional life into the area of the result. Even well-trained craftsmen have fallen into this trap, and even though the surrounding life might be realistic, the end result is contrived. If in the training process, or even beyond that point, the actor develops a BEING consciousness instead of a DOING consciousness, the moment-to-moment reality is never violated for the sake of the result. Furthermore, if the impetus is so strong that the needs and desires of the actor overwhelm the concern with "acting" or the results of the scene, then he will behave as naturally to the circumstance as he would in life, and not as if he were on stage.

At this point the hackles rise in all of the critics to this kind of approach: "What do you mean, he will forget he is on the stage and behave as if he were in life? What about acting? Is this an art form, or do we abandon our responsibilities to the theater?"

Of course not! Reality is the highest form of art! That is the actor's responsibility, but on a deeper level of consciousness. If on the first ten levels of his consciousness the actor is totally involved in the flow of reality, but on the Eleventh Level of Consciousness he knows he is "acting" on the stage, then the play is serviced. He says the proper words in the scene, he doesn't really strangle the leading lady at the end of the second act, and so on. This concept of the "Eleventh Level of Consciousness" is something I have been working on for many years, and I will go into it in greater detail later in the book.

As part of "result consciousness," the actor is very often seduced into contriving the feelings of the character and "going for the emotion," because, as actors, we want to fulfill what is expected of us. In a real-life situation, a person actually experiences *the reverse*. For example, the actor works toward, and wants to experience, the grief in the scene, while the person in the real-life situation is experiencing the grief and wants not to. Another example is the man with a limp who tries not to limp, and the actor playing a man with a limp who works feverishly for the handicap.

The trap of result consciousness can be avoided along with many other such pitfalls. If the actor starts from a real state of life and works for a choice that really affects him as the real-life situation would affect him, then the natural response would be to avoid the impact of trauma rather than to encourage it. Where the tendency to achieve result exists, there is an interference with involvement with the choice and a lack of belief in the existence of the reality. What actually occurs is a "split" in consciousness. Instead of the actor being totally related to the life being stimulated by the choice, a part of him is involved in an awareness of the resulting emotion, or the desired resulting emotion.

In order to create a threshold for this kind of reality, the actor must first achieve a BEING state and, from that foundation, be totally willing and available to believe in the circumstance and reality. He must irreverently follow his impulses wherever they lead. By approaching the obligations of the material in this manner, he is actually functioning as he would if the circumstances were really happening. In that case, the instrument takes care of itself. That is to say, the normal instinctive human response occurs, thereby fulfilling the material organically with dimension and unpredictability.

Trust plays an important part in the overall process, since it is very important to allow all your impulses to be expressed. When an actor is halfway through the scene and begins to experience impulses that were never there before, there is the tendency to panic or become terribly insecure about the outcome of the scene. If the choice has been previously successful in fulfilling the scene, then you must *trust* the inclusion of these "new" impulses and include them as part of the whole picture. The philosophical commitment to "the work" is an important part in the success of it. After years of experience with the creative process and an exploration that has taken you on the journey of failure and success, the commitment to irreverence isn't quite as difficult as it is in the beginning stages.

If the actor knows how the scene ends, it will affect the way he approaches the entire scene from the beginning. Let us suppose that the scene is about a man and a woman who have been married for a couple of years and have come to a point where the relationship is no longer working. She wants to end it, but he, still very much in love, wants them to stay together. The scene involves a discussion about divorce, and he pleads with her to give it more time; in the end, she refuses and leaves. Since both actors have read the play, they certainly know how the scene ends. Knowing the outcome of the scene or the play, the actor cannot truly believe that he can change it, unless he does believe that he can! If, in reality, a person knows what will happen and that nothing can change it, he will not go after his desires and needs in the same way as he would if he believed that he honestly could change the outcome. *If the choice, the need, or the reality is strong enough, the actor, as a person, will attempt to change the outcome of the play!*

So, you say, we are now writing new plays, new endings, and becoming our own playwrights! No, of course not! If the actress is equally committed to her reality, she will have to fight harder to maintain her resolve. In that contest between the two realities lives irreverently exciting and unpredictable ensemble work.

Several years ago, two actors, a man and a woman, were doing a scene in my class. She was obligated to stop him from leaving, and he wanted to get away from her. As it is written, she does not succeed in keeping him there. As it turned out, the actress was not really dedicated to stopping him. So, when he said, "I'm leaving," she made very little real effort to stop him, and he left the room and didn't return to class that evening. A little extreme, you may be thinking. Perhaps so, except that it taught the actress and the rest of the class the need to be involved in the reality of the needs of the characters.

How, then, is it possible to know and not to know what happens in the play? Part of being irreverent to the material, particularly in the rehearsal process, is to explore the various possibilities of approaching it. One very important element in reality is to go after what you want, if indeed you really want it. If the actors and the director are collaborators in the creative process, then all concerned will attempt to fulfill their desires, even if the play says otherwise. In the rehearsal framework it is certainly permissible to take liberties with the material, and if the actor who has a stronger thrust than his partner can reverse the results, he should. Everybody involved learns and grows from such an occurrence. The actress realizes that she must make some adjustments in her choices in order to avoid being so vulnerable to the other actor's needs. They both experience the ultimate possibility of achieving or not achieving their goals. The dynamics between them as people takes on elements of behavior that do not exist in actors who know what is going to happen. They are both much more energetically committed to achieving what they want, and out of this kind of life comes electrifying theater.

The actor must have the courage to create reality and absorb himself in that reality above and beyond his concepts. Then he can irreverently follow his impulses and feelings to where they take him. He must be willing to do battle with the conventional and often provincial concepts of acting and theater—to stand up for what he believes in and commit to his approach, no matter what!

REHEARSAL IRREVERENCE

Perhaps in the rehearsal stage the actor is the most irreverent. It is in this stage of the creative process that most of the exploration and experimentation takes place. After several readings of the material, and possibly discussions with the director and the other actors, you begin to form some ideas and concepts about the play and your character. The director more often than not will proffer his interpretation of the play and of the characters' interaction and relationships. By the time you come to the first "standing-up" rehearsals, you are filled with concepts about your character's behavior, desires, and actions. In addition to all of the intellectual activity taking place, you must usually confront other actors who are "acting" and are trying to reach the complex resulting behavior of the character in the script at the very first rehearsal. They are not trying to find the impetus and the realities that produce the behavior organically but are assuming and imposing behaviors and attitudes that are not real at all. At this very point, the craftsman stands at the precipice of truth! In fact, this is *the moment of truth!* Is he seductively drawn into the web of deception, or does he acknowledge what is happening, allow himself to be affected by it, express his moment-to-moment impulses, and launch into the craft that journeys to reality? It is a rhetorical question.

If you wondered about the seeming contradiction in the use of the word "concept," let me explain. Certainly, you form ideas about what the play is about, what the elements of your character's personality are, and how the character evolves throughout the action of the piece. That is as it should be! An actor must have a *mind,* an intellect that curiously explores and deduces the obligations of his character. Once you have some solid ideas, the creative process begins. Where you start depends on the most important criterion. If it seems that the place the character is in has a very impacting effect on his behavior, it would be wise to start with creating a place that affects you in the same way as the character is affected by the place in the play. If the relationship elements seem to be the most impelling element in the scene, then you should begin dealing with the relationship obligations. No matter which of the major obligations you start with, you begin by identifying what you hope to experience. You make a choice selection and decide on a way to realize your choice, and essentially you have begun. The actual exploration depends on the nature of the choice approach. If you were using Sense Memory as a choice approach, you would be asking sensory questions and responding sensorially while you expressed your moment-to-moment impulses through the lines of the material. If, on the other hand, you were using Available Stimulus as a choice approach, you would relate to whatever the object was and encourage a specific exploration of the "available object" while irreverently allowing all your impulses to be expressed through the lines in the scene. What you use the rehearsal for is to explore and discover where choices lead. In order to find that out, you must allow all responses to be expressed. It may take the better part of an entire rehearsal to explore a single choice before you make a decision on whether or not it is a good choice. If you decide to disregard it and try another one, take an inventory of how it affected you, and file this information for future use.

Many directors start to "block" the play immediately. While you are involved with the process of exploring the choices, you must also assimilate the blocking, write it in your script, and so on. Don't let that involvement get in the way of your more creative endeavors. Rather, you might relate to it like someone who reads the newspaper while eating breakfast. When I direct a play, I do not block the actors, since I firmly believe that it interferes with the natural movement of the created realities. If the actors are working properly, the behaviors will find their own physical expression. If you mechanically impose moves on an actor, it inhibits and interferes with the impulsive flow of his reality.

It is the director's responsibility to "stage" the play, and, in that framework, he must guide its physical action within the restrictions of the environment in which it takes place. That is, if the characters are on the balcony of the apartment, that is where the actors must rehearse the scenes. If the characters do not leave the balcony, the actors cannot take it into their heads to move into the living room. The physical action of the play must follow the script. However, within the environment of the play, the actor should be given the freedom to allow his impulses to impel the physical action of each scene. For example, the characters in a scene are having a heated argument; the director tells the actor that on a certain line he should walk away from the other character. However, in the midst of rehearsal and in the throes of emotional impulses, the actor feels strongly impelled to go to the other actor and not away. If he follows the blocking, he runs a big risk of short-circuiting the reality and being left with nothing but an awareness of the awkwardness of the moment. If, on the other hand, the actor honors the real impulse and goes to the other actor, that expression is followed by the next real impulse and the next and so on. Irreverence is a commitment to truth and does not really have an alternative.

When an actor is working with a director who wants to rigidly block the action, the actor must find the creative adjustment for dealing with those physical responsibilities and, at the same time, maintain the authenticity of the moment. This may be accomplished by supplying creative impetus for moving someplace other than where his impulses lead. In the above example of the heated argument, when the actor is really impelled to go to the other actor but is instead directed to walk away, the actor's adjustment might be to create the need to retreat from the other actor rather than to go to her. That might be accomplished, for example, by selectively emphasizing the violence of the anger in her eyes and body. This is a sensory process relating to Available Stimulus, and the adjustment can be accomplished in a matter of seconds. An adjustment of this kind would organically impel the actor to move away, rather than toward, the other actor, supplying an organic impetus instead of a decision to do what the director has asked of him.

Rehearsal irreverence depends on a definite structure. It is not a license granting an undisciplined helter-skelter rambling through a rehearsal period in the hope that something miraculous will occur. Quite the contrary, irreverence is part of a very specific and disciplined process of work that has rules and structure. It depends on the identification of creative responsibilities and the exploration of techniques that ultimately fulfill those responsibilities.

The rehearsal process is like following either a detailed road map or a specific blueprint. The actor (usually from previous experiences with the work) identifies the major "roads" and begins to follow them. He starts by asking very important questions about the material: What is happening in this scene? What is my character experiencing? How does he feel, and what is causing him to feel that way? What are the major elements in the scene? Where is the best place to start dealing with the responsibilities and obligations of the scene?

Wherever the actor starts, the reality of every single moment is what must be established and maintained. If he decides that the most pressing obligation is his emotional state at the beginning of the scene, then he would identify the desired emotional state, make a choice, create the choice, and go moment to moment with the impulses stimulated by the choice he is working for, supposing that it will encourage the life of the character in the play. The actor at all times includes all of the peripheral life that is stimulated by the choice and what is happening on the stage. By so doing, he functions on a dimensional and organic level, avoiding the conceptual traps of picking and choosing impulses that supposedly fulfill the play. By being irreverent in this manner he stands to gain a variety of important things: reality rather than representation, discovery of where the choice leads, the incredible satisfaction of experiencing real life on the stage, and the facets and dimensions of life that can come only from reality. If, in the exploration, the actor discovers that his choice is leading him far afield of the play, he then must acknowledge this adjustment by including it in the behavior of the scene. Then he must make a new choice, hoping that this one will lead him in a better direction for the piece. Of course it is always an option in the rehearsal to stop and take some Inventory before continuing.

The rehearsal period can be a very adventurous and exciting time for the actor, loaded with experimentation and discovery. It is not just a period of great intensity and drudgery, as it is so often for so many actors. Being in love with the creative process and embarking on the incredible journeys that your choices take you on are related to the original reason why people choose to be actors in the first place. Do you remember when you were young and filled with the joy of pretending? We all looked forward to our fantasies and the pretend games, alone or with our friends. There wasn't any fear or insecurity about our being successful with pretending; we did it because it was fun and exciting. It is the same with acting: we do it, hopefully, for the same reasons. When did pretending stop being pretense and become reality? At that point we really believed in our game, and if we pretended to be frightened, we were; if we pretended to be sad, we cried; if we pretended to be angry, we felt the anger creeping up our bodies. When are the rules any different for the adult actor? The game is the same; or if it isn't, it should be!

In the example I gave earlier about the husband and wife splitting up, she wants to leave, and he wants her to stay. As it was written, in the end she leaves. The actor makes a choice that he hopes will stimulate intense love and need to hang on to this woman. The actress, although having loved the man, is now in a place where she no longer wants to be in the relationship, either because she no longer loves him or because she has no faith that the relationship will ever bring her happiness. These separate realities create opposing needs and desires, which is the basis of most drama.

If the actor uses a choice that is very meaningful to him, taken from his own life experience, then the choice should really impel him to fight to keep her. As the actress creates her reality, her anguish and need to escape from the relationship should become equally strong. What then can be accomplished is a very promising foundation for ensemble work.

Let's say that he chooses to work for the woman he is in love with now, in his real life. His choice approach is to endow the actress, sensorially, with that woman's features, coloring, and manner. As he uses this sensory process, the actress becomes more and more a conglomerate of his girlfriend and herself, saying all the things that he fears she might someday say, telling him that she is going to leave him; and if the actor is successful in creating his choice, he may expect to be enormously affected by what happens in the rehearsal. The more he really believes his choice, the more he may panic and attempt to dissuade her from leaving. If, in turn, she has a choice that is equally impelling, they both struggle to get what they want. Herein lies the element of reality, truth, and irreverence. If their belief is far greater that their concern with "acting" the scene, the kind of behavior they will both experience will be filled with a large variety of impulses that go beyond the conventional qualities of the piece. At first, he may beg her to reconsider, she remaining cold to his pleas. He, feeling her coldness, may get very angry. She may respond with greater anger and more threat. He then may take a softer approach, and so on. If both actors are totally committed to believing and having their way and they both include all their individual impulses irreverently, this tug-of-war becomes an electrifying spectacle for an audience that really has no idea how it will turn out.

Being irreverent in rehearsals means that you follow each impulse wherever it leads. In retrospect, if it is indeed wrong for the play, you make other adjustments or choices. You never *make* something happen; instead you create a climate of stimulation and *allow* it to happen.

PERFORMANCE IRREVERENCE

The rehearsal period may last anywhere from two weeks to two years, depending on whom you are working with and where. Stanislavsky and the Moscow Art Theater worked for very long periods on a play, sometimes as long as two years. Recently I directed a production of Tennessee Williams' *The Glass Menagerie* and spent seven months on it. I like a long rehearsal period; it gives everyone a chance to really explore the material. I had the advantage of working with four actors whom I had personally trained. The luxury of time allowed us to work in many areas that would be impossible to address if we had only weeks to rehearse. We didn't deal with the actual text until the beginning of the fifth month. Even if you have a relatively short rehearsal period, that is the time to explore, irreverently; set your choices and know what works and what doesn't, and develop trust in the approaches you have decided to carry into performance.

The main difference between rehearsal irreverence and performance irreverence is that by the time you have reached performance you have arrived at the proper choices and approaches to fulfill the material. The "seeking and exploring" have borne the fruit that we call creating the role. In every performance you know where and when you are going to execute what you have found in rehearsal. That is to say, you know what choices you are going to use and when to leave one choice and start using another. You know where the specific adjustments are and when to begin shifting from one choice into another in order to make a transition. In the performance, experimentation is over and you are involved in creating a variety of emotional states, impulses, thoughts, and behavior that sculpt a character that is alive and real for eight performances a week. The irreverent actor continues to be irreverent during performance by honoring all his impulses, expressing the moment-to-moment realities as they occur on the stage. The play must be serviced, and that responsibility rests on the choices and the approaches you have picked. Within that framework, all the feelings that come from your process and all the stimuli that occur at any given moment in the performance are to be included and embraced as part of the total reality that is taking place on stage.

When you have reached performance, the responsibility to service the author's intent must be met. If the actor has used the rehearsal period fruitfully, he can hope that he will not only have met the demands of the material but also brought new and original dimensions to his character. Another important by-product of irreverence is that it allows and encourages the actor to ventilate many facets of his personality that could never surface as a result of a more conservative and conventional acting approach. If he goes with where the choices take him and allows every impulse to be expressed, his life flow is not inhibited the way it would be if he were facilitating a specific desired behavior. What I mean by that is what happens when an actor "plays" an emotion. He is playing anger, or he is playing sadness, etc. If an actor "plays" anything, it is a false state, an unreal state, and can only *represent* an emotion without really BEING the entire emotional state. Every emotion we feel is part of an entire network of impulses. When a person is functioning honestly, every expression has a multitude of variations in emotional color. Anger is filled with hurt, disappointment, frustration, or whatever the stimulus impelled the person to feel. A facilitated emotion has a beginning, a middle, and an end. It does not authentically give way to another impulse, whereas in the case of reality one emotional impulse gives way to the next and the next and so on.

The actor can expect that, by the time he has reached performance, his technique will produce the results he wants. The choices will take him in the same area of emotional life each time, with, of course, some variations, since it is impossible for him to feel the emotion exactly as he did before. The variations in impulses *do not* threaten the reality of the play. They add the element of unpredictability to the work, and they keep the performance fresh and new each time. Every time an actor steps onto the stage or in front of the camera, new things happen and unexpected things occur. Instead of being thrown by them, the actor should relate to them as the "food" of creative impulses. Without the unexpected, without the moment-to-moment inclusion of realities, there can never be an ensemble state.

When the choices are fresh and new, it is quite simple for a trained craftsman to follow the impulses stimulated by them. However, after he has been in a play for a long time, several things may happen: the actor can fall into the trap of expecting certain emotional responses and quite unconsciously begin to repeat expressions that felt good in earlier performances. He can begin to anticipate results and respond from an intellectual place rather than going with the real impulses. When that occurs, he actually "dams up" his organic flow and gets "stale," so to speak, and becomes presentational. No matter how well-trained or practiced a craftsman he is, the human element cannot be overlooked. The actor must constantly be aware of the traps of performing. He must not become complacent in his work, not for one moment! When I work in a film, I am constantly aware of the need to be prepared. When I am not in a particular shot, I use the time to get ready for my next responsibility. I don't socialize until my work is finished. A while back, I was in a film, and a group of us were inside a trailer rehearsing a scene we were about to shoot. It was a serious scene which dealt with some life-and-death issues. My character was upset and dissenting with the group, challenging their feelings and decisions—a kind of alarmist with justification. We were running the scene, and most of the other actors were joking and not really involved in the obligations of the scene. It bothered me personally, and I used that reality to enhance the choices I had already been exploring. I was angry and upset that the scene, the film, seemed to mean so little to those people, and I let them know how I felt through the lines of the scene. When we moved onto the soundstage to do the scene, I was ready, since I had been using my time from the beginning of the rehearsal. I didn't care about winning friends by joining their jocularity; my commitment was to my work. There are many actors who fear the judgment of other actors. They don't want to be considered too serious or "uptight" about their work, so they become a part of the "gang," and their work suffers. How can you be taken *too seriously* about one of the most important things in your life?

If, after a period of time doing a show, the actor begins to anticipate responses or leads himself to certain kinds of emotional life, he must quickly identify what is happening and immediately deal with it. Whenever the impulsive flow is interrupted, one knows it right away. The intellectual commentary starts, the actor becomes self-conscious and often awkward. At this very juncture, a lot of actors begin to cover their tracks; in other words, they start to compensate and affect a "comfort state," which then becomes epidemic. When this occurs, their performance goes down the tubes. The antidote to this kind of trap is immediate acknowledgment that it is happening, Personal Inventory, and the expression of the moment-to-moment responses elicited by the Personal Inventory process. The Personal Inventory goes on as an Inner Monologue, under the lines of the scenes and in between working with the choice.

Example:

HE: (Entering.) What are you doing with that suitcase?

SHE: I'm leaving, Jack, and I want you not to make it any harder than it is!

HE: You mean for good?

SHE: Yes. We've talked; you know it's over; please let go.

(At a point in the beginning dialogue, he might become aware that he is anticipating her answers and planning the emotional content of his next line. It is at this very point that he must start to deal with the problem.)

HE: (Inner Monologue: *I'm listening to myself. I know what she's going to say, and I even know how she's going to say it. I feel very aware of my body all of a sudden.* Including all of his responses to the above Inner Monologue in the next line of the play.) Please, Joan, stop and let's talk! (Inner Monologue continues under the lines and into Personal Inventory: *How do I feel? I'm uncomfortable*—that is expressed in the very next line.) I DON'T WANT YOU TO LEAVE . . . PLEASE!

SHE: You can't stop me this time. I've made up my mind, and I'm leaving!

HE: (Personal Inventory continuing: *I feel as though I don't know what to do next . . . I'm insecure.*) I love you . . . Doesn't that mean anything to you?

(All the impulses experienced in the framework of the Personal Inventory now become a part of the emotional life of the scene.)

If the actor continues the Personal Inventory and carries it on as an Inner Monologue, he will climb out of the trap he fell into and become more impulsive and organic as he goes on with it. After getting back into an organic groove, he should then reinvest in the original choice he is using for the scene and irreverently continue to express his impulses through the lines.

Another frequent problem that occurs is that choices sometimes lose their strength. What once had great impact loses its thrust occasionally with a lot of use and over a long period of time.

When the actor begins to notice this, he should first explore the possibility of adding fresh elements to the choice. If, for example, the choice is being created through a sensory process, the elements he might add are different, new, and exciting sensory questions—the kinds of questions I call "Jelly-Bean Questions" because they are designed to appeal to the actor emotionally as well as sensorially.

The choice adjustments can actually be made during a performance, since the actor is using essentially the same choice as always, only now he is adding new elements which strengthen it but do not distort the original thrust of the scene obligation.

If the adjustments just aren't enough, he may have to introduce a completely new choice and, in that case, would have to do some homework. The actor may ask the other actor to meet him and have a short rehearsal, or it may suffice to just work with the choice at home.

TECHNIQUES THAT PROMOTE IRREVERENCE

The key to irreverent expression is that whenever you allow your real impulses to be expressed, unencumbered, you are experiencing an organic BEING state. If you then deal with material and continue to honor your own reality, you are in an irreverent state. Any exercise or technique that stimulates impulsiveness encourages irreverence.

The nature of an exercise or technique that will promote irreverence depends on the area of irreverence you are dealing with. Some of the techniques that you might use in rehearsal are definitely not right in performance, since they take too much liberty with the material. So, for the sake of clarity and application, I am going to separate the techniques into three categories: *philosophical, rehearsal,* and *performance.*

TECHNIQUES TO PROMOTE
AN IRREVERENT STATE PHILOSOPHICALLY

Since the entire concept of irreverence is a way of thinking or a state of mind, the first step in moving toward an irreverent state would be believing that the approach is the best way to work as an actor. Once the concept is accepted by the actor, the next step is feeling that he has the right to explore and experiment irreverently.

EGO PREPARATIONS

Any of the wide variety of ego exercises will help the actor to establish a state where he feels that he has the right to BE who he is and take the risks and chances that produce exciting and unpredictable work on the stage.

MAKING MY STATEMENT

A good ego preparation to promote irreverence is to largely express your personal point of view about all the things that you see, hear, and feel around you and to include your personal statements about life.

Example:

"I don't like feeling pressure. I will take all the time I need in this rehearsal . . . I like you; I like working with you . . . I want to have fun with this. I think too many actors work from fear and tension; I will not tolerate that in myself; I will demand that I am given the room to explore the creative process no matter what the insecurities are . . . Acting is what I do, and the way I work is the way I work . . . I like this play. I want to contribute to it and not just mouth someone else's words like a puppet . . . I see you all staring at me strangely. I accept that, and you can think anything you like . . . I am doing this for *me,* and I have the right to be who I am! The world is filled with people who run scared, and I am not going to be one of them . . . I believe in the theater, I believe in my creative process, and I believe in the artist's right to use the rehearsal for what it has been intended."

This exercise can continue for as long as necessary. It can be done before or during rehearsal, at any point where the actor feels the need to elevate his courage level to the point where he can be irreverent in the rehearsal. It is important for any actor using the above technique to apply common sense to the circumstance in which he is using the preparation. Since the purpose of the exercise is to free himself to function, he does not want to create hostility with the director or the other actors. Therefore it would be wise to let everyone know that you are doing a preparation and why you are doing it. Make no compromises in your statements! Be honest and direct in the expressions of what you feel, and stand your ground with your beliefs.

DUE-TAKING PREPARATIONS

This approach is done simply by acknowledging your right to work creatively. It can be done silently as a preparation before starting a rehearsal, or it can be done audibly at any time during the rehearsal. The actor can express his feelings in this area so that others can hear them if he feels that "going on record" will free him to risk more.

Example:

(As an inner stream of consciousness or audibly.)

"I deserve to take my time. It's OK for me not to be heard at this point in rehearsal, since that is not my concern at the moment. I am going to bring myself into this role, and in order to do that I must explore choices that pique parts of me that I am not totally familiar with. I deserve to stop when I think it is necessary. I deserve the respect of my fellow artists, and I deserve their support in my journey as they deserve mine. I need a benevolent environment within which to work, and I am going to demand that!

"I love acting, and I deserve to make this experience wonderful! I have the right as an actor to fail while I am looking for the right approaches to this material! I must be willing to fail in order to succeed organically."

The Due-taking technique is designed to make the actor feel good about working irreverently and using his time profitably.

FEELING SPECIAL

If the actor gets in touch with being special and unique, he will be much more willing to take chances expressing his impulses. Since accepting irreverence as an approach to acting starts with the intellect, convincing yourself that there isn't any alternative is a good starting place.

As an Inner Monologue or out loud, express all the things that you feel are special, unique, and exciting about yourself.

Example:

"I feel a lot. I am very colorful, and I must allow myself to express the variety of things that I feel. I care deeply about all living things, and I must not be intimidated by the expression of those feelings . . . I am very impulsive by nature, and I must encourage that in my acting . . . I am extremely vulnerable, and that is a great gift that I want to share with others . . I have a fine sense of humor. I will include it . . . I have a contribution to make to the world. I am special because there isn't anyone in the world exactly like me. I move in a certain way. I sound different from anyone else. My reactions are uniquely my own. I see things in my own very special way, and I must explore all these things and expose them in my work!"

Achieving a sense of specialness allows the actor to courageously risk the expression of all his impulses and at the same time opens doors to embracing impulses that promote his unique individuality. This allows him to bring those things into the role and, by doing so, dimensionalize the character beyond the author's original concept.

Any technique the actor uses to promote more ego and self-confidence is encouraged. The first major step in accomplishing the work is to believe in it!

TECHNIQUES AND EXERCISES TO PROMOTE AN IRREVERENT STATE IN REHEARSALS

Perhaps the rehearsal period is the time and the place where the actor can be the most outrageously irreverent. I think that rehearsals are designed for the adventurous journey, and if they aren't, they should be. The actor should be encouraged to try almost anything in the quest for the character. Being irreverent to the material is a way of unshackling oneself from result concerns and taking the freedom to stimulate a multitude of impulses and emotional life. This forms the clay from which the actor finely carves the lines of the character.

SOUNDS, WITH A CHOICE

At any time in the rehearsal period, either close to the beginning or even after several rehearsals, the actors can approach the scene by using their choices to relate to each other, but without words. They relate on a moment-to-moment basis; only, instead of the words of the play, they express their impulses in sounds, allowing the sounds a full range of vocal expression. Some very interesting things happen when actors substitute sounds for the words! Immediately, there seem to be infinitely more emotional color and variety. The actors break connection with any intellectual concept or description of feelings, and there is a much greater level of unpredictability and freshness. Also, by using sounds, the actors stimulate a flow of uncensored impulses that don't have to fit into the logic of the scene. Even when the actors return to the words of the scene, there is a carryover of the impulsive vocal variety produced by the sounds.

GIBBERISH, WITH A CHOICE

This exercise is very much like the preceding one and is approached in the same manner. Both actors work for the choice they have decided to use in the scene and relate to each other with gibberish words rather than the written dialogue. At all times they encourage a moment-to-moment reality and respond to each other in gibberish. What it might look like to an objective observer is two actors speaking in some undefinable foreign language. As it is with sounds, the Gibberish technique eliminates concept and premeditation. It allows for the unexpected and fills the scene with emotional colors that it might not have had before. The value of gibberish, in addition to or instead of sounds, is that it allows the actors to form abstract words and sentences, even if the words have no meaning. It is more like talking than making sounds is, and it is a good interim technique between sounds and the written dialogue.

Example:

HE: (Working with his choice and including all of the life he is experiencing.) CARBOG . . . JONGOLA PROCOCO, FORBITS . . . KEEGIC NOLGIINOLGITZ?

SHE: (Also working with her choice.) FAGELAGITIS ANDRITOFF. . . NORTOFITZ ANG GOLOITS . . . NIGIC CANTOPLOTS FORG NOFITS MALTANA. ITDRIGIC MOLOTOS NOSITGOS!

HE: (Responding to her.) YALITS . . . ARA MOLITS ANGRA GIFFITS . . . BEGAGITS NALA SHLIGITS!

SHE: NGA NGA ITSAFIL NGA NGA!

The gibberish scene can go on for as long as, or even longer than, the written scene. Whatever the actors discover by doing it in gibberish will almost surely carry over to the written material.

MOMENT-TO-MOMENT PARAPHRASING IMPROVISATION

A more conventional way to promote irreverence is to use your own words in the scene instead of those written by the playwright. Of course, this is encouraged only as a rehearsal technique, and no actor should take liberties with the script without the playwright's personal permission.

When paraphrasing the material, the actor can not only insert his words, but add words to the material. By so doing, he can experience and express all the impulses that are generated by the relationship with the other actor. The actor does not paraphrase verbatim; that is, he does not proceed line by line. The improvisation is based on paralleling the content of the scene and achieving the essence of the material. Verbatim paraphrasing creates another trap for the actor, since he must think of each line as written and then come up with a suitable paraphrase. He becomes trapped in his head and begins to premeditate new words and the behavior that might go with them. Nonverbatim paraphrasing frees the actor to allow, permit, and include all of his impulses in the scene without being tied to the logic of the words. By expressing all of his personal feelings in the framework of the material, he can then approach the written material with the same feelings of irreverence.

Example:

(The scene as written.)

JOE: Why does it always have to be my responsibility to make the decisions in this family?

ALMA: That's the way it has always been. Why change it now?

JOE: Cute, Alma, real cute! But it doesn't solve the problem about what to do with Dad! I can't take him home with me; I have a house full of kids and a wife who's not well!

ALMA: We've all heard it before, Joe. We know it by heart!

JOE: You know, Alma, all you have to do is open your mouth and you piss me off. Why is that? Why can't you discuss something rationally and with intelligence rather than being a wiseass?

ALMA: I don't like you, Joe. I never did. And what's more, I don't buy your excuses. I don't have it any easier than you, but you don't hear me crying on everybody's shoulder, do you?

JOE: No, Alma, you don't cry on everybody's shoulder, but you also don't contribute a nickel to the support of your own father. I have been doing that for years. Where have you been when it came to reaching into your pocket?

ALMA: Boy, that's dirty. You know how hard it's been for me!

JOE: OK, I'm sorry—but you really make me angry. Listen, Alma, I can't afford to send him to a home, and he doesn't want to go away. (Pause.) Could you take him for a few months?

ALMA: And what good would that do, Joe? In a few months we would be right where we are now!

JOE: So what do we do?

ALMA: If I had an answer, you think I wouldn't tell you? Listen, Joe, I gotta go home. Harry is there, and I have to make dinner for him and the kids. Look, I'll talk to Harry. I don't know. . . maybe I could take Dad for a month or two and then we could deal with it. (Starts to leave.) I'm sorry, too, Joe. I love him, you know that.

JOE: Yeah, Alma, I know that . . . Well, OK, talk to Harry and see if Dad can come and stay with you for a while. I'll send the same amount as I do now. That might help some, huh?
(She crosses to Joe, they embrace, and she leaves.)

The above is a hypothetical scene written to use as an example of how to use paraphrasing. The actors, while paraphrasing, would deal with the relationship obligations and the emotional obligations of the piece. The choices would address the conflict between the two characters. The only difference would be that they would use their own words to parallel the scene.

The actor doing the scene will do whatever preparations he would ordinarily do before beginning the scene. He would work for his choices in whatever order is usual and begin to paraphrase the scene.

(Paraphrasing the scene.)

ACTOR: (Relating to actress.) I'm sick of being in this position. I don't want to be responsible for making all the decisions. (Feeling he is getting no response from actress.) Don't just stand there with your mouth open, say something!

ACTRESS: What would you like me to say? . . . You seem to be doing all the talking!

ACTOR: You know . . . I don't like being the one who carries everything and everybody. (Feeling angry and unseen.) And I'm not going to take your wise-mouth shit anymore. I've been shelling out support money for years, and you sit on your ass and cheer me on —

ACTRESS: (Interrupting, feeling all kinds of things—angry, attacked.) Now, just a minute, HERO. I'm not taking any abuse from you; I've done that for too many years —

ACTOR: (Jumping in on her line.) Look, Alma, we're not getting anywhere this way. Let's stop all the ugly shit and get down to cases . . . (Feeling ambivalent and not sure how to proceed, the actor includes all these feelings in the paraphrased lines.) You know my situation. I can't take Dad home, and, goddammit, you know why. And, for Christ's sakes, I'm not a millionaire, so I can't afford to send him to a home either. So what the hell is left?

ACTRESS: Don't throw it in my lap, Joe. I hardly make it through the month on the money we have.

ACTOR: You could take Dad home for a few months. That would help!

ACTRESS: (Feeling really manipulated and split between that feeling and the emotional response to the choice relating to her father.) What good would that do? We would have to go through this all over again— Hey, wait a minute, I'm allowing you to push me around again. FUCK YOU, JOE! I'm sick of your manipulations. I'm getting the hell out of here. (The actress starts to leave the stage.)

ACTOR: (Stopping her; steps in front of her. Softer.) Wait a minute— I'm sorry I upset you . . . Listen, we both love the old man. Why are we fighting each other?

ACTRESS: (Starts to cry—really hurt.) I feel helpless and unable to do anything, and you . . . you, my own brother, back me into a corner and start kicking the shit out of me.

ACTOR: (Really affected by the actress, goes to her and embraces her, visibly moved by her feelings. Holds her.) I'm sorry; I understand how you feel. I love you too! Please, Alma, talk to Harry; see if anything can be done.

ACTRESS: (Pauses. Looks at him. There is a real exchange of caring between the actors.) I will, Joe. I love you too. (She kisses him on the cheek and leaves.)

In the above example of paraphrasing the material, both actors essentially stayed with the circumstances of the scene. However, there was a lot more life in the exchange than the words of the written script would indicate. Including all the moment-to-moment life they experienced and allowing themselves to express it verbally in their own words freed the actors to be more irreverently expressive in the short scene. The technique is also an excellent way of exploring the subtext of the scene and finding out where the choices will lead. It enables the actors to add elements and impulses to what might be a very thinly written scene. Paraphrasing is a very good rehearsal technique in that it takes the actor "off the spot" with the written words until he has had time to build his realities to a point where the lines won't get in the way.

NURSERY RHYMES

To avoid the trap of logic and concept and also to promote irreverence in a scene, the actor can use a nursery rhyme in place of the written words. Continuing to work for the choices and encouraging the relationship obligations, the actor simply relates through the words of *Mary Had a Little Lamb*.

Any nursery rhyme or poem will do, just as long as the actor avoids falling into the trap of the meter of the rhyme. If that occurs, the use of the rhyme becomes much less effective because, in a sense, you are servicing the nursery rhyme and not expressing your own moment-to-moment impulses.

Example:

HE: Mary had a little? . . .

SHE: Jack and Jill went up . . .

HE: Lamb and its fleece was white as snow and . . .

SHE: The hill, to fetch a . . . pail of—

HE: (Interrupting.) Everywhere that Mary went the lamb . . .

SHE: (Emphatically.) Water!!! Jack fell down . . . and broke his crown . . . and Jill!!!

HE: Was sure . . . to go . . . It followed her to school one day and that . . .

SHE: Came tumbling after, Jack and Jill went . . .

HE: (Feeling empathy for her and expressing it in the next line.) Was against the rules . . . All the children laughed . . . and played . . . to see . . .

The nursery rhyme replaces the written lines and removes the tendency toward concept and leadership. The actors are free to explore their choices and express their real impulses through the rhyme. When they return to the script, they usually feel much more impulsive and irreverent in the scene. The use of this technique transfers the emphasis from the meaning of the words to the impulses, which encourages not only irreverence but a wider spectrum of emotional colors.

TWO-PEOPLE TRICK IN CIRCUMSTANCES

This is a technique that starts out very arbitrarily. Using the lines of the material, both actors attempt to "trick" each other by doing unexpected and unpredictable things while doing the scene (in rehearsal). This irreverence technique works best when both actors are working for their respective choices in an attempt to fulfill the demands of the material. Tricking each other may take a variety of forms: they can physically do unexpected things or say their lines with a completely illogical and unexpected expression. Either actor may move toward or away from the other without reason or cause or, depending on how far you want to take the technique, be completely illogical in behavior. If both actors agree to use the technique in rehearsal and allow themselves to go with the way they are truly affected by each other, the results can be quite exciting and fruitful.

INNER–OUTER MONOLOGUE

This exercise will be discussed many times in this book in relation to irreverence, since it immediately focuses the actor on the reality of the moment. The technique can be used in a variety of ways and for several different reasons. As a rehearsal technique to promote irreverence, it can be done audibly or silently. The actors, relating to each other with the lines of the scene, will, in between the written words, express what is going on within themselves. Thus they can stay with the expression of their real feelings in the framework of the written scene. Every time either actor exposes the inner life in between and through the words of the material, he or she is not only being irreverent, but also bringing the dimension of his/her own personality to each moment of the scene.

Example:

HE: Where would you like to have dinner? (Inner Monologue: *I feel awkward. Wow, she is really pretty! I would really like to take her to dinner.*) Do you feel like going someplace nice, or do you want to send out for something?

SHE: (Inner Monologue: *I'm really hungry. I wish we could eat before doing this scene . . . He's looking at me very strangely.*) I don't care, whatever you feel like doing is fine with me.

HE: (Inner Monologue: *I'm afraid to tell you what I feel like doing!*) Well, if you're going to leave it to me, I'd rather stay home and get comfortable in front of a nice fire!

SHE: OK. I'll change into something more comfortable and you can send out for some Chinese . . . (Inner Monologue: *Ugh . . . I hate Chinese food . . . Now, I could eat some lasagna!*) Be back in a moment.

This technique can go on throughout the entire scene, and the life stimulated by the expression of the Inner–Outer Monologue becomes a part of the scene. If the actors choose to express their Inner Monologues out loud, then they will certainly be affected by what is expressed, and their response will come from that. If, on the other hand, the actors do not express the Inner Monologue audibly, it will only affect their behavior, and the response of the other actor will be as a result of the way he or she is affected by the behavior rather than from hearing the words of the Inner Monologue. Both techniques are valid, depending on what the actors want to accomplish in the rehearsal. If they want to "stick" to the script, taking no liberties with the written lines, then they would not express their impulses out loud. If they want to explore their inner life and be privy to what the other is thinking and feeling, the audible technique would be a better choice. The Inner–Outer Monologue is a very good way to keep the actor honest in the scene, and it is a perfect antidote to premeditation and logic.

CHOICE IRREVERENCE

Promoting irreverence in rehearsal is often approached with the exploration of the choice itself. While it is always a creative practice to be adventurous and experimental with the choice, being irreverent stimulates a greater thrust in the process of exploring.

Being irreverent with the choice is affected by the specific choice approach. If, for example, the choice is a particular person and the choice approach is Sense Memory, the irreverent element would be in the way the actor approaches the Sense Memory creation of the choice. Besides the normally structured Sense Memory questions, the actor would encourage unexpected or even outrageous trick questions related to the choice he is in the process of creating!

Example:

(The actor works sensorially to create a woman he knows.) *How tall is she?* (Visual response after each question.) *How wide are her shoulders? . . . What is the shape of her body? . . . How is she standing? . . . Where are her arms? . . . What is the color of her hair? . . . the shape of her hairline? . . .*

The Sense Memory exercise can go on very conventionally for a while until the actor has satisfactorily created the choice, at which point he can begin to ask irreverent questions related to that choice.

Example:

How far apart are her eyes? . . . What color are they? . . . What color is the left eye? . . . What color is the right eye? . . . What would her eyes look like if they were looking in totally opposite directions? . . . When she opens her mouth, what would I see if all her front teeth were missing? (The actor responds to all of the irreverent questions sensorially, actually attempting to create the sensory responses.) *If one of her eyes were bright red, how would that contrast with the other? . . . If she started to pick her nose, with which finger would she do it? . . . How far into the nostril does the finger penetrate?*

In this example of irreverent sensory exploration, the examples are somewhat outlandish on purpose to make it clear that you should encourage unconventional explorations.

By taking liberties like this, the actor not only excites his interest in the choice-approach process by making it more fun, but also stimulates a great variety of impulsive responses. All this leads to unpredictability and irreverence.

If the actor was using Imaginary Monologue as a choice approach, the irreverent process would exist in the things he said in the monologue. If it was a Believability choice approach, the adventure would take place in the direction the actor took the Believability.

In every choice and approach, it is possible to be very irreverent in the execution of the particular technique. The ingredients are imagination, courage, and a real desire to adventurously promote irreverence in the choice process.

ANTITHETICAL EXPLORATIONS

The rehearsal period can and should be used for a large variety of creative purposes, such as finding all the elements of the character, picking those elements in your own personality, and discovering the "underlife" that may motivate a character to behave in an opposite manner from the obvious. Antithetical Explorations is a good way to discover unusual facets in behavior while at the same time fragmenting concepts and encouraging irreverence in the work. Suppose that the character you are exploring is a volatile, angry person, spewing hate in every scene. He seems without a soft place in his body, is angry and violent throughout the whole play. *For a rehearsal technique, you, the actor, can choose to go in the opposite direction!* You can make choices that stimulate love and affection, that produce humanity rather than violence. You can surround yourself with choices that make you feel warm and loving toward the world and everyone in it.

Naturally, if you are successful in this quest, it will certainly not fulfill the demands of the material, at least not in the beginning. What it very well might accomplish is to open a lot of doors into why this character turned out the way he did. At the same time, the Antithetical Exploration will establish an anticonceptual involvement in the scenes of the play.

Going in the opposite direction from the obvious behavior of the character in the piece is a very interesting way of avoiding "on the nose" acting. That is to say that you avoid making a character black or white and one-dimensional. Adolf Hitler was a beast and a disciple of evil; however, he thought he was doing wonderful things for his people and the world. He had a reputation for loving children and obviously had moments of softness and charm. An actor attempting just to portray the beast would not, obviously, create a complete person. Hitler believed he was right and a savior of the world; the actor playing him must also believe that. Therefore, exploring the antithetical elements of a character is almost always necessary in fulfilling the obligations to the character and the piece. Let us say that in the early rehearsals the actor goes in the antithetical direction of the play, and as the rehearsals proceed, he finds ways to frustrate and deny the loving impulses he has stimulated. He finds ways to be discounted and rejected by the other characters in the play. He then begins to form resentments and hostilities toward the other actors and begins to *really feel,* from an organic origin, the impulses that the character in the piece feels. By using his time well, the actor not only creates an irreverent BEING state, he also builds a strong foundation of organic reality from which his behavior comes. He also avoids the trap of superficial behavior that expresses the emotion of the character without creating the impetus from which that emotional life comes.

SWITCH-TRICK EXPLORATION

This is another arbitrary technique used to stimulate an accelerated impulsivity. Because this exercise so obviously does not promote the obligations of the material, it should be used *exclusively* in rehearsals. The purpose of the approach is to suggest so many different stimuli to the actor, so quickly, that it tends to throw him off balance in such a way as to create a state of high impulsive irreverence. When he returns to the lines of the scene immediately after a Switch Trick experience, the actor seems more in touch with his real impulsive inner life. The exercise is done by very rapid suggestions and encouraging an immediate response to those stimulus suggestions.

Example:

(The actor starts the exercise after he gets into the written words.)

HE: The trouble with you, Harry, is that you're lazy. You want the world to dance to whatever tune you play, and when it doesn't, you sulk and behave like a naughty child. Well, it's time you grew up, old chum.

At this point the actor might feel very aware of himself and the next line. He might elect, in rehearsal, to try a Switch-Trick Exploration. He could start the technique by audibly, semiaudibly, or silently suggesting objects to himself.

HE: You have been living off your old man since the year one... *In the doorway he has a knife; he's after me ... On the sofa, my wife, she's hurt ... Oh no, she's bleeding ... My mother is in the chair, crying ... The dog is dead on the carpet ... He's lying down on the floor and sticking his tongue out at me! ...* (Suggesting that there is someone there he doesn't want to see.) *Nude pictures all over the walls. Everywhere I look, I see nude people ... in the wings ... on the walls ... Harvey the six-foot rabbit just came on stage ... Oh, there's my grandmother in a bikini ... She's winking at him! ...*

I'm sure you get the idea. The important thing is to suggest these things in a rapid-fire manner and encourage a response to each suggestion, even if the response is arbitrary. Some of the responses will be real and lead to other authentic feelings. It would also be advisable to let the other actors know what you are doing, or they might think that you have lost your mind right in the middle of the monologue.

OUTRAGEOUS EXAGGERATIONS

The title describes the approach. The actor, feeling stifled, might decide simply to exaggerate all of his behavior, vocally, physically, and verbally. This brings incredible flamboyance and music to the lines as well as turning a very serious scene into something that resembles a ballet. Since it is blatant exaggeration and not all meant to deal with the responsibility of the material, the actor can go as far as he likes with the outrageousness of the exercise. At a point where he feels freer, more impulsive, and irreverent to the material, he can return to the choice he is using and carry over that impulsive freedom into the written scene.

As you use the craft and become increasingly familiar with the techniques that promote irreverence, you will discover your own ways to be irreverent. Rehearsals are a place where the actor has the freedom and license to experiment, explore, and be irreverent to the material for a period of time. Perhaps the rehearsal period is the only time that affords such complete freedom. If that opportunity passes without being taken advantage of, then the actor really loses.

TECHNIQUES TO PROMOTE IRREVERENCE IN PERFORMANCE

As I have already stated, a different kind of responsibility and discipline exists in the performance phase. *The actor is obligated to service and fulfill the demands and obligations of the material!* I am certain that I would get into disputes with many "theater people" about how much latitude an actor has in performance. The more conventional thinkers would staunchly defend the premise of the "Speak the speech, I pray you" philosophy. In other words, once the lines have been said in a certain way, they must always be said exactly in that way. I think that is ridiculous and have always thought it ridiculous! It is that kind of limited thinking that leads to staid, predictable, and superficial performances that an audience has to overlook in order to justify the forty or more dollars they spend to see a Broadway play.

The actor has to fight that kind of antiquated thinking and stand up for the truth—his personal truth as well as the truth of the play. What are the actor's guidelines? How do you know what the perimeters of irreverence are in performance when you are walking a tightrope between irreverence and misinterpretation?

Several years ago at the Actors Studio, I directed Joan Hotchkis in a play that she had written. Again, we had the luxury of a long rehearsal period, and we were doing it as a work in progress in the directors unit at the Studio. I told her to express everything that she felt, moment to moment, through the lines of the scene. We were in a frustrating period of development, and she was grappling with her fears and insecurities in the scene and as an actress in general. She had expressed to me that she often felt like screaming right in the middle of a line, and I told her to do just that! The role was that of a middle-aged woman living in upper-class suburbia, going through a most severe middle-age crisis, totally frustrated and contemplating suicide. On this particular evening, Joan was working in a scene where she was making telephone calls and talking to herself. The emotional obligation of the character in that scene was enormous frustration, confusion, and a kind of uncontrolled terror. Somewhere in the middle of the scene, Joan gave out a bloodcurdling scream that was full of everything she was feeling, up to and including that moment. Then she went on with the rehearsal, carrying into the scene everything that the scream had released in her.

When the scene was over, we launched into a discussion of the work, which was customary at the end of a rehearsal. There were a lot of questions about the work, some positive feedback, and some not-so-positive feedback. One of the playwrights in the unit asked me, the director, if the scream was written into the material. I told him that it was not and that I encouraged Joan to include all the impulses she experienced during the time she was working in the scene. That answer started a huge controversy among the writers, as well as the directors. The playwright wanted to know who had granted me the authority to take such liberties with the material. "It was irresponsible to misinterpret a writer's work," he said. "How dare anyone think they had the right to change the character's behavior in a piece of material?" Some of the writers were up in arms over the whole thing, when I asked him (the playwright), "Was it not possible for that character to behave that way in that scene?" He paused for a long moment and then reluctantly admitted that it "might be possible" but that that was not how he saw the behavior. I very quickly told him that I did not care how he saw the behavior. I added that if it was possible for the character in any play or scene to behave that way, then it was acceptable. I also said that even if it was not likely or probable that she would scream at that moment in the scene, it was strictly a matter of interpretation and individual taste as to whether she might or not. Besides, a very important fact of reality that everyone seemed to overlook was that the actress, filled with frustration and insecurity, feeling that she did not know where to go at that moment (which, incidentally, was right for the character), purged all that was happening internally. The unacceptable alternative was to deny the reality and continue to struggle (as the actress) with the emotional block. This would only have allowed her to impose unreal behavior over the problem. By including her reality and purging the conglomerated emotions, she freed herself to function organically throughout the rest of the scene.

The guidelines of irreverent expression in a scene are based on whether an actor or a director can justify and include impulses not indicated in the text by asking this question: Is it not possible for the character to behave or respond in that way at that moment? If the answer to that question is Yes, then it is permissible. As you work with the craft and encourage all your real impulses into your work, you will find that it is an extremely rare occurrence when the answer to that question would be No.

THE INCLUSION OF ALL IMPULSES, FEAR, AND CONFUSION

In the midst of any scene, when the actor becomes aware of any obstacle, it is very important that the emotional life of that moment become a part of the expression of the character through the lines. Is it not true that people in everyday life have emotional blocks and obstacles? Don't we suffer confusion and insecurity, and don't we often express it even though we do not refer to it directly? So why should it be any different for a real character in a play? If the actor conditions himself to honor all of his impulses as part of the total life of the character, he is then, in a sense, never really in trouble on the stage.

Example:

"To be or not to be: that is the question . . . " *(I feel awkward and somewhat self-conscious . . . I am aware of my body . . .)* At this point, is it not acceptable for the actor to manifest his real internal feelings in the next line of his soliloquy? After all, Hamlet was a mere boy in his teens. Is it not possible that at this moment, grappling with a life-and-death matter, he might be uncomfortable? No, it is not possible if you deify Shakespeare with a never-to-be-tampered-with reverence that makes his characters unreal and not human! I have a feeling that old Bill was more irreverent than all of us.

PERSONAL INVENTORY

This is a way of finding out what you are feeling at any moment in the scene. It is a technique that an actor can use in performance to identify and then express the impulse. Earlier in this section there is an example of how it is done in the midst of a scene.

INNER MONOLOGUE

This is a very similar technique to the Inner–Outer Monologue exercise in rehearsal usage. The major difference is that the Inner Monologue remains silent as a stream of consciousness under the lines that the actor expresses. By encouraging this kind of flow, the actor stimulates an unbroken and unpredictable impulsive life on the stage. In fact, we in life always have some kind of internal monologue going on. The nature of the Inner Monologue will be decided by the kind of stimulus by which the actor is being affected. If the choice for the scene is affecting to the actor, it will impel him to think and feel very much as the character might. So, in effect, the Inner Monologue will become the flow of life of the character, creating a collaboration between the actor and the character. This allows the character to inhabit or become the actor. Again, what I am saying is that the actor does not become the character; the character, in effect, becomes the actor.

IMPULSIVITY EXERCISES

While in the midst of a scene, the actor can activate any number of impulsivity exercises. Let us imagine that everything is going along just fine, and, as sometimes happens, the actor gets into trouble. He begins to lead himself to certain kinds of behavior and expressions and becomes aware of it only when he is already well committed to it. He may try a number of antidotes such as Inner Monologue, Personal Inventory, acknowledgment and inclusion of all the problems, which will probably help to remedy the situation. But suppose he continues to lapse backward into a repetition of the problem. Disconnected Impulsivity is a very good technique for stimulating very quick impulsive responses and a particularly good approach to eliminate leadership of any kind.

THE DISCONNECTED-IMPULSIVITY EXERCISE

The exercise is done first by making yourself aware of your real moment-to-moment impulses, then encouraging the expression of those impulses within the lines of the scene. As the word "disconnected" indicates, the impulses need not, and usually *do not,* relate to each other. They can go from a logical response to a completely unrelated thought.

This process takes place internally. The actor can activate the impulses under his lines, in between the lines, or even when he is listening to the other actor.

Example:

(Lines of a Scene.) "If you don't study for that test, you're going to flunk the class—and you know what that's going to mean!" (At this juncture, the actor starts the Disconnected Impulsivity technique.) *Looking at me . . . I don't like it . . . blue walls . . . he's talking . . . feel cold chills . . . light. Aha, the camera . . . action . . . don't be funny! I feel excited . . . love it, love it . . . I think words . . . see the furniture . . .*

The actual expression of these impulses is very subtle and usually eliminates premeditation immediately.

It would seem by the above description that Disconnected Impulsivity would take you away from the relationship and the scene, but it doesn't. In fact, what it looks like is a person responding to the environment, to the other actor (character), and also to his own personal thoughts. Besides being very natural, it stimulates an openness and an energy which excite the relationships on stage. In fact, it can charge a low-energy scene. Any impulsivity approach in a scene is employed only for the length of time it is needed. The important goal is a moment-to-moment involvement with the other character, hopefully leading to an ensemble relationship. The technique is a problem solver and should not be used indiscriminately.

TWO PEOPLE TRICK EACH OTHER

This a very useful involvement and is often a great deal of fun. A lot of actors during a long run of a show have been known to do unexpected things during a scene just to keep each other on their toes. Without an awareness of what you are doing, it can be dangerous to the play. First of all, it should be decided between the actors that you are going to employ the technique and why. It is not a game but a very creative approach to keep the reality from lapsing into predictability. It promotes a performance irreverence and keeps the play fresh and impulsive. Just as any of the other exercises, it should not be used unless the actors or the director has good reason to do so.

During the scene, either actor can begin doing unexpected things— only, of course, if this does not violate the logic of the play. They might touch each other physically in a moment where this has meaning or expresses an emotional impulse quite unlike anything expressed before. Either actor can exaggerate moments, fondle a prop, stare at the wall at a most unlikely time, or not relate to the other thereby forcing him to work to gain attention. All of these actions and involvements *must* fit into the scene; they *must not* distract or violate the reality of the moment or the scene!

An interesting theater story is one about the famous Lunt and Fontanne, who, I am told, used to take delight in tricking each other. One night during the run of a play on Broadway, he arranged with a stagehand to have a telephone ring in the middle of a scene where there wasn't supposed to be a telephone ring. After the ring, he immediately turned to her and said, "Telephone, darling." I'm sure she was surprised, but, immediately and without batting an eyelash, she walked to the table with the telephone on it, picked up the phone, said hello, and turned to him, saying, "It's for you, darling." Whatever their reasons for this kind of trickery, I am quite certain that it stimulated great fun and a fresh impulsiveness to the play and each other.

Eric and Ange doing an Irreverence Preparation

Chapter 3

THE CRAFT
PREPARATIONS

There are actually only three major categories related to craft. Preparation falls into separate areas, instrumental and craft, whereas obligations, choices, and choice approaches are pure craft. Since this book, however, is devoted exclusively to the exploration of craft, the preparations in this section are mainly craft preparations.

Preparation is the largest part of acting, since your ability to function with a craft is totally dependent on your being ready to do that. In the instrumental area, you must reach a state of BEING in order to create truth, so the first preparational steps are the most important. When you achieve readiness, then your responsibility shifts to the material and what you are obligated to deal with. At this point you might move from the instrumental preparation to the craft preparation.

There are endless numbers of preparational possibilities, and as you work, you will discover and invent new ones that work well for you. However, there are a number of important categories of preparations that I use which cover a wide spectrum of needs. These major areas exist for specific reasons and should be used on an as-needed basis. It is important, however, to practice the various techniques and exercises in order to master the process.

A mystery of the ages has been: What does an actor do when he is acting? Equally as mysterious is: What does the actor do to *prepare* to act?

There are eight major categories of preparation: the standard relaxation cluster, involvement preparations, emotional preparations, ego preparations, the large expurgatives, relationship preparations, interim preparations, and irreverent preparations. Each of the preparations can be used in two ways: instrumentally and craftually.

The basic difference between using a preparation instrumentally and using it craftually is that when you choose a preparation and emphasize the instrumental, it is specifically used to eliminate emotional blocks and obstacles to expression, whereas when you use the very same technique as a craft preparation, the emphasis and the usage are directly related to affecting and changing the emotional state (either by taking you from one emotional place to another or by stimulating a completely new emotional life).

Take the example of the Exorcism exercise. Used as an instrumental-therapy exercise, it purges tension and conglomerated impulses. It dumps all the blocked emotion, thereby freeing the actor to function from a BEING place. The very same exercise, with a slight change of emphasis, can stimulate large emotional responses—anger, rage, frustration—which can then be carried directly into a scene or to the choice you are using for the scene.

The thrust of a preparation depends on two things: first, you must be instrumentally ready to use a preparation or choice so that you can change an already existing BEING state; second, you must know why you are using the particular preparation and what you hope to accomplish by exploring the technique. Using a preparation for theatrical purposes is just like using a choice in a scene, while purging the instrument of tension is a pre-preparation state.

As I mentioned earlier, each of these preparations can be used in both areas—either dealing with the instrument with an eye to achieving a readiness to act, or specifically related to a piece of material focusing on the obligation at hand.

THE STANDARD
RELAXATION CLUSTER

This is the start mark and definitely deals with the instrument! Relaxation is the only point from which an artist can create, so that's where you begin. There are a number of very good relaxation exercises, and you should find the ones that do the job best for you. Some work better than others, depending on a variety of factors—how tense you are, what *kind* of tension you are experiencing, and so on.

PHYSICAL RELAXERS

Using an exercise to relax you when you are about to shoot a scene is quite a different experience from lying on the floor with no immediate obligation to "deliver." There are several relaxers you can do that are unobtrusive.

WEIGHT-AND-GRAVITY RELAXATION

You start this technique by slowly exaggerating your own body weight, doing this until you feel quite heavy—almost as if it would take a great effort to lift your arms from your side. Continue doing this, and, at the same time, slowly move your arms upward and then allow them to fall with the exaggerated weight and the pull of gravity. Gently do the same thing with other parts of your body. Remember to breathe deeply while doing this technique, since deep breathing helps the entire relaxation process. You can do this exercise while waiting for the crew to adjust a light or while the director is talking to another actor, while you are working with a choice. No one need know what you are into. What separates this technique from an instrumental approach for "getting ready to get ready" is that you do all of these craft preparations while you are involved with a craft obligation. It is a matter of making an adjustment in the emphasis of the exercise.

TENSING AND RELAXING

By tiring the muscles in your body you can force the physical tension to dissipate. You accomplish this by tensing or constricting the muscles in your body to the extreme, flexing, and slowly relaxing the tension in each area. Repeat this a number of times until you actually feel more physically relaxed. There are two ways you might try the exercise: first, as an overall experience, tense the whole body at once so that you become rigid with muscular tension, and then let go in the same manner; or start with the top of your head, and slowly work down the body until you are tensed to the soles of your feet; of course, when you relax, just reverse the process and slowly relax upward, letting go in the same manner in which you tensed the body. This is a more extreme approach to getting rid of tension; but in some cases, especially while you are on the spot, it can work rather quickly to alleviate tension which accumulated during the scene.

DEEP BREATHING

As the name of the exercise implies, you progressively encourage yourself to take air into your body more deeply. Being aware of the tendency to hyperventilate slightly while doing this technique, you slowly increase the amount of air you take into your lungs, making sure that you exhale evenly. A good way to approach this exercise is to imagine that you are an empty vessel which can be filled from the bottom up, and each time you take in some air, you are filling yourself up from the bottom of your feet to the top of your head. With that extra, imagined possibility, it is simple to breathe on a deeper and fuller level. This process accomplishes good things for you. It definitely works to relax you, and it oxygenates the blood, making you feel better and giving you a burst of energy.

All of the physical-relaxation techniques can be done either before you start dealing with the material or at any time during the rehearsal or performance process. In the instrumental framework you can take more time, make loud sounds, and generally approach the exercises as an overall physical preparation. When you are using them exclusively in a craft involvement, it is often necessary to work much faster and less obtrusively.

STRETCHING AND YAWNING

What is more natural than to stretch and yawn? It may sound strange, but both activities serve a really important physical function. We often yawn because we are not getting enough oxygen, so it is the body's way of taking what it needs. Stretching allows the body to adjust itself into its normal position and to eliminate the kinks caused by fatigue and tension. When you yawn, you not only take in more oxygen, but you open the voice box and release tension in the throat. If you want an interesting experience, say some lines from a scene and then yawn for a few minutes. When you return to the lines after yawning, you will find that your voice is much richer and several octaves lower. Some of the preparations work better than others, particularly when they are intelligently chosen to fit the circumstances and the need.

SENSITIZING

Sensitizing is part of the relaxation cluster and is done with all five of the senses when you are relating to it as a basic instrumental involvement. However, as a craft technique the exercise is used more selectively—and only when you find it necessary. Let us suppose that you are involved in the process of exploring a sensory choice and you discover that your senses are sluggish and unresponsive. You could continue to plug along and hope that things will change, or appeal to your senses with more inspiring questions. But if none of this works, you could intersperse the sensitizing preparation while you are actually working for the choice in the midst of the scene. That might sound like an interruption in the flow of the reality, but, quite the contrary, it becomes *part* of the reality. Sensitizing while you are working operates in a similar way to just sensitizing as an instrumental preparation, except that you isolate the sense or senses that you are having difficulty with and concentrate all of your energy into that sense. Let us say that it is the auditory area with which you are having problems; listen with a very heightened concentration to the other actor's voice, and really hear every element, quality, pitch, and depth idiosyncrasy of the voice. "Live" in your ears for a time, and then reinvest in the sensory questions related to your original choice. Repeat the process as many times as necessary.

The process of on-the-spot sensitizing is essentially the same with all five senses, the emphasis of the exercise being intense concentration in the particular sense that you are sensitizing. If, for example, you are experiencing difficulty in a tactile area, you would center your entire concentration in the part of your body where you want to heighten the responses. If it is the hand, then your focus would shift into the part of your hand that you want to sensitize: you would "live" in that part of your hand until you could feel it tingle with responsiveness. Suppose that you are in the middle of a scene and you feel the need to sensitize. You continue working with your choice, saying your lines and including the sensitizing process as part of your entire involvement. You might acquire the habit of sensitizing as a preparation before you start a rehearsal or come on stage. If you are truly willing to be irreverent in your work, the process of preparation is a natural inclusion for your work and will add a great deal of color and dimension to it.

PERSONAL INVENTORY

The last part of the relaxation cluster is Personal Inventory. This preparation is done in order to discover what you are feeling and to get to a place where you can express those impulses on a moment-to-moment basis. It is a wonderful instrumental preparation and necessary for stimulating an organic state. When used as a craft preparation, it is done before the first line and during the scene, whenever you feel that you are losing the connection with the internal reality. Imagine that you have prepared yourself instrumentally and that you are ready to deal with the first responsibility to the scene. You have started to work for a choice, and you begin to sense a separation from what you feel. You begin the scene and become aware that the author's words are not connected to what you feel; instead, you are listening to the words and thinking about how the next line should sound. You continue to work for the choice, hoping that it will help you to become reinvolved with the reality, but instead you get farther away from it and continue to premeditate behavior. Using the Personal Inventory preparation at this point would almost surely restimulate your impulses.

You can do Personal Inventory by simply asking yourself, "How do I feel?" and responding to the question. If you are doing the preparation as an exercise, you would answer the question audibly. If, however, you are in the midst of a scene, you respond to the question either silently or through the behavior and words of the scene. The Personal Inventory process continues as an ongoing Inner Monologue as you are doing the scene, until you no longer need it.

THE SCENE:

HE: We have to sit down and discuss our settlement!

SHE: What's the hurry? There's plenty of time.

HE: I want to get it out of the way. I want to feel settled in my life.

Suppose you are doing his lines and you become really disconnected from the real life behind those words. You might then start the Personal Inventory process:

SHE: Do you want to talk about reconciliation?

HE: I don't think so, Helen; we tried for years to make it work . . . (Personal Inventory: *How do I feel?* . . . *I feel stiff* . . . *I feel uncomfortable . . . wooden . . .*)

As this is happening and you get more in touch with your authentic inner life, you encourage the expression of all those feelings through the lines and behavior of the play. At this juncture, most actors would want to immediately deny all of those uncomfortable feelings, thinking that they don't belong to the material and, furthermore, that it would be embarrassing to let anyone know they were this insecure and uncomfortable on the stage. Most actors, if indeed they are fortunate enough to be aware of their inner feelings, would at this point sweep them under the carpet and go on presenting the desired concept of the character's behavior.

The alternative—and the right decision—is to include as part of the scene all the impulses you become aware of. If you feel stiff and uncomfortable, even wooden, isn't it possible that the character could feel that way *exactly?* Even if he didn't, to deny your real impulses for your intellectual concept means that you short-circuit the flow of reality. This is a perfect example of how performance irreverence works. If you continue to do the Personal Inventory under the lines and include the responses to "How do I feel?" you establish your personal emotional point of view in relationship to the other actor-character, and pretty soon the excitement of ensemble becomes possible.

THE INVOLVEMENT GROUP

There are a large number of involvement disciplines and exercises. The area is enormous, for without being selflessly involved the actor cannot achieve the kind of relationship that is so important in stimulating reality in theater or film.

THRESHOLD OF INTEREST

Understanding this concept will save you a lot of time and energy when you are doing involvement techniques. It is always much easier and more fun to relate to things that interest you than it is to force some kind of involvement with something that doesn't mean anything to you. In preparation terms, you might start by looking for the things that particularly hold some interest for you. Sometimes it is just a part of a place or a part of an object that fascinates you. In that case, just relate to the part of the place or object that stimulates involvement.

Threshold of Interest is simply looking for the things that mean something to you. If you apply this theory to all of your work, it will lead you right into the heart of the object or choice.

AVAILABLE-STIMULUS SWEEP

This exercise can be done anywhere, and it is very simple. Start by looking around the room or the stage, and allow your eyes to "sweep" the entire place. Stop at the objects that appeal to your interest and explore them. If it is possible, go to the object and satisfy your curiosity by holding it or smelling it. Use as many of the other senses as possible in the circumstance. When you have explored the object to the point you want to, move on to the next one. Continue to investigate and explore the environment until you are totally involved and out of yourself. This technique works best when you *allow* interest and not when you obligate yourself to be interested. The beauty of it is that you can do it silently and call no attention to yourself while doing it. If you incorporate this into your everyday life, it will also raise the level of your awareness. You will see more in the world, and when you see more, you experience more.

Remember that involvement is the natural enemy of tension and self-consciousness, so if you practice involvement and use it to prepare, there will be *no* tension.

WONDER, PERCEIVE, AND OBSERVE

This is a wonderful way to get right into the other actor. Start your involvement process by gently easing into observing your scene partner. What is she doing, how is she dressed, what is she holding in her hand, and how does she seem to feel? The observation part of the exercise deals with everything that is obvious, things that are there to see if you look. You can go quite deeply into observing the other person. You can look for things in her that you have heretofore not been aware of—her features, the colors in her eyes and hair, the way she moves her head when she speaks, the color of her eye shadow, how her hair hides her ears, and so on.

To perceive is another kind of involvement. To do this you must look deeper, ask more questions, and challenge your powers of observation; it is a more complex form of involvement.

I'm looking into her eyes . . . I see how quickly she avoids eye contact with me . . . Her eyes are darting in all directions. I see fear there . . . and

*possibly a little sadness . . . She's smiling at me . . . but nervously . . . There
is a warmth there and almost a plea for cooperation . . . I perceive a childlike quality in the way she speaks . . . almost as if she asks for you to like
her . . . She holds a lot of tension in her shoulders, and it restricts her movement in the scene . . . I perceive that there is a lot of underlife going on and
very little of it gets out in her life and in her acting . . . It is really interesting the way she will avoid contact with another person, particularly when
she feels something that might be seen . . . The more I look into her eyes,
the more fear I see . . . There is a goodness there, too . . . It is interesting to
see how she will tighten her mouth just when it looks as though she is going
to express something important . . . She avoids close physical proximity.*

This process takes place as an Inner Monologue and is not usually
shared with the other actor, unless you are doing the exercise together. It
can continue throughout the entire scene.

To wonder is to encourage yourself to curiously explore anything you're
really curious about. You wonder in the same way you observe and perceive. If you are doing the exercise by yourself, then you do it silently; if
you are doing it with another actor, then you ask your questions out loud to
each other and respond to the questions if you want to.

*I wonder what she's thinking right now . . . I wonder if she knows what I
am doing . . . I wonder how old she is . . . Has she ever been married? . . . I
wonder if she finds me attractive . . . What does she do when she isn't
acting? . . . What kind of place does she live in? . . . I wonder if that is
really sadness I see . . . What does she want to express that she
doesn't? . . .*

While you are doing the exercise, go back and forth between the various
parts of it. You perceive, then you might wonder, and then observe for a
moment or two.

It is a very useful preparation, whether you do it by yourself, silently, or
with the other actor out loud. It takes you into each other and establishes
the foundation of a relationship. The advantage of doing it silently is that
you can perceive and wonder on a more private level, which sometimes
excites real curiosity.

SENSORY EXPLORATION

This is a very good involvement exercise because whenever you are
working sensorially, you must be involved in order to be successful. You
can begin your Sensory Exploration by asking sensory questions about the
other actor or any of the objects on the stage.

Let us say that you have three or four minutes before you are to start the
rehearsal and you want to heighten your level of involvement as a prelude
to exploring the first choice in the scene. It would be a very intelligent

decision to do some kind of sensory involvement that would be consistent with your first emotional obligation in the scene. The first emotional obligation might be that you feel concern and empathy for the other character. So you do a Sensory Exploration related to the actress with whom you are doing the play.

Example:

What do I see in her eyes? (This sensory question is responded to visually.) *What is it in her face and expression that tells me she's hurt and sad?* (Again you are appealing to your visual sense, so encourage your eyes to see and respond to all the facial elements that answer that sensory question.) *What is it in her body, the posture, that I see?* (Another physical question appealing to your visual sense.) *What does her voice sound like? What are the specific emotional elements that I hear?* (This is a sensory question aimed at your auditory sense, so that is the sense that you respond with.) *How does the voice sound different from what it is usually?* (Answer the question with your ears.) *What is it exactly that I hear that communicates the emotion?* (Be demanding in your response to that auditory question.)

By continuing to ask sensory questions related to the actress, you are getting increasingly involved with her and thereby becoming more ready to deal with the scene. You might ask thirty to forty sensory questions before starting to work for your first choice. The amount of questions and time that you spend doing a Sensory Exploration is totally dependent on how quickly you reach the desired level of involvement.

If, while you are doing the exercise, you encourage an emotional state of life that is not really there in the actress, then you would respond sensorially by endowing her with the qualities and emotional stimuli that you are attempting to create. That is to say, if she is not hurt or sad in reality, but it would serve your purpose to see her that way, then you would, through your sensory process, "endow" her with those elements.

SAYING A SENTENCE BACKWARD

This is a really easy involvement exercise and one that comes in handy when you are on the spot and are so tense that nothing else seems to work. You do this exercise by saying a sentence to yourself backward, verbatim. It should be a moderately lengthy sentence, since it is important for you to "reach" for the backward order. A sentence I have used for years, since I was a very young actor, is: "Yesterday at four o'clock I went to the zoo and stood in front of the leopard's cage."

That is a fairly simple sentence. Now say it backward: "Cage leopard's the of front in stood and zoo the to went I o'clock four at yesterday."

Thinking about the order of the words forces a kind of concentration that takes you away from your concern with self. This exercise works immediately and allows you to take the next involvement step. Make up your own sentences; have fun with it.

MAKING UP STORIES ABOUT PEOPLE AND OBJECTS

This is a good involvement preparation that deals with what exists in the environment. Look around the room or stage and pick out inanimate objects or people and create a story about them. The stories can take any form: they can be pure fantasy, they can be serious tales, or they can be very funny.

You might look at some innocuous prop made of an old dime-store pitcher and papier mâché and weave a tale of Russia: "It came from the house of the last Czar, Nicholas, and was smuggled out of Russia by one of the servants who worked in the palace and narrowly escaped the Bolsheviks. This servant, Andreiovich, worked his way across the world and finally ended up in New York, where he fell on very bad times and had to pawn this priceless heirloom. Fearing that the pawnshop owner might recognize the piece as a priceless historical find, Andreiovich disguised the piece beyond recognition, planning to redeem it at the first opportunity. He died before he could. A young actress, seeing the pitcher in the pawnshop window, thought it would make a nice vase for her New York walk-up and bought it for fifteen dollars. Later, after moving to Hollywood to pursue her career, and while in a play in Glendale, she loaned it to the theater for a production and never took it back. For the past ten years the piece has been kicking around from theater to theater and play to play. Now here it sits at the rehearsal of my play which opens next week."

It may take three or four minutes to make up such a story, but it does encourage a selfless involvement and is a good addition to the category of craft involvement exercises. An additional bonus of this particular technique is that it also stimulates the imagination. Don't limit yourself to inanimate objects; people can be a great deal of fun too.

There are other good involvement preparations, and I'm sure that as you work with the craft you will discover many for yourself. Remember that the purpose of craft involvement preparations is to involve you outside yourself. The selfless-involvement emphasis is dependent totally on appealing to your interest, so, when using any kind of selfless-involvement exercise, make sure that the thrust of the exercise is *outward*. All of the preparations in all the categories can be done either alone or with another actor. Some of them can be done by a whole group of actors. The decision on how to use each technique should be based on the requirements of each given theatrical circumstance.

EMOTIONAL PREPARATIONS

If you take it down to the bottom line, an actor sells emotions. If the actor, for whatever reasons, either is not in touch with his emotions or feels a block between himself and what is happening inside, then he needs a preparation to stimulate the free flow of his emotional impulses. The nature of the preparation is dependent on some variables: How numb is he? What are the instrumental conditions—meaning does the actor have difficulty in this particular area of his own life? What are the obligation factors? What are the specifics of this particular circumstance? Once he understands where he is, then he can pick the right emotional preparation. Personal Inventory is a good way to find out what is happening and how to antidote it.

VULNERABILITY WORKOUT

This technique, however you approach it, is designed to raise the level of your vulnerability. Being vulnerable or accessible is the foundation to establishing a creative flow. There are a number of ways to heighten your vulnerability.

TALKING TO PEOPLE ABOUT MEANINGFUL THINGS

If you decide to do this as a preparation, you simply choose to "selectively emphasize" all the meaningful things in your life, and, in a conversational framework, you choose to talk about them. You can really discuss things with whoever is around—the other actor in rehearsal, someone you know backstage—or you might do it as a "self-monologue" relating to yourself. You can also do this exercise while you are in the midst of a scene. At that time it would be approached as an Inner Monologue which you would carry on between the lines of the scene. Wherever you elect to use it, you will find that it does stimulate a change in your emotional point of view, and, depending on the content, it will affect your level of vulnerability.

COFFIN MONOLOGUES

As the title might indicate, this exercise is done by imagining that you are talking to someone who has died. You are with the person at the funeral parlor or at the cemetery talking to the dead body lying in a coffin. The person whom you imagine does not have to really be dead. You encourage yourself to talk about things that you know will affect you, things that you may never have had the opportunity to express while the person was alive. By dealing with a meaningful person and talking about very meaningful things, you can pretty well depend on becoming vulnerable.

A Coffin Monologue can be done out loud or silently. It can be used just before you begin a rehearsal or a performance or anytime you might want to elevate your vulnerability.

Example:

(You can do this either sitting or standing.) *I never told you how much I loved you . . . You were never around . . . and I used to feel that you didn't care . . . until you would do something warm and loving for me . . . like that time I wanted a new bike like all the other kids had and you said we couldn't afford it . . . but when I woke up the next morning it was standing shiny and new at the foot of my bed . . . Oh, Dad, I wish we could have spent more time together to just hang out and laugh with each other . . . I remember how you would hold me when I was little, and I used to wish you would have done that when I was grown-up.*

Allow yourself to feel and express everything that the monologue stimulates.

SHARING AND DOUBLE EXPOSURE

This is one of the preparations that you do with another person, and it lends itself quite well to a pre-rehearsal or pre-performance situation. If you have the cooperation of the other actors in the play or film, then you will have no trouble doing craft preparations of this kind. You don't need a special place or setup to do the exercise; you can do it in the dressing room or in the coffee shop down the street. Talk to each other, preferably one at a time, and share the most meaningful things in your life. The person listening should try to draw the other one out, asking pertinent questions and, hopefully, being concerned enough to really care. When the first person to share is finished, the other one begins the Sharing-and-Double-Exposure process. This should all be done in the simple framework of conversation and should not take on the obvious structure of an exercise. What you talk about is up to your discretion. It should be very meaningful but not necessarily private. Your right to privacy should never be violated. As you do the exercise, you will notice that you are much more involved and related to each other than when you started it. You will also be aware of how much more emotional you have become and how much closer you are to each other.

EMOTIONALLY MEANINGFUL IMAGINARY MONOLOGUES

Imaginary Monologues is one of the twenty-two choice approaches and, in terms of approach process, will be discussed and explored in great detail in a later chapter. But for now, please understand that an Imaginary Monologue is a very simple technique wherein you talk to a person who is not really present at the time. You talk to the person as if he were there saying things to you that are affecting and meaningful and would serve the desired response of the material. It is similar to the Coffin Monologue, only the person you are talking to isn't in a coffin and isn't dead. You put the person anywhere in the room and *imagine* his presence. It is not necessary when dealing with an Imaginary Monologue to create the person so that he really exists for you. You intelligently choose to creatively manipulate the monologue so as to stimulate strong emotional responses.

This exercise is unlike a Coffin Monologue in that you allow for the imagined responses of the person you are talking to. Place the person somewhere in the room—in a chair facing you or standing against the doorjamb.

Example:

Why is it that I can't get anything I need from you? . . . You say you love me, but you never touch me! I love you. I tell you that all the time. When I come near you, you seem to want to move away. If you don't really love me, then tell me so. I think that would be easier to deal with! Please don't say anything; just listen to me . . . You're smiling—what does that mean? You think I'm making trouble again, right? . . . Why don't you ever tell me that you love me?

This monologue can go for any length of time, depending on when it does what it is supposed to do.

When you choose to do an Emotionally Meaningful Imaginary Monologue, it should be to a real person who exists in your life, and you should talk to the person about real things. You might want to selectively emphasize one element in the relationship, but it should be a reality.

Again, you can do this in almost any setting—as an out-loud workout, as an Inner Monologue, or as an exercise done with the other actor. When you do it with the other actor, you must talk to him as if he were the meaningful person in your life and, just as a courtesy to him, tell him what you are doing and why.

SENSE MEMORY WITH
EMOTIONALLY IMPACTING OBJECTS

There is a wide variety of preparations in each category because certain preparations work better in certain situations. When you are dealing with a piece of material, selection of choice and approach is extremely important. Choosing the proper preparation is equally important, since it sets up the entire system of work.

The theatrical use of Sense Memory has a very large advantage for the actor. It can be done silently, it does not interfere with anything you are doing or saying, and it does not call attention to itself. Therefore, it makes a good approach to the creative process. When using it as a way to elevate your emotional state, you do it in the same manner as if you were using it as a choice approach in a scene. (Choice approaches are defined and explored in the next chapter.)

Emotional preparations can be done anytime or anywhere. Picking the right time depends on what level of emotional life you want to attain and how long you want to maintain the emotional pitch stimulated by the preparation.

The meaningful or impacting object that you choose to create can be anything: an important person, your dog, a place, a photograph, an old love letter, a telephone call, a sound, a meaningful piece of music—in fact anything that you can work for and create sensorially.

Example:

If I were using this to stimulate a heightened emotional state, I would work sensorially to create my father, whom I loved dearly. He died in 1969, and every time I think of him I become vulnerable just from remembering.

I would start the preparation by deciding where in the room I would place him, then I would start the sensory process:

How far away is he sitting? (Respond visually—only with what you see.) *How much of the chair does his body occupy?* (Let your eyes tell you.) *How wide are his shoulders?* (They are as wide as you see.) *What is the shape of his body? What is the physical attitude of his body as he sits there? How is his weight distributed?*

Up to this point, you might just be asking visual sensory questions. As a good practice for starting any Sense Memory involvement, ask spatial questions in order to establish where your object is in space: if the object is placed in a particular place, and you establish that at the beginning, it will stay there.

What is the shape of his face? (You are still responding visually. You attempt to see the object.) *What is the texture of his skin? Where does his hairline begin? What is the color of his hair? its texture? How would it feel if I touched it?* (This is a question aimed at your tactile sense, and that is where you would respond, in the hand.)

At the point where you bring in this sense, you might go over to the object and touch his hair:

As I touch his hair, what do I feel in my fingers? (Tactile response.) *As I look down at him, what do I see? What is the texture of his skin on his bald head? the temperature of his skin? How does he smell?* (This is a new sense, the olfactory. You respond by attempting to smell.) *What is it about his odor that tells me it is my father?* (Again the olfactory sense tries to remember.) *What color are his eyes? What is the shape of his eyes? How far apart are they? How many colors do I see? Is there a difference between his eyes?*

My father had a cataract in his right eye. That last question was asked to establish a visual response to the difference and to "see" the cataract.

I would go on with the process of creating my father in the chair. I might ask as many as three hundred sensory questions, using all five of my senses, before he became a reality that existed in the room with me. At any point in the sensory exploration, I might begin to respond emotionally. I continue the process and encourage myself to express what I feel.

Using Sense Memory in relation to meaningful objects is a very good way to prepare while waiting to work. There are endless hours of waiting when you do films, and, as a result, you "ebb and flow" emotionally. There are a great number of objects in everyone's life that are meaningful and impacting, so you never run out of possibilities.

MUSIC

There is an old saying, "Music has charms to soothe a savage breast," which makes quite a statement related to the impact of music and how it might be utilized in an acting framework. When you stop and think of all the different pieces and kinds of music that have been important in your life, the number would probably be staggering: music related to movies you loved; songs that were popular when you started going to high-school dances; your first love song and how you shared it; pieces you were forced to plunk out in your early piano lessons; the Top Ten; etc. You could go on forever thinking of how music has affected your life. As a craft preparation, music can be used in a variety of ways. Once you decide on what kind of emotional life you would like to stimulate, you pick the piece of music that you think would produce that kind of response. If it is at all possible to actually play it, then listen to a cassette or a record in the dressing room.

You might prepare before each performance in this manner. If that is not possible or you need the preparation after you are on stage, you could work for the piece sensorially. Remember, Sense Memory results in *really hearing* the piece.

As an actor, I have many times called upon music to prepare or to fulfill the obligation in a scene. You must be in touch with the specific areas of music that you are sensitive to and how they make you feel. It would be advisable to become increasingly aware of music in your life and to take inventories about music in your past. Every time you notice a response to something you hear, ask yourself what you feel and see if you can relate it to an event in your life, past or present. If you "catalogue" your music, it will make it much easier to pluck out the right piece when you need it.

Another way to use music is to hum to yourself. Incidentally, this is not cheating. Many of my students think that if something is too easy it is cheating and not doing the craft. Nonsense! If it works to stimulate an organic response and is not intrusive to the play, *use it!* Music is a very rich choice area and one that should be explored by every actor. Play with it; make it an enjoyable experience; listen to a wide variety of music, and be aware of the impact of each experience.

OTHER MEANINGFUL SOUNDS

Like music, there are an endless number of sounds that stimulate emotional responses—sounds that we have learned to take for granted. Unfortunately, most of us have learned to tune sounds out. In a high-tech society, it would be impossible to function, or even survive, if we allowed every sound to affect us. Imagine living in New York City and allowing yourself to respond to all the offensive street noises. Three blocks and you would have to be hospitalized. So how do you relate to sounds and, at the same time, protect yourself from injury? The first step in the process is to acknowledge the importance of sounds in your acting technique. Then you must start the inventory process of listening and responding to the various sounds that you encounter each day. If a sound is offensive, acknowledge your response before you shut it off. Know that it bothers you and file it for future use. Listen with a new ear to everything that hits your ears, and allow for the emotional response, no matter how subtle it may be. Go back in time and try to remember things that have strongly affected you. How many of these things were specifically sounds?

Here are some examples:

the sound of rain starting to hit the roof

your mother singing in the other room

a scream from somewhere out in the streets

the wind whipping through the trees

a baby crying in another apartment

a voice on the telephone

a dog barking in the distance

a train whistle far away in the night

laughter

the teakettle whistling in the kitchen

the sound of conflict and arguing

chalk screeching across a blackboard

blasting automobile horns

crickets on a summer night

the sound of burning wood popping in a fireplace

thunder

waves hitting the beach

birds singing in the morning

the school bell

the hum of a jet engine in the distance

the chattering of voices in an auditorium

the applause of an audience

When using a sound as a craft preparation to promote an emotional state, you can approach it by re-creating the sound sensorially or by exploring its availability at the moment. Often the very sound you need to use is there somewhere in the environment with you. In that case, selectively emphasize it, and allow it to affect you. If it is a very special sound from way back in childhood that is clouded by time, re-create it by asking sensory questions and encouraging your auditory sense to respond. You can support the auditory recall by using other senses to re-create the place where the sound existed.

As an emotional preparation, sounds are related to events and experiences that had impact on your life. Using a particular sound or combination of sounds to create an emotional foundation for the scene is often necessary to the success of your choice in that scene.

Let us say, for example, that you are in a play, doing the part of a returning war veteran (any war, pick one). The first scene in the play centers around you in the living room of the house in which you grew up. The action of the scene is to take place in the room with all the familiar objects from a time past. You are to pick up things and to nostalgically remember a better time in life and to experience a sadness from the loss of youth and innocence. Those are the emotional elements in the scene. In the rehearsal process you have experimented with a variety of choices and settled on a couple of really impelling ones. The play opens with you on stage as the lights come up. As a craft preparation, you might prime your instrument by working for a piece of music that makes you feel nostalgic and reminiscent of times past; or you could create a variety of sounds from a similar period in your life: sounds like the neighbor's dog barking and your sister talking on the telephone to her friends, the sound that the big clock in the hallway made as it chimed the hour, or your father's laughter as he sat watching television. You could do these preparations in the dressing room before the five-minute call, or you could create them as you stand alone on stage just before the curtain rises. The extreme value of such craft preparations is that they make it much easier to be transported by the choice you use. If you are in the right state of emotional preparedness, the time it takes for your choice to work is a fraction of the time it would take without the preparation.

PASSIONS WORKOUT

In an instrumental framework, the Passions Workout is designed to get the adrenaline going, to excite and elevate your energy level. By switching emphasis in almost all the preparation areas, you can use the same technique with a few adjustments to accomplish a different goal.

If you feel that your emotional state is below the level of the obligations of the material, that the character feels things more deeply and passionately than you do at this particular moment, then you might elect to do a Passions Workout as a craft preparation in an emotional area.

Start by relating to the things in this world that you feel passion for: the people, the ideas, the principles you hold dear in your life. If it is possible in your surroundings, approach the exercise as a large commitment; express your impulses both vocally and physically.

Example:

"I love to feel good! I love to be on the stage with that incredible wall of light in front of me, knowing that there are hundreds of people out there... I love my wife... I love the way she looks and feels... I love to be surrounded by beauty... to eat the best foods... to be pampered and waited on... I love to laugh... to ride my motorcycle really fast with the wind blowing in my face and the total freedom as if I could fly!"

As you do this, feel free to jump around the room or the stage. Be as loud as the environment permits.

If you succeed with this preparation, you will feel much more energy throughout your body, and you will be much more accessible and expressive. Even if the character you are doing isn't passionate, the Passions Workout gets you prepared for the next step by making you much more emotionally available.

The entire area of emotional preparations is specifically used to affect the actor's emotional state, to elevate emotional accessibility, to change the emotional state from one place of emotional being to another, to seduce the instrument into emotional surrender, and, generally, to manipulate the actor into the area of emotional reality that the material demands.

JOY AND EUPHORIA

This is an exaggerated state, one of large experience and flamboyant expression. The purpose of the technique is to stretch the instrument to expressive extreme. It is a very good instrumental preparation and a superb craft technique. By committing to the exercise in the extreme, you create a state of internal excitement and external expression that produces a very compelling visual experience. It makes you feel very good, to say the least. If the exercise works the way it usually does, you feel that anything is possible and that no task is too difficult. *Acting should be fun,* and this is a fun exercise. It is a very simple exercise to do. It should have a very large beginning and a big voice supported by very flamboyant gestures.

Example:

"I feel fantastic! Oh, yeah! I feel the earth's energy climbing up my body from the soles of my feet to the top of my head! I feel like King Kong!" (Opening your body to its most expanded place.) "I feel magnificent! Oh, yeah! I can do anything!" Leave the ground as much as you can, and encourage yourself to stretch your entire body upward.

You can do this exercise for as long as it feels good and then go to your next involvement. It is an excellent emotional preparation, since it makes you feel as if you could experience almost any emotion freely.

When working with emotional preparations, remember to pick and use the specific technique you need on an as-needed basis. Each of the techniques has its own unique result and will work wonders for you if used intelligently.

EGO PREPARATIONS

Probably the most important ingredient of an artist is a healthy ego. The ego governs the outcome of the creative process. If you feel good about yourself and that you deserve to succeed, then you usually will. If there is doubt, then you find an incredible number of ways to sabotage yourself.

In my other books, I have already explored the instrumental ramifications of ego preparations and how necessary it is to "get ready to get ready." In this book, and specifically in this chapter on the craft preparations, I want to emphasize the use of the following techniques for theatrical purposes.

If an actor comes to the theater or to the film world with a heavily damaged or abused ego, then it might be necessary for him to get into some form of psychotherapy, while at the same time studying acting. That, of course, depends on the severity of the blocks and problems.

A very good gauge of what kind of craft preparation is in order is to ask yourself about the character in the piece. What is he or she experiencing or feeling? What is the ego state? How does the character feel about himself/herself generally? in the world? in this scene? Once you determine that, ask yourself where *you* are at this moment in life. What are the parallels between you and the character? What are the differences? After you clearly establish that, you can pick the right preparation, if indeed a preparation is needed at all in this case.

Let us suppose that you are in pretty good shape, generally, and that you are even fairly optimistic at the moment. You feel that you can allow yourself to act without much terror. However, the character in the piece is a superachiever in the world of business, has an ego larger than Yosemite, and feels he could do anything. There is quite a separation between the two of you. While you are feeling pretty good about yourself, you certainly don't share the character's worldly confidence. So what do you do in order to establish a place from which to begin?

It is a good idea with almost any choice or approach to try to "sneak up" on what you want to feel, a step at a time. Often, if you go for it, the stress and stretch are so great that an otherwise good choice just snaps and fails to work because of the size of the obligation placed on it. It is always a good idea to identify the parallel of the ego state between you and the character. If you start there and deal with any separation, then you will find it much easier to do what is next necessary.

SUPERMAN

This is also a large-commitment type of technique. Jump in, and, with great vocal and physical commitment, say, "I am Superman! I can do anything! I can fly! I can leap tall buildings! I'm faster than a speeding bullet!" etc. As you do the exercise, using the lines of the comic strip, slowly inject the super things about yourself: "I am superintelligent. I'm a good friend and can do anything I decide I want to do. I came to California to act, and I am doing just that. I support myself, and I feel super about that. I have always done what I set out to do! I am a Superman!" You can go with it for many minutes or however long it feels right to you. At the conclusion of the exercise you should be in a very different ego state and, hopefully, closer to the obligated state of the character in the play.

There are variations on the Superman exercise, so feel free to experiment with it. The Superman approach is designed to meet the challenge of large ego obligations, but of course there are subtler ego states. If you use a Superman preparation in those other instances, you might end up with overkill.

COUNTING YOUR BLESSINGS

This technique can be used anywhere and at any time. It can be done audibly or in silence. You can do it while on stage as an Inner Monologue or in your dressing room before a performance. As the title of the exercise indicates, you "count your blessings"—that is, list all the good things in your life and about you.

Example:

"I am healthy. . . I care about people and the world . . . I am a good person . . . I'm talented and growing . . . There are a lot of people on this planet who love me . . . I'm intelligent . . . For the time I have been around, I have accomplished a lot . . . I graduated from college . . . supported myself . . . started a career that is building . . . created two children who are healthy and happy. . . I'm in a film at the moment . . . I like my work, and so do other people I respect . . . I'm honest . . . "

The exercise can continue until you reach a desired state, and each time you do it, you can add new "blessings." You may decide to use the exercise to stimulate a sense of well-being or a feeling of accomplishment. A lot depends on the content. If you selectively emphasize certain areas of blessings, the results of the technique will have those emotional colors.

SENSORY SELF-ENDOWMENTS

This involvement depends on the actor's ability to do Sense Memory, since it is approached exclusively through the use of Sense Memory.

You have undoubtedly heard people say that they wish they had been born with a better this or nicer that: "I wish my nose were a little smaller or had a better shape," "If only my hips were smaller," "I wish I had bigger breasts," "What I wouldn't give for a full head of hair," and so on. I'm sure you have had such complaints about something. So, for the purpose of affecting the ego state, you *can* change whatever you wish.

Through Sensory Self-Endowments you can work to change or create the desired feature. You do this not only to feel better about yourself, but to establish a foundation of how the *character* feels about himself. If you personally carry a dissatisfaction around and the character has quite a different opinion about himself, then the dichotomy will interfere with the fulfillment of the piece.

The Endowment process starts the same way any Sense Memory exercise does, by asking the first question. Let us suppose that you are a very attractive woman who has always wanted rich, full, and long hair but was not blessed with it. So let's begin the process of "building" that beautiful hair.

Example:

Where on my head do I feel a change in weight? (Respond sensorially by creating the weight in specific areas.) *How is the weight different on the back of my head from what it is on the front?* (Respond sensorially to the question; attempt to feel the extra weight of long hair down your back.) *What do I feel around the sides of my face?* (Answer that sensorially.) *Around my ears?* (Relate to the different weight and mass.) *Do things sound different?* (That is an auditory question, answered by the same sense.) *As I touch my head with my right hand, what do I feel?* (Respond with the surface of the right hand.) *What is the texture I experience?* (Respond to the mass and weight and thickness.) *As I run my hand along the hair down the side of my body, where does it end?* (Allow your hand to go down the body, all the while creating sensorially the response to the hair.) *As I move my head from side to side slowly, where do I feel the movement of the hair?* (Answer that question sensorially in all the places where you create responses.) *How does the weight all around my head affect the way I move?* (A Sensory Exploration is in order here: move your head slowly from side to side, and deal creatively with the changes.) *When I put both hands on my head, how much larger does my head feel?* (Again with both hands, trace the difference in the size and shape of your head.) *As I lower my hands along the surface of the hair, how does it feel slipping through and along my fingers?* (Respond to the question in the various parts of each hand and finger.) *When I hold the hair to my cheeks, what does it feel like? its texture? temperature? on each side of my face?* (Take time to respond to all parts of that sensory question.) *What does it smell like? How many different odors are there? Where in my nose do I smell it?* (Respond to all of the olfactory questions in that sensory area.) *When I put a piece of hair into my mouth, what does it feel like on my lips? What does it taste like? How many tastes do I experience?* (Another sensory area. Respond with the gustatory sense.)

As is true with any Sense Memory involvement, you employ as many of the five senses as possible in the exploration.

You naturally would go on with the process of Sensory Exploration until you really had the sense of long, thick, and luxurious hair. The amount of time it would take to accomplish this is dependent on a variety of things: your expertise with Sense Memory, the nature of the questions, your sensory availability at the start of the exercise, and so on.

The above example of Sensory Self-Endowment might produce some very interesting theatrical results. If your purpose was to elevate your ego to the state of the character, you probably would accomplish that. If the character was a bit more vain or self-involved than you tend to be, then the process you just experienced would probably supply that preoccupation.

Sensory Self-Endowments can be used to add or eliminate almost anything about the body. When using the technique as a craft preparation, you would obviously "endow" yourself with enhancements that made you look better and more attractive. However, as a choice approach, Self-Endowments could relate to negative things like overweight, having larger features than you actually have, and so on. Used properly, Sensory Self-Endowments has limitless possibilities.

ACCEPTING THE ACADEMY AWARD

Every actor I know has secretly, and in fantasy, rehearsed an acceptance speech at the Academy Awards presentations. It is almost as widespread a fantasy as the proverbial "actor's nightmare" in which the actor forgets his lines upon entering the stage or, in fact, forgets what the play is.

This fantasy stimulates a feeling of euphoria and excitement. It creates a high that is indescribable. I started using the exercise in class to affect the ego in a positive way and later used it while directing actors in scenes and plays. What it does is remarkable! Immediately after using the technique, actors seem to take on a stature that affects every part of their being. It virtually transforms the voice, the body, and the essence of the person. If this technique is used at the right time and in the right circumstance, it can take the actor into an ego dimension that could fulfill the character elements and the emotional obligation of a piece of material.

The exercise is done simply by delivering your acceptance of the Academy Award statuette, thanking those people who you feel deserve appreciation. Talk a little about how long you have worked for this and how happy and grateful you are to be honored in this way. The speech has to be your own, and what it contains must, of course, be very meaningful and personal. The exercise can be done in any place, either as an Inner Monologue or out loud.

FANTASIES AND SELF-AGGRANDIZEMENTS

You can approach this preparation in a variety of ways: as an Inner or Outer Monologue, as a sharing technique with the other actor, or, if time and environment allow, you can "walk yourself through it." As is true with all the techniques in this section, Fantasies are used to make you feel better about yourself.

The best way to start a Fantasy is to sneak into it. Children have fantasies all the time, and they hardly ever make the decision to start having one. The kind of "fantasy trip" that you take depends on what turns you on in the ego area. The Academy Award exercise has a categorical appeal; however, what works best is always personal.

You might imagine or selectively emphasize that people around you are looking at you with great admiration and approval or that the opposite sex is strongly attracted to you. The Fantasy can take place as a running Inner Monologue while you are doing other things.

Suppose you are in the waiting room at the studio before an audition and there are several people with you in that room. You could approach the Fantasy through an Inner Monologue:

Everybody in this room is aware of my presence. I can tell by the way they look at me and sneak glances in my direction. The secretary was quite taken with me when I walked in; I could feel that from her. In fact, she seems to be having trouble concentrating on her work because of her interest in me! . . . I know that when I get into the interview, they will have either seen my work or heard of me favorably. I have always been respected as an actor and every time I read for a part I can see how impressed they are.

The Inner Monologue may continue for as long as needed, or it may take other directions. You might fantasize that you have already done the part you are waiting to read for and, in fact, are reading incredible reviews of your work. You can take your Fantasies into superstardom if you like. You might fantasize giving interviews to the press, being on the most prestigious talk shows, lecturing to young actors at your old alma mater, signing autographs, and so on.

The Inner Monologue is particularly valuable when you want to do the preparation undetected. If you are alone, however, or with other actors who know and understand what you are doing, you might want to "give the interview" out loud, allowing yourself to get caught up in the preparation as in improvisation.

I personally have had hour-long improvisations with *myself,* improvising a situation that I put myself into, usually for the sheer pleasure of having a Fantasy. I do this on airplanes quite a bit, since I spend many hours flying around the country. It helps to pass the time and is really very enjoyable.

I usually start such a Fantasy by imagining that I am flying to a film location. I create the film sketch in the story and a tour-de-force role for myself. I begin having semiaudible conversations with the director, who is usually someone like Elia Kazan, and we collaborate in this fantastic creative involvement. I am then sitting in the theater at the preview, and, of course, everyone is shattered by the brilliance of my work. I very graciously accept their compliments and go on to the next project, which is usually greater than the last. When I finish one of those airplane Fantasies, I feel great, and that nice sense of myself maintains itself for several hours after. Whether you do the Fantasy work as a preparation for acting and using craft or for the pleasure of it, the process is the same. One of the advantages of doing it anywhere and for fun is that it becomes really easy to do and to look forward to doing.

Another approach to the Fantasy area of preparations is to do an improvisation with the other actor before you rehearse the scene. You can either decide on the circumstance or just start to relate, both of you taking a self-aggrandizing position and role. This kind of improvisation can elevate the ego states of both of you as well as create a sense of reality and fun as a start to the rehearsal. When I was directing *The Glass Menagerie* a couple of years ago, I would have the actors improvise the "unwritten scenes" of the play—the evenings when they would all be at home together doing their different things: Tom would be writing his poetry, Amanda making her calls to sell subscriptions, Laura playing and fantasizing about her glass animals—talking about things not written in the play itself. We spent quite a lot of time doing improvisations like that with excellent results. While they were not specifically ego exercises, they were Fantasies about themselves, their relationships, and what they wanted in life. The improvisations stimulated a sense of reality and ensemble and dimensionalized the written material.

PROGRESS REPORTS

Almost the antithesis of Fantasy, Progress Reports are based totally on reality. This is an organic technique which emphasizes your progress and growth. You may do this preparation out loud, silently, or to a group of people, whichever promotes your purpose best.

Settle on a time frame—the last three years, the last six months, or whatever—and talk about your growth.

Example:

"The major change in my life is consciousness. I am much more conscious and aware. I earned it. I worked very hard on myself in this last year. I am no longer so self-critical. I acknowledge my problems but don't beat myself anymore for having them. My relationships have improved across the board, I'm much less self-involved, and my work as an actor shows that. My discipline has improved. I can set goals for myself and work toward them . . . " and so on.

Make very sure that you don't embellish reality, since it is very important to believe in your progress. The Progress Reports can cover any area of living, from your personal relationships to your work, to having fun, or even to your hobbies. You can make lists and add new things to them every day. The value of this preparational technique is that it helps put your ego into proper perspective and serves as a very good craft preparation if you happen to have the tendency to be hard on yourself.

THE MAGIC-POCKET EXERCISE

Also of a fantasy nature, this exercise is a great deal of fun to do. It stretches the imagination while it builds the ego. Imagine you can have anything in your pocket that could actually fit there: a contract to do three pictures a year for the largest studio in Hollywood, signed by the head of the studio; a cashier's check for ten million dollars drawn on the Chase Manhattan Bank and made out to you; the keys to a brand-new Ferrari which is sitting out in front of your house; a letter informing you that you have been chosen for an award you have always wanted; the key to a safe-deposit box containing anything that you can imagine; pieces of King Tut's treasure; and so on.

The preparation can be accomplished by the use of pure imagination, or you can work with the Sense Memory process to establish a greater sense of tangible reality. The choice depends on your willingness to believe that the object really exists in your pocket.

As an ego craft preparation, the technique stimulates an elation and a sense of specialness that allows you to bridge that life into the choice necessary for fulfilling the scene. The Magic Pocket exercise can be done before or during the performance.

Remember that any of the craft preparations is chosen on an as-needed basis. In any area of preparations there are a variety of techniques that fit into that category. There are a number of alternative choices because one preparation will take you where you want to go when another in the very same category will not work for you. Picking the right one is dependent on knowing yourself and experimenting with various techniques.

TWO-PERSON VALIDATIONS

This is a very good preparation in any category. Before starting to rehearse the play, or before a performance, two actors can sit down together and do this exercise. It is based on truth and can be selectively emphasized, which simply means to isolate and relate only to the good things about each other.

Do the exercise conversationally, and don't structure it in such a way as to make it feel unnatural. It can even be done while the two of you are putting on makeup or getting dressed.

The purpose, of course, is to feel good about yourself and each other, and all the better if it deals with the material obligation.

Example:

HE: I think you're beautiful—and you're doing really fine work in this play.

SHE: I get an awful lot from you. You've helped me enormously.

HE: You know, just your presence makes me feel good. That may sound a little mushy, but it's true. When you walk into the theater, I notice the change in the way I feel.

SHE: Thank you. That makes me feel really good.

HE: I like the way you relate to the other actors too.

SHE: You give a lot to everyone, not just on the stage but all the time. I'm going to miss you when the play ends.

HE: Me too...

It is very important that everything be authentic; don't exaggerate, and don't make things up in relation to each other.

Do the exercise as long as you want to and anytime you think you need it.

Since the thrust of this approach is essentially positive, be careful not to qualify or infuse any negative elements—like, "I didn't like you at first, but I do now," or "You are much nicer than I thought you were."

This craft preparation can be used in between takes or before you make your entrance on stage.

THE LARGE EXPURGATIVES

This group has been largely regarded and used as an instrumental preparation to expurgate tension. The various exercises are large and somewhat violent in movement and are used when most other tension relievers do not work. I call them the "Jackhammer Group," since they work like pushing your way through tension as solid as cement. With a slight adjustment of emphasis and content, this cluster of techniques can also be employed as craft preparations.

Each of the exercises starts very arbitrarily. You must jump in and start the exercise, hoping it will accomplish what you desire.

THE TERRIFIC TRIO

These are three exercises in a cluster of expurgatives, done very energetically. The first is:

ABANDONMENT

When doing this as an instrumental exercise, you lie down on the floor and proceed to have an all-out tantrum, moving your body with abandonment in all directions and with no physical interference or leadership. At the same time, you scream and make huge uninterrupted vocal expurgations, so that the whole thing might look like someone who has gone stark raving mad. The exercise is done for however long it takes to purge the tension or, in the case of a craft preparation, until you have stimulated the proper or desired emotional state. If the exercise is used as a craft technique, it must have a specific goal: what emotional state you want to stimulate and what the content of the Abandonment must be. Let us say, for example, that you are playing a very volatile and irrational character prone to outbursts of irrational behavior and that, in order to use a choice that might stimulate that kind of life, you need a craft preparation that builds a foundation for such a choice. In that case, an Abandonment preparation accompanied by irrational thoughts and expressions might set you up for the right choice. The exercise can be done in a standing position and, as a craft involvement, may include words and other expressions. It creates a very high-energy vibration in the actor and is a very good preparation for stimulating any large emotion.

VESUVIUS

This is a very large verbal eruptive expurgation of feelings—frustrations, anger, rage, dissatisfactions, euphoria, and other big emotions. Craftually, you start yelling about things that are disturbing you at the moment, dumping your frustrations and dissatisfactions and allowing the purge to go anywhere it wants to. As you feel the flow become easier, you might inject, through "creative manipulation," thoughts and feelings designed specifically to stimulate a desired emotional state.

Example:

(With large vocal volume.) "I'm tired of not doing what I want to do with my life. I want to work at acting . . . I'm frustrated with not having the things I want in my life. . . I want to be comfortable. . . I am angry about what people think! I don't care about that . . . I want to have more fun. I don't like being broke all the time! . . . I hate obligations. I don't want to have to do anything or be anywhere on time. I'm sick of all of it." At this point you could begin to interject a specific kind of expurgation aimed at producing a specific emotional response. "I'm really sick and tired of people who complain and whine as I'm doing right now. I hate people who think that the world owes them something, and I hate to have to work hard so that other people who don't want to work can live on welfare. I'm exhausted by dependency, and I don't like people who expect anything from me. . . " and so on in this vein.

Now, the reason for this kind of creative leadership in this case might be to create a threshold of resentment for the other characters in the play. What started as an expurgation of your here-and-now realities turns into a vocal and verbal tirade against a type or group of people who affect you in a certain way. The content of any Vesuvius depends totally on the emotional obligation you set for yourself.

Naturally, any of the large-expurgative-type preparations is structured to produce large expressive emotions, and if you want to reach subtler levels, the expurgatives are not the right choice. Vesuvius is a very good preparation for stimulating a "hot blood" state and encouraging that kind of expression.

EXORCISM

This one is also done with great volume and with large physical commitment. With large and violent pushing movements, you thrust the unwanted people and other things out of your life and environment. You start the exercise by thrusting your open palms forward and screaming, "Get out! Get out of my life! Get out of my way! Get out of my sight! . . . " As you continue the approach, you can specify exactly what it is that you are exorcising: "Get away from me! I hate your criticism! . . . Get out of my house! I hate stupidity! Get away, stupid people! Go, get away! . . . You have spent your whole life putting me down! Get out; get away from me!" As you express these things, you continue to thrust violently forward with your arms.

There doesn't seem to be a great deal of difference between the Vesuvius and the Exorcism in regard to the kind of emotional life that each of them yields. However, if one emotion is predominantly verbal while the other has more physical characteristics, then there can be quite a difference in the essence of the two exercises. As you will find out when doing the work, experimentation will determine your choice in every area. The Exorcism preparation will get the adrenaline going and stimulate aggressive impulses. If that is the kind of preparational state you are after, you will find the third part of the Terrific Trio the right one to use.

CONFRONT AND ENCOUNTER

This is another in the category of large expurgatives that is a bigger-than-life type of commitment. It can be done with people who are present or with an Imaginary Monologue approach. Usually the people around you do not stimulate the need to confront them aggressively, and, if the occasion should arise, you certainly cannot depend on its happening just at the time when you would be preparing to start a rehearsal or a performance. Therefore, using "imaginary people" (real people in the world who are not present at the moment) would be much more expedient most of the time.

To do this preparation you must pick the people in your life, past or present, whom you could justifiably confront, people with whom you have unfinished business or toward whom you have strong impulses. The exercise can take the form of an indictment, or it can be quite conversational, depending on the content of the Imaginary Monologue and how you feel about the person you are talking to.

Example:

Why is it that you never told me that you loved me? . . . You never hugged me or even touched me affectionately. I loved you a lot, but it was hard to get close to you . . . I know you loved me, or at least I think you did, but you never expressed it . . . When you were dying and I came to the hospital, I held your hand, and you began to cry. That was the first time I ever felt love from you. But why, oh God, Daddy, why did you wait so long to let me see it? . . .

The entire monologue can become a two-person version of the exercise. It can deal with a real issue between you and the other actor, or you can relate to each other as other people in your life. If you choose to confront each other over something real, agree to do the exercise for the right reasons. Don't irresponsibly use the play as an excuse to dump some incubated bile on the other person.

If, indeed, it is done as a two-person preparation, then decide what it is you want to accomplish with the approach and what is the specific issue that you will explore. If you want to create conflict between you and the other actor, confrontation is a very good way to establish this. If you use each other to really confront other people in your life, you can bounce off each other's responses. In either case, Confront and Encounter is an excellent preparation.

GO CRAZY

A funny title for a serious craft, you say, huh? Well, if you do the exercise properly, that is what it looks like: someone who has completely lost it, freaked out, gone bananas. You start the preparation with a large commitment, going from moment to moment with every impulse you experience. Feel very free to interrupt a sentence in midstream and go in an entirely different direction.

The exercise doesn't have to make any sense at all, but it must be large and exaggerated. You can make sounds, say words, do just about anything you feel. Jump around, roll on the ground, and encourage all of the outrageous thoughts and impulses toward expression. You can relate to things and people in the room, mixing expressions from external to internal stimuli. You can go from a serious place to the absurd in the space of a second or two. The exercise can take two or five minutes, depending on how much of a roll you accomplish by doing it.

This particular craft preparation accomplishes a number of wonderful things at the same time. It frees you of any restrictions you may have started with, and it encourages irreverence in everything that follows. It creates an unbroken flow of impulses and can set up the foundation for a very free-flowing and expressive character. It structures a foundation of flamboyance and colorful behavior. Go Crazy may sound like a funny name for a craft preparation, but it stimulates some very serious and important results. Try it; play with it, and see where it leads.

ANGER-AND-RAGE EXPRESSION

This is a very good approach for stimulating your anger. It can start with an arbitrary decision as simple as saying, "I'm angry." Then, with increasing volume and conviction: "I'm angry. . . I am angry! . . . I'm angry at what is going on in the world! . . . I'm angry at war and killing! . . . I'm angry! . . . I'm angry at all the people in my life who have hurt me! . . . I am livid . . . I hate insensitivity, cruelty, and the hurting of animals! . . . I'm angry at my brother! I hate the way he has treated me since I was a child!" As you do this exercise, it elevates in volume, energy, and physical involvement until you actually are in touch with your anger and rage. You can continue to "rage" for as long as it feels right before taking the next craft step.

Used as an instrumental preparation, the exercise purges your pent-up feelings and eliminates tension in the process. When used as a craft preparation, it is chosen with an eye to stimulating a particular emotional life, to creating an anger-and-rage state. Your choice is based on what you want for the material or what basic BEING state is the foundation for taking the next step in dealing with the text. There is also the intelligent choice of what you are going to express anger about. Unlike an instrumental preparation, which can be done by expurgating anything that even resembles anger and rage, the craft preparation must have the kind of content that will ventilate the right kind of emotional life.

There are times when the life of the character does not express his inner emotional state. Let us say that the character in a play appears composed and rational, seeming to measure every expression with a kind of modulated mellowness. However, in reality the character is seething with rage inside, covering the anger with a kind of rational control which disguises it completely. Before an actor can or should deal with "cover behavior," he should first create the underlying reality—in this case, anger. This would be a very good place to use the craft preparation of Anger-and-Rage Expression. Once you have successfully stimulated the underlife (anger and rage), you could find an organic justification for covering it so it will not be seen by the other characters in the play.

When using any of the craft preparations, remember that there are a large number of them and a lot of different kinds. When one tool fails to work, another will do the job perfectly. The above example of how to use the technique opens the intellect to understanding that any preparation can be used in a variety of ways and that you should not be literal in its employment.

RELATIONSHIP PREPARATIONS

There are three major elements that are paramount to acting: reality, relationship, and ensemble. The playwright or screen writer has the responsibility of creating interesting, compelling, and theatrical material. The actor must fulfill the writer's content with truth, reality, and an involved relationship to the other characters, as well as to the time and place. If the actor succeeds in establishing the truth of emotion and reality in the relationships, he is well on the way to accomplishing ensemble work. The relationship between two or more people on the stage is uppermost in promoting the reality and impact of the piece. Therefore, an actor must prepare for this relationship; he must create an atmosphere of involvement, affectability, and responsiveness. The following group of preparations is designed to accomplish all of that.

NONVERBAL COMMUNICATION

There are several good techniques in the nonverbal area. First, let's discuss the purpose of nonverbal communication. Words and the use of words as a system of communication often take the place of emotional expression. We learn through the use of words to describe our feelings rather than express them. Over the years, the habit of doing this becomes subtle and insidious. In addition to that phenomenon, when we relate verbally we also spend a lot of time thinking about what we are going to say next, which interferes with our involvement with the other person. So, if you remove the obligation to verbalize, that energy can be transferred to other kinds of relating. As a result of that transfer of concentration, you become more aware of the other actor, more related, more involved, and more emotionally communicative rather than just descriptive of what you feel.

A NONVERBAL RELATING EXERCISE

In this exercise, two actors sitting and facing each other attempt to relate without words, gestures, or mime of any kind, simply allowing whatever is going on in the moment to just happen between them. As the exercise proceeds, the level of involvement deepens, and impulses begin to stir in each of them. As this happens, they begin to respond to each other in a moment-to-moment way, allowing themselves to be affected by each other and to respond in turn to the responses. For example, an actor feels something for the person he is relating to and expresses that feeling (without words or gestures); they both respond, and so on, in an unbroken chain of emotional responses. The exercise continues until both actors are ready to go into the scene or start working for the first choice related to the scene. Watching a Nonverbal Relating exercise is almost as exciting as doing it, since you can see a panorama of changing emotions, almost a kaleidoscope experience. The preparation stimulates a collaboration between the actors.

TELEPATHY

This is not an extrasensory exercise; that's just the name. This too is a nonverbal exercise, slightly different from the above preparation in that you attempt to explore what the other person is feeling beneath the expression. The major difference between the two exercises is that in Telepathy you look deeper, dig deeper, and exercise your perception muscles. Still facing each other, you look into each other's eyes and beyond into what lies behind them. At the same time you attempt to respond to what you perceive is there. This exchange creates a very deep and meaningful involvement, and it is not unusual to see actors experience deep and meaningful emotional life.

Both nonverbal exercises establish a relationship that you carry right into the scene. The value of these kinds of preparations is that they force the actors to relate to and with each other rather than *at* each other. We have all seen actors staring glassy-eyed at the other person or relating to the other's chin, oblivious to the person's existence. There is a truism that says, "A well-written play moves from the first word, with every word, toward its conclusion." The relationships on the stage are an integral part of that organic movement toward conclusion.

LOOKING FOR THINGS
IN THE OTHER PERSON
THAT YOU HAVEN'T SEEN BEFORE

It is phenomenal how much we take for granted, how much we look and do not see. You can work with another actor for months and sometimes be in class with someone for years and not really see many things about that person. I am referring to the obvious features: eye color, the shape of a person's ears, and so on. It is not only a question of being observant; it relates to caring, interest, involvement, and what is important to you. Most people experience a very limited threshold of interest, limited to the things that they find important to their survival and pleasures.

The actor is a student of life and behavior, and he never knows when he will be called upon to experience something quite foreign to his experience. Therefore, *everything* should hold interest to the actor! People, in particular, should be important and interesting. A very good preparation and a good discipline is this technique of involvement and relating.

You can do this verbally or nonverbally, whichever way seems to promote the exercise best for you. Sit and look at another actor from across the room. Do this in the dressing room before the curtain goes up or before any rehearsal. What you do is look specifically for all the things you have never noticed about the other person: eye color and shape, hairline and hair color, the shape of the person's nose, the complexion, blemishes or scars, teeth—their color and regularity—mannerisms, behavioral traits, the existence of any self-consciousness, the sound and peculiarities of the voice, the individualities of sounds and enunciations, body language and the story that the body tells, the person's shape and skeletal structure, and so on almost into infinity. You'll be surprised at how much time you can spend just seeing things you never saw in the person before. Besides being very educational, this technique promotes involvement with the person and stimulates a varied emotional point of view, which is one of the most important ingredients in a relationship, on or off the stage.

This is a very good exercise to start off with, since it takes you out of any of the preoccupations you came in with and relates you directly to the actor with whom you are about to work. It is also a great living exercise, because it helps you to see more, experience more, and elevate the quality of your life.

WONDER, PERCEIVE, AND OBSERVE

This technique has already been discussed in the "Involvement Group" section of this chapter. It is also an excellent relationship preparation and can be used in either area with great payoff.

The chief difference in its usage is the emphasis of the exercise. In the involvement area, the main purpose is to achieve involvement with the other actor. When dealing with the promotion of a relationship, we consider the ingredients of the relationship and the component elements. Once you have decided what it is you want to feel and experience, you can adjust the exercise in such a way as to promote the life and emotional point of view you are after.

Consider, for example, that the play you are doing calls for your involvement with this woman. You are to be loving and affectionate and have great affinity for each other. In truth, you like the actress you are working with, but the real relationship falls far short of having an affinity for each other. A necessary step in "getting ready to get ready" is to build a foundation of affection and affinity. Therefore, you choose, as a craft preparation, to work in the relationship area because that is where the demands are. Starting with Wonder, Perceive, and Observe, you embark on an involvement that will hopefully stimulate a kind of love relationship or, at the very least, a foundation to be built upon by other techniques.

THE EXERCISE AS USED IN RELATIONSHIP PREPARATIONS

It is probably better to do the preparation silently, since it would afford more latitude in private exploration of the other person.

She is looking at me expectantly. . . I perceive a very childlike quality under her sophistication . . . She keeps looking away from my eyes. I think she is a little nervous with this . . . I wonder what she was like when she was a child. I see evidence of hurt behind what she covers up. I perceive, in the way she moves, a tentativeness which indicates fear. She really is very sensitive . . . I wonder if she cares about me. I see a warmth in her toward me . . . Her chin is quivering ever so slightly. I wonder what that is all about. When I look at her fear and the things that tell me she is easily hurt, I feel caring toward her . . . Her smile is lovely . . . I wonder when she started to protect herself . . . and why . . . I can see evidence every once in a while that she finds me attractive. I can also see that she is afraid of that . . . She is smiling at me now . . . I see how much more open that allows her to be . . .

Continuing the exercise with some creative leadership and manipulation, pretty soon you might begin to experience the elements related to the obligation. To emphasize does not, however, mean that you distort the truth. You don't perceive things that do not exist. You don't observe behaviors that are not there, so in fact the exercise is not a lie but the truth with an intelligent, creative emphasis to promote your goal.

FEEDBACK

There are several kinds of feedback that can be used in this area. The simple approach is to relate to the other actor and, in a conversational framework, ask each other for feedback.

The kind of questions you ask should relate to important things; don't waste time asking for unimportant feedback.

There isn't a rigid structure to the technique, but it *is* structured. You can ask one question apiece, or you can go on for several minutes questioning the other actor.

Example:

HE: What do you find interesting about me?

SHE: The way you look . . . and talk. What did you think of me the first time you met me?

HE: I thought you were attractive and stuck-up!

SHE: Did that turn you off?

HE: No, it kind of interested me, actually. When we act together, do you get a lot from me? Let me rephrase that: What do you get from me when we work together?

SHE: I think you relate to me well. I believe you—but I wish you listened better.

HE: What do you mean listened better?

SHE: I think that sometimes you are preoccupied with the next line or whatever.

HE: Yes, that's true sometimes. I'm . . . I'm afraid that I won't remember sometimes! Why haven't you said something about this before?

SHE: I just didn't think that unsolicited advice or criticism would have been appreciated. What do you think of me as an actress?

HE: Oh, I think you're fantastic! I am sometimes intimidated at how easily you get there.

SHE: Do you always believe me?

HE: No, not always—but I can tell when you believe yourself!

SHE: You are much more perceptive than one would think you are. If you could give me a critique on the scene we are doing now, how would it go?

HE: I think what you are doing is essentially good. The one thing that I miss is that I wish you as the character, which is you as the person, would be more interested in me the character and person. Ditto for me—give me the same feedback!

SHE: Well, don't take this as a retaliation of your critique, but if I got more from you, maybe I would give more and want more, too.

HE: I'm not offended by that, and, as before, I think you have a valid point. Would you want me as a friend if we were not working together?

SHE: Yes—definitely yes! I think that meeting you and working with you has been one of the better things in my life.

Of course, the exercise can go on for however long you want it to. The nature of the curiosities and their importance will decide how good a relationship preparation it will be. If you are courageous and go after the nucleus of your desires to know the answer to your questions, you stand a really good chance of building a relationship that will stand up to any kind of material obligation.

LIKE-AND-DISLIKE FEEDBACK

This is done in the same manner as the preceding exercise, but the thrust is different. In this approach, you remain exclusive to what you like about each other and what you like least. You should not use the term "dislike" or "not like"; rather, use "like least." The simple reason for that rule is so that you keep the exercise positive and avoid any tendency toward defensiveness.

Example:

HE: What I like most about you is your seriousness and dedication.

(As part of the structure of this particular exercise, each statement must be repeated verbatim by the other person.)

SHE: What you like most about me is my seriousness and dedication. What I like most about you is that you tell it the way you see it.

HE: What you like most about me is that I tell it the way I see it. What I like least about you is the way you protect yourself from intimacy.

SHE: What you like least about me is the way I protect myself from intimacy.

And it can go on like that for ten or fifteen minutes. If you go on any longer than that, you might have to get married! The value of the Feedback exercises is that they deal with everyone's favorite subject—himself—and because of that they are enormously involving and yield great emotional responses.

INTIMATE SHARING

Again, there is a similarity between this preparation and the Double Exposure technique in the "Emotional Preparations" section. There is enough of a difference, however, to make including it in this section worthwhile.

In the emotional preparation, your desire is to elevate your vulnerability state to a higher level, while in the relationship area the goal is to establish intimacy and involvement with another person and to create a state of closeness and sharing. As you can see, the goals are different, and so are the thrust and content of the exercise.

You can agree to do the exercise as a preparation together, or one of you can just start sharing intimate and meaningful things with the other.

Example:

"You know, I'm forty-five years old, and for the first time in my life I feel mortal. I'm in touch with the fact that I'm going to die—I mean for the first time I really believe it. It is no longer something that happens to your grandparents! . . . I'm not actually afraid of dying . . . I'm afraid that I'll die and I won't have accomplished anything with my life. It isn't that I want to go down in history and be read about by schoolchildren, but I would like to have some of the success that I thought I would have by now. I get depressed when I think of how long I have been chasing the brass ring, and I'm really tired of the crumbs and not the bread, if you know what I mean. Don't misunderstand me: I'm not bitter. I chose the theater, and I'm not sorry about that. I love it. But . . . I sometimes feel hopeless about the future. You know, if I had wanted to do anything else I might be very successful at this point in my life, and I feel that I sacrificed a home and a family to be an actor. I'm not sure that I made the right decision in that area."

Hopefully, the person you have been sharing all this with is still listening and emotionally involved, because her response is as important a relationship element as the person talking. You, of course, could continue; she might ask you some questions anywhere in the sharing process, or she might share some things with you.

Example:

SHE: I'm younger than you, but I feel a lot of the things you do. I have been asked to get married several times and have always refused because my career was more important. I think that would be a very selfish way to go into a marriage, don't you?

HE: I don't know. . . There are a lot of married actors in the world. I don't know how many of them are happily married, but I must say I do know some.

SHE: All that talk about death makes me depressed . . . I think about it once in a while, and when things get really heavy, I sometimes think how nice it would be to go to sleep easily and sweetly and not wake up anymore—but I don't really want to die!

HE: We all have thoughts like that, but you want to know something funny? I never even suspected that you were anything but deliriously happy.

SHE: Well, it ain't exactly what it looks like. I am, for the most part, happy, but, believe me, I have some real down times.

The sharing process can or will continue until it reaches its important point, and most likely both actors will be able to identify that moment. The value of this one is that it really can draw two people in very close to each other and establish the foundation of a very personal relationship, and if that is where you want to go, there isn't a better technique for getting there.

ENDOWMENTS

This preparation is totally dependent on the Sense Memory process; you cannot execute an Endowment any other way so that it is effective. Simply, Endowment is a technique for changing elements or features of an existing object—adding things to it or distorting it in some way. Suppose that you are working in a rehearsal with another actor and you want to stimulate a foundation of distaste leading to repulsion. You really don't feel that way about the other actor and, in fact, find her rather attractive. So what can you do in order to stimulate an antithetical emotional response? You can endow her with bad and offensive body odor and a disgusting complexion. You can change her features so that she is much less attractive and even ugly to you.

It is possible through Endowments to create different behavior and distort the sounds in the voice. Even the words the other actor says can be changed. As a matter of fact, you can do almost anything with the Endowment process. You can create an entirely different person in relation to the actor you are working with.

If, for example, there is someone you know who would affect you the way you want to be affected, then you could create that person in relation to your scene partner. If you are proficient with Sense Memory, then the process is really rather simple. As a relationship preparation, it is a very powerful tool, since it embraces an almost unlimited group of possibilities.

Going in the opposite direction, let's say that you are doing a scene where the obligation of the relationship dictates a wild attraction to the other actor—the kind of attraction that stimulates overwhelming lust, desire, and even obsession. The actress with whom you are working, while very attractive and pleasant, does not begin to affect you that way. A perfect opportunity to use Endowments! Starting anywhere, you can sculpt the fantasy of your dreams. It is very much like using Sense Memory the way a sculptor uses clay. You just add a little of this and take away a little of that until you see a body that drives you mad; feel skin that has existed only in your dreams; smell the fragrance that up till now related only to the goddess Diana. Every movement is sheer beauty.

INTERIM PREPARATIONS

An interim involvement is space between the BEING state and the obligation to the material. It is the priming emotion leading to what the character is experiencing in the scene. In a sense, all of the craft preparations are interim preparations, since they are all designed to get you to a place where you are ready to deal with the first emotional responsibility of the material.

The specific difference and the purpose of this category relate to "stretch and difference"; if an obligation is so extreme or distant from where you are emotionally at the moment, then you must build a bridge that leads to that emotional state.

The play opens with the main character having an explosive and irrational tantrum. In the space of a couple of minutes, he almost destroys the entire stage setting. He is ranting and raving at the peak of his energy. That is the way the play begins, and *you* are playing the part! How do you get to that point? What do you do that will kick off that kind of explosion? And how do you maintain it? Coming from a place of relaxation, a place of comfort, a BEING state where you are doing no more or less than what you feel, but are light-years away from flipping out, you can definitely use an interim preparation.

What is a stimulus to irrationality? What could kick off behavior like that? Those should be your first questions. In the case of an extreme emotional obligation like an irrational outburst, the interim preparation can be chosen in order to "sneak up" on that emotional state. You might start by stimulating irritation. Using available stimuli or working sensorially for a choice, you progressively build a state of extreme irritation. By concentrating and selectively emphasizing all the jarring sounds in a place, like shrill automobile horns, loud laughter, children creating a racket, loud voices, and so on, you establish a foundation from which to structure the irritability. Once you have indeed accomplished that state, it can be the springboard to the next interim preparation.

From a place of extreme irritation, you might encourage a large expurgative expression of all the irritating and irrational impulses that you feel, all the while getting larger and more irrational, "dumping" all of the otherwise antisocial feelings that we all incubate and don't usually express. If this works, you can go right into the major choice for the scene. If it is not quite enough, you might select some of your favorite "hate people" and do some outrageous Imaginary Monologues with them.

Whatever the obligation of a scene, the interim preparation should be intelligently selected in order to create a bridge to the emotion that you are after. Knowing your instrument and having experience with the craft teach you when and how to use the various preparations, and, as in everything else, you don't use something if it is not needed. If the emotional obligation in a piece of material is not a stretch for the actor, then there is no need for an interim preparation. Because of insecurity and a lack of experience, actors often do too much, hoping that, if there are enough preparations, the "miracle" will occur. Try to remember, "More is less, and less is more," and "If it isn't broken, don't fix it!"

Let us suppose that you are doing a role of a very "together" and sexy person. All the characters of the opposite sex respond with great attraction. The author describes the character as an incredibly attractive "catlike creature" whose every expression is sensual. A good interim preparation might be to get in touch with your own sensuality. Do a variety of sensualizing exercises elevating your sensual awareness and physical connections. (The sensuality exercises are described in the next chapter.) You might add to this process the awareness of your own sexual attraction to the others in the play, allowing yourself to fantasize in that area. Even though the character in the piece may not be overtly expressive of his or her sexuality, the interim preparation creates a foundation for the embodiment of your own sexuality.

A good test as to whether you need an interim preparation relates to the way you feel about the obligation. If it seems like a stretch or if you are intimidated by it, then it would just be sensible to make it easy on yourself by using something that would get you closer to the desired state. Remember, extreme emotional states and real "stretch and distance" usually call for interim preparations.

IRREVERENT PREPARATIONS

Allowing yourself the right to be irreverent in your work is not an ability that once accomplished is always maintained! It often depends on the circumstances, the environment, and the people you are working with. If you are dealing with a director who has rigid concepts about the piece and all the performances, you will be infinitely more resistant to taking chances in your exploration. If you are surrounded by actors whose every rehearsal is a mere duplication of the previous one, you will find it more precarious to call attention to yourself by being impulsive and irreverent. The irreverent preparations are designed to encourage an irreverent behavior foundation so that you will allow yourself to trust the truth of every moment and not impose other, less authentic behavior over that truth in order to "fit into" the circumstance.

Most of the irreverent preparations are large or exaggerated in nature; they are meant to stretch expression and stimulate courage in the actor. Depending on the specific circumstance you are involved with, it is often more intelligent to do them privately.

Prepare alone, in the dressing room if there isn't anyone around, or at home. If, on the other hand, you are involved with a group that wants exploration and is organically oriented, it is better to do the preparation in front of others or with them. Use discretion.

Keep in mind that the irreverent preparations are just preparations to be irreverent! They are meant to open your instrument, expand your expression, encourage you to trust the unpredictability of each impulse, and imbue you with courage to take risks.

THE ANIMATION WORKOUT

Even though this exercise is done with great exaggeration, all the impulses expressed in the body of the preparation are totally organic and are to come from the actor's moment-to-moment real impulses. Starting with wherever you are, arbitrarily animate all the thoughts and feelings that go on; exaggerate the vocal and physical elements so that you might be shouting and jumping all over the stage. Encourage the full color of your vocal range, and use your body with great flamboyance.

Example:

"I feel scared to begin this!" (This first expression can even sound like the beginning of a song.) "I am going to start by jumping into the air." (And doing so.) "Wow! I feel as though I don't know what to say! . . . I am looking at all of youuuuu . . . and I wonderrr what you think of whaaat I'm doing! . . . I feeelll . . . silly as hell! But I don't care! . . ." (At all times during this preparation, the actor should exaggerate everything physically, facially, and vocally. It is almost impossible to stretch too far.)

"I feel better now. . . I feel that I could say or do anything! And I might, so look out, all of youuuu! . . ." (Spinning around and cavorting in all directions.) "I'm crazy! I love the feeling! I don't care what anybody thinks right now! . . . "

The exercise can go on for many minutes. It can get into the expression of very serious thoughts and feelings, just as long as they continue to be of animated expression. I have seen actors in my classes start on a very humorous level and move into heart-wrenching grief and vulnerability. The value in the preparation is its freeing quality. It sets you up to allow whatever you feel to come out, to encourage an emotional abandonment of expression, which is then carried into the rehearsal.

Once the actor feels the permission to allow reality to be expressed, it is like a chain reaction of impulsive flow. The impulses flow into the choice, the choice in turn stimulates new impulses, those new impulses are expressed through the lines of the scene. As long as the actor does not interfere with that organic and impulsive flow, the resulting behavior is unpredictable and exciting.

THE FREEDOM WORKOUT

This one is similar in nature to the Animation Workout except for the physical requirements and the freedom to be less organic in expression.

The preparation can take a variety of forms, depending on the individual doing it. It can look like a scene from *Swan Lake* with the actor appearing much like a ballet dancer, leaping and twirling through the air, or it can appear more basic and animal-like in body movements.

Very large and vigorous movements are part of the structure of this exercise, and the actor can create an outrageous fantasy in the vocal and verbal expression. He can take it from one subject into another, without warning or loyalty to logic. It can be a gourmet feast of ridiculum.

Example:

"I am going to leave the ground . . . and fly." (Assuming the physical attitude of a giant prehistoric bird.) "I flap my wings." Doing what appears to be a choreographed flight dance, the actor glides across the stage, making outlandish birdlike sounds that seem not of this world. Without any indication that the exercise is about to change, he twirls, spins around again, and, assuming a French accent, begins to flamboyantly paint with imaginary brushes on an imaginary canvas: "Aha! Thees is magnifico! Ze texture . . . ze perspecteeve! . . . Ah! I am a geniuus! . . . I see life! . . . I interpret life! . . . " Again, all the movements are incredibly exaggerated.

At this point the actor can take the exercise in another direction, all the time allowing himself to feel free of all logic and restrictions. The main obligation of this preparation is size and stretch. The more inventive and creative your efforts, the richer the rewards.

THE GO-CRAZY EXERCISE

This is also a good preparation for irreverence. It is described in detail in the section "The Large Expurgatives," which are also a craft preparation. You do the exercise in the same way. It is amazingly freeing and promotes a feeling of irreverence.

THE OUTRAGEOUS MONOLOGUE

Take any monologue you might be working on presently, and approach it with a complete disregard for meaning, content, or logic!

Unlike what you do in an irreverent monologue, you don't have to honor or include your real impulses; you can be completely outrageous in your attack on the material. You could approach the piece characteristically, i.e., speaking peculiarly, distorting the words, and taking it out of the realm of any reality at all.

You might take a Shakespearean soliloquy and approach it like a punch-drunk fighter delivering a speech. There are no limits to where the preparation can be taken! It can, and should, be a blasphemous expression of outrageous theatrical license. The value of such a preparation is that it allows the actor to cut the cords of logic, expectations, and preconceived notions about the material. At the same time it creates a superstructure of trust in the allowing of impulsive expression. The critics of an irreverent approach to acting would cry that this kind of indulgence is masturbation and blatantly distorts the integrity of the playwright and his material. What they fail to understand is that the actor does not treat the material this way in performance but is just using it as a framework within which to do a preparation which will free him to fulfill the author's intent totally.

The Outrageous Monologue can be done with any kind of material and with any free and nonconceptual approach. The actor might use this exercise as a craft preparation just prior to beginning a rehearsal, in the dressing room or actually on stage. It can be employed as an antidote to a rehearsal stalled in concept and logic. That is to say, if you find yourself imposing behavior that does not come out of the moment, or repeating behavior successfully achieved in a prior rehearsal, then you might, in the middle of a rehearsal, stop. In such a case you might do the material outrageously, distorting all meaning and making a sham of the whole thing. After a brief exploration in this area, reinvest in the choices for the piece, and continue the rehearsal, dealing with the demands of the material as written. You will be amazed at how that preparation will lift you out of the logic rut and breathe new and fresh impulses into your work and the scene.

THE NONVERBAL APPROACH

A very strange thing happens to actors as soon as the words are removed from a scene. All of a sudden a new kind of freedom replaces the careful and trepidant behavior associated with the logic and meaning of the words. It is as if the actor is no longer responsible for conjuring up the right kind of emotion for a given moment in the piece. A new variety of expression replaces the former and more conventional behavior of the actor, there are infinitely more colors and kinds of life, and the scene takes on dimension it lacked but a few minutes ago. Why does all this occur? How can this be used to free the actor to be just as exciting with the words as he is without? Words have meaning associated with feelings and emotions. There is a predictable or expected emotion associated with the verbal statement "I am angry with you." This is a line from a play which immediately connotes the expression of some kind of anger or dissatisfaction, when, in reality, that single line can be filled with a wide variety of impulses from humor to disbelief. The content of emotion in that line, or any line, depends on the internal, impulsive flow of the actor expressing it. The emotional flow is governed by the choice the actor is using, the way he is being affected by the other actors in the scene, and the inclusion of all the stimuli present in the moment.

If, by using a nonverbal preparation, you can remove your loyalty to meaning, then you can really explore and experiment with your honest emotions as they accumulate throughout the piece.

Using a piece of material you know very well or, in fact, a scene from a play you are involved in, work for the choices that you have been using up to this point, and relate to the other actor(s) without words—in gibberish or in sounds. Allow everything you feel from one moment to the next to express itself through the sounds or the gibberish, including your responses to the other actor(s). Don't allow yourself to get caught in the trap of a line-by-line, nonverbal relationship, because that in itself creates a kind of logic you want to avoid. Instead, allow the nonverbal expression to communicate the overall content and feeling of the material. By doing the scene in this way, you will make many discoveries about the limitless possibilities of emotional life inherent in the material. It is a good way to free yourself of logic and to promote an irreverent state.

PARALLEL IMPROVISING

Taking the circumstances of the material and finding your own real-life parallel (using real things in your life that resemble the circumstances of the character), do an improvisation with the actor(s) in the scene. Use your own words and include the flow of your Inner Monologue as part of the improvisation. Encourage a total freedom to go wherever the improvisation takes you, with complete irreverence to the written material.

Example:

In this scene from *The Glass Menagerie,* Tom argues with his mother about taking his books back to the library. He resents his lack of privacy and her general interference in his life. Here the actor can choose a similar circumstance in his own life and do a Parallel Improvisation in relation to the scene. The actor's choice doesn't have to be his mother; it can be anyone with whom he has a relationship with similar emotional elements.

Example:

"I can't ever find anything in this house . . . Why is that? Things have a way of disappearing around here, and I'm sick of it . . . Just last week an important telephone number just vanished . . . And don't tell me that I'm sloppy and to take responsibility for my things! I don't like the way you push things off on me . . . I don't seem to have any rights in my own house." All the while the actor should be including all the Inner Monologue impulses. "I'm having trouble believing that I feel angry at this moment . . . but it does upset me that you have such little regard for my feelings and my things . . . and I'm sure that if you were really present you wouldn't let me go on like this without interruption!"

The value of Parallel Improvising is that it allows other impulses to surface in the behavior. It stimulates the actor to include impulses that might be interpreted as irreverent to the material, which, in reality, deepen and enrich the emotional life and the relationship.

All of the irreverent preparations encourage the actor to allow, permit, and include everything in the work. If the goal is to expose the uniqueness of your emotional point of view in every part that you play, then you must encourage that individuality to expose itself in the face of possible rejection and ridicule. This is the only way you will ever develop the courage to trust and believe in what you are and what you have to contribute.

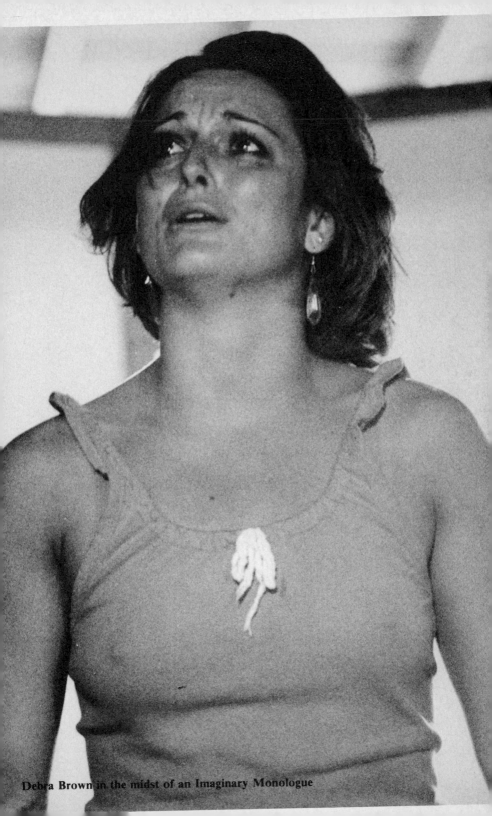

Debra Brown in the midst of an Imaginary Monologue

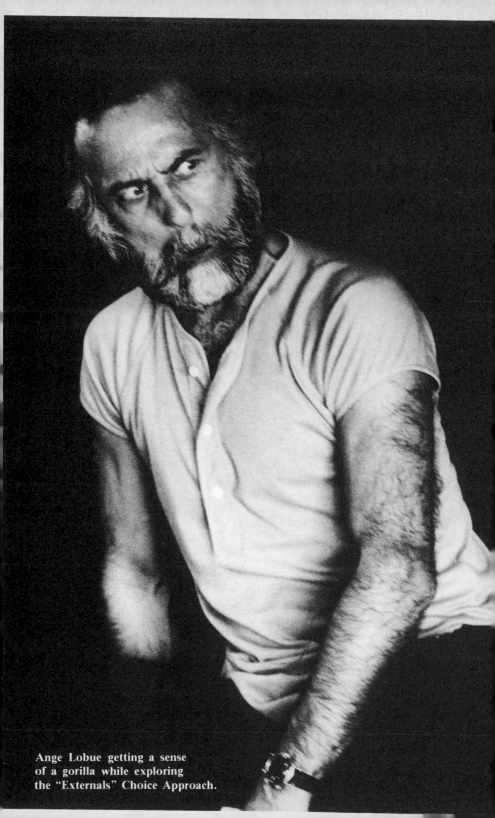

Ange Lobue getting a sense
of a gorilla while exploring
the "Externals" Choice Approach.

Chapter 4

THE THREE MAJOR CATEGORIES OF CRAFT

The heart of the craft consists of three major parts: obligations, choices, and choice approaches. After preparation, the actor must deal with his responsibilities to the material. What are those responsibilities? They are the various obligations of the material: what the character feels, where he is, who the other characters in the play are, how he feels about them, what his statement in the play says, his relationship to the environment, what kind of person he is, and so on.

OBLIGATIONS

The obligations in a piece of material are the elements that the playwright has stated as the realities of the material: the place, the time, the relationships between all the characters, the theme, the emotional involvement of each character, and the impact the characters have on each other. These are some of the realities of the piece that the actor must make equally real for himself. How the actor does that is what craft is all about.

I would like to say a few words about objectives, superobjectives, actions, activities, and why I have eliminated these techniques from the work that I do. I am aware that a lot of Method teachers use and believe in these approaches. In fact, for many years, I, as an actor, attempted to employ them, without much success. I believe they are countercreative involvements. The reason I am taking the time to discuss them at all is to contrast them with, and make clearer the importance and use of, obligations. An objective in a scene is essentially what the character wants to accomplish, what he wants to get or have. For example, one character wants to borrow a sum of money from the other character. The objective then is to borrow the money, to get it. That is fairly clear, and any actor reading the scene can determine what the objective is. But how does the actor "play" that? How does he create *the need* for the money? Certainly not just by deciding that he must borrow that money.

When the same circumstances are defined in obligation terms, the actor's obligation in the scene becomes creating a need for that money. The obligation, as identified, is *the need* for the money. By defining it in those terms, the actor now can use the craft—a choice approach—to stimulate an organic need for the money. If successful in doing that, he can expect that he will be honestly impelled to borrow the money from the other character. If he really needs it and he knows that the other character has it, he will approach getting it from a completely different place. Obligations depend on adapting yourself to the behavior of the scene.

Example:

(The group is stranded in the desert; they have run out of water and are all suffering from thirst, exhaustion, and exposure. Some of the characters are expending their last bits of energy feverishly looking for water, digging, cutting, and squeezing cactus plants, and so on.)

The objective is to find water!

The action is to look for water!

The action is divided into three parts:

What am I doing?

Why am I doing it?

How am I doing it?

The dedicated Method actor playing this scene then breaks down the action in the following manner:

What am I doing? . . . I am looking for water!

Why am I doing that? . . . Because I am dying of thirst!

How am I doing that? . . . Feverishly, with panic and almost crazed!

After the actor has defined that whole process, usually what he ends up doing is imposing behavior that he has not organically created. His entire process of identification is cerebral and does not stimulate behavior or impel him to anything except understanding what is happening in the scene.

The obligation of the scene is to be thirsty!

If the actor can successfully create a state of real thirst, thirst that is extreme—complete with a sense of dehydration and a swelling tongue—then he doesn't have to think about anything. He will damn well feverishly be impelled to find water, and all the life that surrounds that need will evolve organically!

If the actor, through his craft, really creates that state, everything will fall into place honestly, and all the behavior will come from the intense need and not be filled with intellectual contrivances. If the actor is really desperately thirsty, he doesn't have time, energy, or inclination to plan behavior or do little things to convince the audience that he is there in the desert.

The obligations in a scene are the impelling elements that stimulate behavior organically. Once the actor identifies the various obligations, he can go about the process of stimulating those needs and realities from his own life experience.

In this example dealing with the obligation of intense thirst, the process involved would be a Sense Memory choice approach. Instead of imposing a frantic and desperate behavior, the actor would begin the sensory process by asking sensory questions related to thirst, questions that appealed to his senses. Everyone has experienced thirst in one form or another, and the responsibility here would be to sensorially re-create that experience and exaggerate it. The process goal is to actually physically and sensorially experience thirst. If the need is real, the behavior will be dimensional and unpredictable. It will be filled with variety and change. If a character needs to borrow money because his child is critically ill and needs an operation for survival, and the actor makes that real to himself, the behavior will come out of the intensity of that need. When confronted by refusal and other obstacles, the actor will organically adjust to taking another approach to getting the money. The way he responds and changes in emotional intensity will be real and will follow a natural path of reality. His actions will not be facilitated or contrived.

The bottom line in human behavior is that we respond and behave as a result of the impulses that we experience. If the actor uses his energy and his craft to "set up" the stimulus, then the instrument functions naturally, as it does in a real-life situation. When that occurs, the behavior is as colorful and multidimensional as it is in life.

The "blueprint" is very simple:

What do I want to feel or experience in the scene?

What would make me feel that way or relate that way?

How can I make that real for myself?

What you want to feel or experience is the *obligation*.

What would make you feel that way or stimulate the experience is the *choice*.

How you create it or make it real is the process called the *choice approach*.

Everything that exists as a responsibility in a play can be identified by the above technique. All of the actor's responsibilities can be met by these three categories of craft.

THE SEVEN MAIN OBLIGATIONS

Time and Place	Emotional	Thematic
Relationship	Character	Subtextual
	Historic	

The order in which they are listed above is not necessarily their order of importance or approach. The importance of any of the obligations and the order in which you work to fulfill them vary with each piece of material. It is important to note that the seven main obligations are categories that "blueprint" an actor's responsibility to a given piece of material. However, there may be variations or other refined elements in any of the seven areas. There can be other obligations or amendments to the already existing ones. Be open and aware of this, and use the seven categories as a blueprint for approaching material.

TIME-AND-PLACE OBLIGATION

Every scene in a film or a play takes place somewhere, at some time of day or night and at some time of year. Why a playwright chooses to place a scene in a certain location depends a lot on what he or she is attempting to communicate or promote in the scene. Most often, the time and the place are very important and have a significant effect on the characters. For instance, a love scene on a deserted beach in the middle of the afternoon, two people having an argument on a crowded street in the middle of the day, a secluded weather station in the Antarctic—cold and lonely—and so on. All of the elements of a place at a certain time have an effect on the people in the scene. The actor's responsibility is to identify and understand what the time and the place mean to the character in the piece and find a time and a place of his own life that will stimulate the same or similar feelings for him. If, for example, he is really on a beach about to do a love scene and the character is seemingly affected by the wind, the surf, and the smells of that environment and not only responds to those stimuli but has lines that relate to the environment, then the actor must stimulate similar emotional responses. But let us imagine that this particular actor feels this way in the forest and not at the beach. What then? He can, through his process, work for and create the forest, and, by doing that, he, the actor, will experience what the character does. The audience sees the beach; they relate to what they see. But if our actor feels that way about the forest, then he should create that environment for himself because it fulfills the obligation to the place. Sometimes the time and the place don't seem to have a distinguishable impact on the scene. No matter, it is still very important for the actor to create a time and a place for himself, if for no other reason than to be someplace other than on the stage. The moment-to-moment life of the character and the actor is fed by his relationship to the surroundings, and when he naturally glances away from the other person, what he sees must somehow affect his personal emotional point of view.

Identifying how a place and/or time affects the character in a scene should be one of the actor's first questions when approaching a piece of material. There are a few questions you can standardize when preparing to work on a scene:

Where does the scene take place?

How does the place affect or seem to affect the characters?

Do the characters make references to the place?

What do the characters say about it?

What does the author say about the time and place?

Why do I think it takes place here?

Are the characters' behaviors directly related to either the time or the place?

Would the characters relate or behave differently in another time or place?

Ask any question you can think of that will help you to understand the impact and importance of the time and place as an obligation to the scene and the play.

Every piece of material takes place in a particular environment at a specific time, and while the place may not be the most important element in the scene, it is never to be disregarded! At times it may not even be necessary for the actor to work for another place in relation to the "set." He may be able to use the available environment and respond much as the character does to that place.

Whatever the reality, it is one of the very first obligations the actor must address himself to. There are times when the place and the time are the most important element in the play. There have been a great number of films about bank robberies, jewel thefts, and breaking into an impregnable vault late at night, attempting to avoid the complex alarm systems. The film *How to Steal a Million* takes place for the most part in a museum after it is closed, with guards making periodic rounds. The action, the behavior, and the emotions of the two central characters are almost totally affected by the place and the time. An actor playing one of those roles would certainly have to deal with creating a similar time and place, replete with all of the dangers and obstacles. The place, in this case, makes up what is at stake and is the major element in the event.

The play *K2* takes place on a mountain. The film *Flight of the Phoenix* takes place in the desert. The characters are stranded without means to survive, and the entire film focuses on survival and getting out of the desert. In this case the place is ultimately important! The actor must create the time and the place so as to be affected just as the character is affected throughout the film. As time moves on, the place must be increasingly impacting on the character and therefore on the actor.

Once the actor realizes the importance of the time and place, he can set out to either use the available stimuli (the existing set) or add elements, such as objects that are meaningful to him; or indeed he may elect to create a wholly different place. Whatever he does, the end result of the work must be that he is really in another place and not on the stage and that the place stimulates different thoughts, feelings, and impulses and affects the way he relates to the other people in the play.

When I was growing up and going to school, Sundays were a mixture of pleasure and pain. I liked the relaxed and lazy feeling of a Sunday morning, lounging in my pajamas and reading the funnies. I hated the thought of having to go back to school the next day, and I always used to say, "The only thing wrong with Sunday is Monday." Sundays were very meaningful, and I felt a very identifiable mixture of strong emotions. If I, as an actor, needed to stimulate those kinds of impulses in a scene, I could break down the component parts of the time and place. I could work sensorially to create the sound of church bells in the faint distance, the quiet in the street, the Sunday papers strewn all over the carpet, the way the sunlight happened to fall on the floor at that time of morning, my pajamas, the odor of the food my mother used to cook, mostly just on Sundays, and all the other elements that made up Sunday for me. If I were successful in creating all of these elements, I could pretty much count on feeling a lot of the same things that I felt on Sunday mornings. If that happened to be the obligation of the scene, I would certainly be dealing with the time element in the material.

Again, a good formula is to ask yourself:

What do I want to experience in the scene?

What would create that experience for me?

How can I work for it?

If an actor has a definite emotional point of view about everything around him, he will never feel that he is just on stage acting.

RELATIONSHIP OBLIGATION

There are two parts to the relationship obligation: the relationship responsibility and the emotional obligation of the relationship.

First, let's talk about what a relationship obligation is. It is that which the actor must experience between himself and the other characters in the piece. Who are they and how does he feel about them? What are the relationships between the characters? How does the emotional life change? The responsibility to make real for himself the realities of the material in this area is what I call relationship obligations.

RELATIONSHIP RESPONSIBILITY

The relationship responsibility relates to who the other characters are to your character. Is that your wife, mother, sister, brother, father, lawyer, doctor, friend, adversary, business partner, neighbor, lover, fiancé, uncle, etc.?

That is my wife! We have been married for fourteen years, eating together, sleeping with each other, sharing all kinds of intimacies, and the audience has to believe that is true! The actor must address that relationship responsibility by creating a stimulus that parallels the reality of the material. If that is his wife of fourteen years and he knows her intimately, then he must create a person, in relation to the actress he is working with, with whom he has had a similar long-term intimate relationship.

In order to substantiate the parallel reality, it is not always necessary to create a completely different person in relation to the actor with whom you are working. Sometimes you can relate to available and existing features and behaviors that are very much like that of people you know well or are close to. Often the actor can selectively emphasize qualities of the person he is working with that remind him of someone very close to him.

Whatever the process is, the responsibility is to make the other actor be to you what the other character is to your character in the scene.

THE EMOTIONAL OBLIGATION
OF RELATIONSHIP

Once you have established who the character is to you, then you must find out how you feel about him or her. "That is my wife of fourteen years." You have made that a reality, and now, how do you feel about her? Suppose you hate her. At the opening of the play you are in a violent argument with your wife. It is quite apparent that you have animosity and hatred for each other, and, as the scene unfolds, it becomes clear that you are tied into this relationship because of children and economics. The emotional responsibility of this relationship obligation then is to create all the elements that have built the animosity, resentment, and, finally, hatred toward her. If you start with a choice that fulfills both the relationship responsibility and the emotional content, you have made a good selection. If not, then first you create the person and then "endow" that choice with personality elements that will stimulate the anger and hatred.

If you have scenes with more than one person in the play, you will have to deal with the relationship obligations to each of the other characters, again by identifying first the responsibility and then the emotional point of view toward that person. Unless an actor is doing a dramatic reading by himself, there will always be relationship obligations.

In this area, the actor's responsibility is to make the other actor be to him whatever the script says the other character is. If you are doing a scene with an actor who is supposedly your father, then you, through your craft, must create a reality which promotes the belief that the other actor is indeed your father or has qualities that make you feel the same way you would feel toward your father. For example, you are doing a play with an actor of great theatrical experience, someone who has been in theater longer than you have been alive. He is kind and considerate of you and is always willing to help you and give you good advice. Throughout the entire rehearsal period you have grown fond of him, and you have even begun to depend on his approving nod after a scene. If that actor is playing your father in the play and he is in fact many of the things you think your father is, you have an available reality in the works, and that is enough to fulfill your responsibility to the relationship obligation.

The emotional elements and impulses usually undergo many changes as the piece progresses, and the actor must adjust, change, and even work for new choices to accommodate the evolvement of the emotional life of the play.

Questions to ask in this area:

Who is this person to my character?

What is the nature of the relationship?

How long have they known each other?

How does my character feel about this person?

How does that change in the play?

What are the growth elements in the relationship?

After answering all the above questions, the actor will find it much easier to select choices and approaches that relate to the responsibilities of this obligation.

THE SCENE (emphasizing only the relationship obligations):

Sunday, the park, children running, playing; a balmy summer day, about four in the afternoon. Al and Debbie sit on a blanket finishing what looks like a very nice picnic lunch. It is easy to see that these two young people are very much in love.

AL: I have twenty-five hundred dollars in the bank. Another couple thousands and we can get married, huh?

DEBBIE: Oh, I love you, Al. Why do we have to wait until you have more money? Why can't we get married right now?

AL: Because I want it to be right. I want to take you on a nice honeymoon and have money to get started, and not have to struggle immediately.

DEBBIE: Yeah . . . I know you're right, but I wish we didn't have to wait.

The scene is a fairly obvious and simple piece of material; all the obligations are very visible. He has known her for some time, she is his girlfriend, and, as it comes out later in the scene, they have been sleeping with each other. They are very much in love and enjoy being together. For the sake of this example, let us assume that both actors have just met a couple of hours ago and that they are going to shoot the scene in the next half hour. They have time for very little preparation and must communicate to an audience that they have known each other for a period of time, have been sexually intimate, and are deeply in love. Both the relationship responsibility and the emotional obligation of the relationship are inherent in the description. After a brief period of relating to the actress, the actor decides to work for his wife in relation to this actress he has just met. He works to sensorially endow her with the features of his wife: her sounds and smells and the way she moves. He does this using a sensory process, endowing the actress with these elements but not disregarding how she also affects him. He might selectively emphasize all the personality elements about his wife that he really loves and attribute them to the actress he is working with. By making the decision to use his wife as the choice in the scene, the actor has dealt with both areas of the relationship obligation—the familiarity and intimacy and the love he feels for her.

EMOTIONAL OBLIGATION

The emotional obligation in a scene is what the character feels. It is what he is experiencing as the scene starts and as it evolves. It is the emotional life of the character in the scene and the variety of changes that take place in his or her behavior. There may be a number of people in the room (on stage), and our character may have a variety of emotional points of view in relation to them. However, the specific emotional obligation is what the character is feeling in the scene.

THE SCENE:

The main character, a young man in his late teens, is surrounded by a group of other characters, older and obviously related to him: his mother, father, older sister, and an uncle. They are in the midst of a heated discussion about the future of our main character. He wants to go to New York and study acting and get into the theater. The others are all adamantly against such a commitment and want him to go to Harvard and study law. He desperately attempts to communicate his love for acting and the theater. His pleas for understanding seem to be falling on deaf ears. He is frustrated, angry, and feels helpless and unseen.

The emotional obligation is frustration, anger, helplessness, and the feeling of not being seen and understood.

There are a variety of relationship obligations in the scene: how he feels about each of the other characters, which ones he feels closest to and has the most love for, and which of the characters are the most understanding of his needs.

In terms of the identified emotional obligation, the main character or the actor playing that part identifies the emotional life and begins to make choices that will create the realities to promote the emotional experience in the scene.

In this particular example, it is important that the actor work for a choice that stimulates a passionate desire to act. If that element exists, the next logical step in the pyramid of reality is to work for choices that create obstacles to his passions and needs.

If the actor stimulates an excitement and a desire to achieve something and needs the support of the other people, but fails to get that support or understanding, then you have the ingredients that stimulate the emotional life dictated by the scene.

A very common trap for actors is to deal with the resulting elements of the emotional obligation. This kind of involvement leads to singularly dimensional emotional responses and does not build the foundation of reality that leads to an entire network of emotional life for the character and the piece.

The emotional obligation in a scene is those feelings, impulses, and inner life that the character is experiencing: love, hate, passion, confusion, exultation, joy, pain, ambivalence, rage, depression, hopelessness, attraction, needs, satisfaction, invisibility, ambition, lust, greed, and so on. It is important to remember that every emotion is filled with a large variety of complex elements: anger can be filled with hurt, confusion, and fear, and so it is with every human emotion. The nature of the emotional combinations is dependent on the specific stimuli that impel a person to experience certain emotions. Identifying an emotional obligation, such as hurt, depends on the specifics of the stimulus. Being hurt by the insensitivity of someone you love deeply will lead to a very specific kind of hurt in contrast to being hurt by a lifelong adversary and critic.

"On the nose" emotions may be organic responses to choices that the actor has created, but they seriously lack the impacting stimuli that justify the character's behavior. If our main character is not driven by the need to accomplish what he wants, there isn't the depth of conflict that exists in the author's intent for the scene.

Let us suppose that the actor neglects to deal with the passions and the need to go to New York and become an actor. Instead, he works to create a variety of frustrating personality elements in the other characters. He endows them with behavior that stimulates anger. He has Inner Monologues with them that make him feel hurt and frustrated, but none of these feelings is the result of having desires that are being disregarded by the others. Therefore, we have an actor who authentically feels anger, frustration, and hurt, but without the elements of need, passion, and desire to get something from the others. The difference in the resulting behavior is monumental!

The emotional obligation is what the character feels in every given scene and in every moment throughout the play and how those emotions change throughout the entire play.

CHARACTER OBLIGATION

There are four parts to this obligation: the physical, the emotional, the intellectual, and the psychological.

These four elements are what the actor must address himself to when dealing with characterization—that is, breaking down the character so that he can fulfill the nature of the person he is to create.

What kind of person is this character?
What is his physical makeup?
Is he physically frail? Is he beautiful? unattractive?
What kind of person is he mentally? Is he stable? insecure?
What is his level of intelligence? Would he be described as bright?
What is the nature of his emotional states?
What about temperament? Is he easygoing or volatile?
Is he suspicious by nature? paranoid?
Is he macho?

All of these factors have a real bearing on how the character behaves and relates to life as well as to all the people around him. Is this character emotionally suppressed or is he extroverted? Is he somewhere in between those extremes? Whatever the elements of the character are, they must be made real in order for the actor to fulfill the character obligations.

When you have read the play and gathered all the pertinent information about the character, the first step is to identify the differences between you, the actor, and the character as drawn by the writer. Isolate each part of the character elements, and begin to identify the differences between you and the character, physically, emotionally, intellectually, and psychologically.

Starting with the physical, let us imagine that the character is much more in touch with his body than the actor is. He relates to the world on a much more basic and earthy level. He enjoys physical contact and spends a lot of time touching other people in the play. The actor, on the other hand, is much less physically aggressive and is even somewhat shy about contact. He tends to make small physical gestures, unlike the character's broad and expansive movements.

To say the least, the actor has a lot of work to do in order to deal with the physical differences between himself and the character. Where does he start? How can you organically change a lifetime of physical habits? *It can be done!* There are choices and approaches that the actor can use which will totally change the way he moves, relates, and even thinks about himself physically.

Just the act of beginning to consciously use your body changes the way you relate to yourself in that area. Lifting weights can immediately change your muscular awareness. Other physical activities will begin to bring you closer to the character. The process of creating a sense of an animal or a more physical person can affect your personality with startling changes.

There are many ways the actor can confront the responsibility of dealing with the differences between himself and the character physically. What if the character has a vastly different emotional fabric? What if he is extremely insecure and believes that most people do not like him, while the actor is exceedingly popular? Here again, the actor must introduce stimuli that will effect a change in the way he relates to the world. He could, for example, do a continual litany of his insecurities, selectively emphasizing all the things in life that he feels insecure about. At the same time, he could emphasize and exaggerate all the rejections he receives, the unaccepting way in which people relate to him. If he spends enough time in these areas, they will soon erode his true confidence. He may also use the other actor in the play to serve these purposes.

I am sure that you get the idea about identifying the differences in all four areas, and when we get into choices and choice approaches, it will become very clear what things you can use to bridge the gaps between you and the character.

The other consideration is to identify the similarities between you and the character. How are you alike? What can you do to pique the expression of the similarities? Imagine that both the actor and the character are very emotionally explosive, only the character in the play seems to blow up more frequently than the actor does in life. Here the adjustment seems quite simple. If the actor and the character have similar traits, then all that is needed is to introduce the kind of stimulus that will cause the actor to respond as the character does and with the same frequency.

Similarities that are very available do not need any attention. The actor is the character, and the character is the actor because in that specific area they are alike. The actor doesn't need to do anything to draw a parallel.

Relating to the area of character obligation is the systematic involvement of identifying the differences and the similarities and bringing them all together so that the character can inhabit the actor.

When a play or a film is cast, the actors chosen for each role are usually selected because of the similarities between them and the characters they have been engaged to play. Often the physical requirements will be overlooked for a similar "quality" of personality or emotional life. Whatever the reality, dealing with this very important obligation is one of the major responsibilities of any actor. If the playwright has been successful in creating a finely drawn character, the actor should have very little trouble identifying the four areas of concern. If, on the other hand, the writer has sketched the character thinly, the actor, in collaboration with the director, will have to fill in the blanks.

HISTORIC OBLIGATION

This obligation area relates to the time in history in which the film or play takes place. It could mean the Elizabethan Period, or it could be the beginning of the Second World War. If the actor hired to play a character at another time in history isn't familiar with the period, then he must research it thoroughly. He must become familiar with the customs, morality, mores, concerns, economics, laws, rules, etiquette, politics, dress, sexual attitudes, awareness, and consciousness of the people of that time and geographical locale. All of these realities must be dealt with when relating to a time other than the contemporary period. The actor should research the time and the place, again drawing parallels with the present whenever possible and finding the contrasts so that he can find ways of assimilating the differences and making them a real part of the character.

The investigative process almost always starts with questions: What were the weather conditions? the climate? How did that affect the people's behavior? What was the language? What were the speech patterns? the mannerisms? What was the people's psychological awareness? religion? How did religion influence their lives? superstition? rituals? How did they feel about birth and death? What was the life expectancy of the period? You could go on almost indefinitely asking and answering these kinds of questions.

All these elements have an impact on how the character looks at life, how he relates to people, speaks, thinks, acts, walks, and talks. Before an actor can deal with anything else, such as the emotional obligation or the relationship obligation, he must understand and confront the various historic obligations that relate to the specific period he is involved with.

The manner in which a character sits, walks, stands, and moves is most often governed by the dress of the period. In this instance the actor can deal with this responsibility through the use of costume. Even if it won't totally inspire him toward that particular physical action, it will go a long way in exciting his imagination and changing his contemporary movement.

Creating climatic conditions is a craft involvement and can easily be accomplished. In almost every instance there is either a substitute or a parallel in the actor's life: something that can be worked for that will produce similar thoughts, preoccupations, impulses, or prejudices. Since the beginning of recorded time, emotions have been universally the same; therefore, anything a character may experience can be restimulated by some personally meaningful choice by the actor playing the part.

We feel the same way about SOMETHING. When he is dealing with a character who is much less knowledgeable, less aware, and living in a time of ignorance and technological vacuum, how is it possible for the actor to know less than he does and have experienced less than he has? How can he have a Middle Ages mentality rather than that of a computerized society? Well, he can't, nor should he fool himself into thinking that he can! If an actor gets totally involved with a certain kind of consciousness, if he becomes preoccupied and even fanatic about something, then he can become almost tunnel-visioned in an area that creates a life that may preclude his other knowledge. It is like the phenomenon of a chicken being hypnotized by a line drawn in the dirt. If our character is a religious fanatic and involves himself in the burning of witches and believes in such things as witches and Satan, the actor surely has other such strong beliefs and convictions. It becomes a matter of translating the substitutions into applicable craft approaches.

If our character lives in the time of Robespierre and has nightmares about the guillotine, our actor can create and emphasize whatever his bogeymen and supernatural terrors may be. If the character is a contemporary person living in the time before the sexual revolution, thinking that every woman who does not bring her virginity to the marriage bed is a whore, the actor can emphasize or ventilate an equal modern-day prejudice of his own. The audience hears him shrieking, "Whore! You are a dirty whore!"

Whatever the realities are that are different from modern time, those are the elements that the actor must address. He must find the ways to assimilate himself into that period and be comfortable being an eighteenth-century man, for example. He cannot just appear to be; he must acquire the manner, speech, thought process, concerns, and beliefs of that time on an organic level. Truth comes from a place of truth, and if the actor fails to create the truth at the very foundation of the character, how can he expect to be real in any of the other obligation areas?

THEMATIC OBLIGATION

This obligation or responsibility carries the "statement" of the play or film. It is what the writer is saying. It might be why he wrote the entire piece. In some instances the responsibility may be divided among several characters in the play, but very often the playwright will single out one character as his spokesman. Shaw was notorious for doing just that: in almost every one of his plays there is one character who spouts the author's thoughts and philosophy or makes his statement.

The actor, when approaching any piece of material, should ask himself, Does my character have a responsibility to promote the statement of this piece? If so, what is it? What is the author trying to say through my character?

An example of an overall statement might be that of a playwright who has written an anti-Communism play. He has chosen the main character, a staunch and fanatic revolutionary Communist, to point out "the evils of Communism" and the hell of living in such a suppressive society. Through the words and behavior of the character, the author succeeds in animating the blind fanaticism of an ideology that enslaves mankind. The actor playing the main character must find a way, in making those statements, to become that single-minded and fanatic so that he believes that the state comes before human rights. Every word and statement that issues from his lips must be the authentic doctrine of the Communist ideology. It is through distorted and blind passion that the actor promotes the author's statement, and therefore that responsibility must become an important part of the actor's art and job. He must include in his list of obligations in this play the thematic obligation.

Sometimes the theme of a film or a play is subtle and expertly woven into the entire fabric of the piece; the relationships, the behavior, the way the characters relate to life, their actual sense of life make the writer's point. At other times, the theme is like a bomb and explodes out of the mouth of a single character in a single statement. Often the writer has several statements, which he issues forth from the mouths of a variety of characters in the play. The theme, however, is what the play says. It is usually why the writer chose to write the material.

SUBTEXTUAL OBLIGATION

Of all the seven obligations, this is the most subtle and usually the hardest to identify. It relates to the unsaid things in the play, the statements and feelings which are inherent in the piece and motivate the character's behavior but are a kind of underlife in the piece. It is sometimes the essence of the material, the quality of the play, the ambiance. It is the underlife of a character actually saying one thing and subtextually meaning something else. In the play *Winterset* there is a quality of despondency, a murky hopelessness, a feeling that one cannot beat the system. The essence of the piece is like a lot of Great Depression plays, plays that attempted to chronicle the period.

The subtextual elements are not necessarily stated by the other characters or the author of the piece, and they might not exist obviously in any of the statements that your character makes. From the quality, or essence, of the play there might be an "understatement"—in other words, a style or a feeling emanating from the material that communicates itself to an audience and produces an overall response to the piece, and can be considered a subtext of the piece. This subtle but existing life sense or emotional ambiance may very well be one of the responsibilities of the character that you are to play. In that case, the quality or emotional element must be approached through the use of choices and choice approaches and dealt with much the same as any of the other obligation areas.

During the turn of the century in this country, when you could buy a good nickel cigar and the men wore straw hats, people would go to the park on Sunday and listen to the band play Sousa marches. They would have picnics and celebrate life. The children laughed and played simple games. There were barbershop quartets, and you could buy a glass of beer for three cents and get free hard-boiled eggs at the same time. There was a lot of hope in this country. We were brand-new.

The essence or quality of the above sentiment is in the play—it is a statement in the piece. It is in the fabric of the play; it is something of hope, a naiveté. The playwright might be saying, "This is when life was worth living." It might be purposely in contrast to our sense of life at this time in America. While the play may be making an entirely different statement, the subtextual statement is also there. The actor, as a part of that emotional and behavioral fabric, would have to promote an overall life quality that was consistent with the rest of the obligations but that at the same time would fulfill this responsibility.

The subtextual obligation is subtle and elusive, but when it is a part of the play and the threads of it weave their way through your character, it must be dealt with as an actor's responsibility. As an overall picture, it is definitely also the director's responsibility.

Once the actor identifies the subtextual responsibility, he can specify his own behavior goals. For example, let's use the above scenario. To be a part of that society which is full of hope and wonder, the actor could work for choices that stimulate a sense of life filled with Pollyanna elements. No matter what his changing emotional point of view might be from scene to scene, his underlife and the personality fabric of the character would service the subtextual requirements.

MATERIAL EXAMPLES OF OBLIGATIONS

For the purpose of tracing the identification of obligations through a specific role from a particular play, I have chosen Amanda from *The Glass Menagerie*.

The Time-and-Place Obligations: Amanda lives in St Louis. As the play progresses, the seasons change and so does the clothing. The time of day and evening and the days of the week change from scene to scene.

The actress would have to relate to the various weather changes; she would have to deal with the heat of spring and summer, and when the fall and winter come, she would be obligated to adjust to those climate changes.

The other realities of time and place are the light and darkness elements of day and night and early morning, as well as the distinctions between a workday and a Sunday, spent sitting in the parlor. All the realities relating to time and place would have to be made real by the actress.

The Relationship Obligations: There are four main relationship obligations for Amanda in this play. They are the relationship to Tom, her son; to Laura, her daughter; to Jim, the Gentleman Caller; and to her husband, who appears in the play only as an old photograph hanging on the wall. There are other relationships she talks about; however, they are not as crucial as the aforementioned four.

The Relationship to Tom: Amanda loves Tom but seems to be in constant conflict with him. He obviously reminds her of her husband, who deserted all of them a long time ago. She fears that Tom will leave and she will not be able to support herself and Laura. She has strong opinions about propriety and comes into conflict with Tom about the way he thinks, drinks, and stays out "till the wee hours of the morning." She thinks he is a dreamer who refuses to face the responsibilities of life. They argue a lot about the books he reads, his poetry, and his love for the movies. There is a great deal of ambivalence related to Tom. There is struggle for control. Amanda relates to the household as hers, and Tom insists that he pays rent.

These are the realities of the relationship Amanda has with Tom. Translating all of these facts into impelling choices and realizing those choices so that they fulfill the obligations are what the actress explores in the rehearsal process.

Approaching the Relationship Obligation to Tom: The choices the actress could explore in dealing with the relationship obligation to Tom might start with any of the available-stimulus realities that exist between her and the actor playing Tom. If, for example, they have areas of conflict with each other, it would be a simple thing to use those realities to promote the realities of the play. If the actress happens to have a son with whom she shares some of the same dynamics, she could work for her son in relation to the actor, using Sensory Endowments. For the dependency that Amanda has on Tom, the actress may emphasize parallel feelings for her own son or work for a choice that will endow the actor with something she needs from him. Another approach to dealing with the dependency on Tom is for the actress to elevate her own insecurities in some real area and then make an adjustment that impels her to look to the actor playing Tom. There are unlimited choice possibilities that the actress can investigate and explore while building her character. The best place for her to begin dealing with her relationship to Tom is to make the blood tie. If he is as important to her as any son is to a mother, she will have the basis for a love relationship. If that is accomplished in the beginning, the needs and conflicts are deeper and more complex as well as more dimensional.

The Relationship to Laura: Amanda has great concern for Laura; she loves her and feels protective of her at the same time. Amanda refuses to accept that Laura is crippled. She insists Laura has only a "slight defect." She thinks Laura is beautiful and often enjoys relating to her. Amanda loses patience with Laura because of Laura's shyness and inability to function socially. She lives in terror that Laura will end up an old maid, living like a hermit, without a profession and unable to support herself. In a strange way, Amanda is as dependent on Laura as Laura is on her. There is a purpose here, and, in an indirect manner, it motivates a great deal of Amanda's behavior. The conflict in the relationship comes from Amanda's expectations of Laura and Laura's inability to rise to them, as is seen with the Rubicam Business College fiasco. There is a mother-hen quality in Amanda's relationship to Laura. There is also the underlying resentment she feels toward Laura. Why couldn't she be a normal young lady who has "gentleman callers"? Why isn't she married and out in life with a family? For how long will she be a burden? Amanda has ambivalence with both of her children.

The actress would confront all of the relationship information and translate it into process: the way she wants to feel in relation to the other actress, the complex and conflicting emotional life, which may be accomplished with one single choice.

The work of dealing with a relationship obligation is much the same as with any of the other obligations: it depends on clearly understanding the inner organic emotional life related to the other character.

The Emotional Obligations: Amanda's emotional obligations in the play pretty well run the gamut. The emotional life of the character is strongly influenced by a Southern upbringing which places a large premium on politeness and manners. Nonetheless, Amanda expresses everything from delight to rage. Many of the emotional obligations come directly from the individual relationships and what is happening in a given scene. Amanda's emotional life is also influenced by the underlying desperation that exists in her character. To identify the specific emotional obligations, you would have to approach the play scene by scene. They are very identifiable.

The Character Obligation: Here we have some strong handles. One could say that Amanda is definitely a "character"—in every sense of the word. Even though she has been away from the South for many years, she clings to the manners, the style, and the behavior of a pampered Southern belle, at least in her reminiscence. She spends much time describing "the good old days on the plantation" to her children, who have heard the same stories over and over again. She places a great deal of importance on manners and etiquette. Underneath this aging belle hiding behind an imaginary fan beats the heart of a strong-willed, single-minded survivor who single-handedly raised two children. She is more than likely filled with unexplored and unexpressed rage—first for being deserted by a man who was originally below her in social position, and second, because her life turned out to be what it is. She keeps the family together and would do just about anything to maintain that unity. Amanda is an actress of a kind. She puts on a good show whenever it is necessary (on the telephone selling magazine subscriptions, with gentleman callers, and, more honestly, when she shares her former life with Tom and Laura through stories). She fights depression rather well, and only in a couple of moments in the play does she allow herself to lose that battle. She is not terribly educated but quite intelligent in the ways of life. She remembers her beauty but doesn't seem to mourn the ravages of aging. Her psychological awareness and her perceptions come from the same place instincts do when an animal is hungry and needs to hunt for food. Her age is beginning to tell in her movements and in the fatigue that breaks through whenever she lowers her guard.

An actress interpreting the character description could pick certain words to use as guideposts leading to the translation of that description into behavioral realities. If an actress could create the underpinnings of the character's reality from her own life experiences, she could add other choices that would come from that foundation and fulfill other character elements. By surrounding herself with people who need to be taken care of, people the actress really cares about, she might excite the "mother instincts." Working for choices that would speak of a better time in her life, she could mirror Amanda's recollections. Surrounding herself with evidence of failure and with people who frustrate her every need is another way to stimulate desperation. Each of Amanda's character elements can be approached through the craft, the parallels drawn, and the character obligation fulfilled.

The Historic Obligation: The play takes place just before the start of World War Two, at the tail end of the Great Depression. Amanda was enmeshed in a survival struggle that was strangling most of the people in this country. There was a "poverty consciousness" which permeated everything. Leisure time was spent looking through family photograph albums and listening to old records on the Victrola. Yet, in spite of the Depression and the unrest in the rest of the world, there was an underlying hope that the people in this country had. They shared a patriotism and a belief in our system of government. There was a naiveté about politics, and there was a great belief in our leaders. Franklin D. Roosevelt was the President, and he would have his radio "fireside chats" during which the people would huddle around their big console radios and digest his every word. Everyone had favorite movie stars, and the movie theaters were the great escape palaces of the thirties. Hitler was in power and threatening all of Europe while we were isolating ourselves from the rest of the world. Amanda ordered dress patterns from Sears, Roebuck and sewed clothes for herself and Laura. It was the time of the work ethic, and pleasures were taken in very simple ways. The styles were very different from what they are today. Not too may startling things had occurred in technology: there was radio; there were movies with sound, and air travel was for the rich and adventurous. The consciousness movement was many years in the future, so if someone needed psychological help, people raised an eyebrow and exchanged a knowing look. There were favorite radio shows of the period, and a woman usually listened to them avidly in the kitchen while attending to another task. When Amanda voiced her dreams, they were not for riches or fantastic things, just that she and her children would have enough to eat, that Laura would find a nice husband, and that Tom could follow his dreams. There was a definite quality of life indigenous to that particular period in this country. The Wingfields lived in St. Louis, which had a Midwestern awareness and manner quite unlike the Eastern awareness, which was slightly more sophisticated. All of this information about the period allows the actress to understand the environment, the lifestyle, concerns, and involvements of the time. The emotional life, the relationship of the characters to each other as well as to the world at large, would be affected by the ingredients of that time in history.

An actress old enough to play Amanda could have been a child at the time of this play. She might remember some of the events and feelings of that time. One way of approaching the fulfillment of the historic obligation would be to go back to the objects, pictures, movies, magazines, music, and dress of the thirties; explore these things, hoping to pique and excite unconscious responses and memories of that time and place. In all of us there are deep and colorful memories and feelings locked in the memory banks of our unconscious, and if the actress spent a considerable amount of time doing this kind of research, I know it would yield good results. In addition to this kind of involvement, there are many substitutions that can be made. By emphasizing existing economical problems the actress can create her own kind of poverty consciousness. In almost every instance, a parallel reality can be used to create the reality that leads to getting a sense of living at that time and in that place.

There are events and conditions in our present lives that stimulate thoughts and feelings and behavior similar to the experience of the people we are trying to play at any time in history. We feel the same way about something as the character does about everything in the play. The job is to find these experiences and events and translate them into craft terms, apply the craft elements, and create the organic experience for ourselves on the stage.

When I directed this play, we spent a lot of time together dealing with the period. For weeks we looked at magazines and books from that era, played thirties music, talked about current events of that time and about movies we had seen that had been produced then. The actors brought in objects and small pieces of furniture from the thirties. Joan, who played Amanda, and I are old enough to remember some of that period. We shared our own personal memories and experiences. We spoke of our families and of how they behaved during that time.

I had the actors wear clothing of that period, and they did improvisations relating to how the Wingfield family spent their time at home. The actor who played Tom read and really wrote poetry; Amanda cleaned, washed dishes, and spoke of former times with great nostalgia; Laura played with her glass collection and made up stories about each glass animal. The actors listened to music of the period and surrounded themselves with objects that came from that time. Essentially, we created a reality that surrounded the play.

I had several reasons for doing this. One was to re-create real elements and stimuli from that time. I hoped to give the actors a taste of the essence of a period that might pique an unconscious relationship and understanding of how these people lived. I felt that if they had that foundation, the choices they made thereafter to stimulate similar feelings and impulses would be more specific, would be selected with greater knowledge of the requirements of the emotional life and fabric. Another reason for this kind of improvisation was to establish relationships that actually happened and were ongoing, supplementing the scenes in the play. I wanted the actors to establish experiences related to each other that paralleled the play and would hopefully establish a foundation for ensemble work. If the actors spent enough time making the environment familiar and personal, while at the same time establishing shared experience in the Wingfield environment, they would create a dimension of relationship that went way beyond the beginning, the middle, and the end of just the written material.

The events and action of the play probably couldn't happen in a time like the present. Our economic circumstances and our mobility, as well as our level of consciousness, are so different that other alternatives to responsibility would be found. Therefore, the impact of the historic obligation on the actors and the director of this play is of primary importance and must be considered immediately.

An actor approaching this obligation area should ask some pertinent questions:

What are the specifics of this period—customs, clothing, etc.?

After establishing those realities, ask the following:

How does that awareness affect the character?

What could I use or work for that will stimulate similar feelings for me?

What kind of objects, people, places could I create that would pique parts of my own personality in order for me to experience a similar inner life?

Once the actor decides on a choice, he can explore it to see how much of the demands of this obligation are satisfied by the emotional life produced by that choice involvement.

The Thematic Obligation: While Amanda makes a great number of statements throughout the play, I believe that the thematic responsibility of this play is Tom's responsibility. When Tom relates directly to the audience in his soliloquies, he carries the message of this play.

The Subtextual Obligation: Besides the obvious subtext of a mother's role in relation to her children, which is a lot of the unspoken thrust of the underlife of Amanda, there is the very obvious texture and quality of this play. It has a dreamlike quality. It is loaded with nostalgia, particularly from Amanda, and even the original music used in this play promotes that nostalgia. It might be said that you are experiencing the characters through a gauze filter, their behavior seeming to be stylized with an almost imperceptible distortion in speech and movement.

The play has a kind of life that seems to exaggerate reality while maintaining the integrity of reality. It is an essence, a quality, a style, an ambiance—a fabric of behavior and life that must somehow manifest itself throughout.

The actress must specify a kind of cause-and-effect understanding before approaching something as elusive as the qualities discussed above. She would start by determining specifically the nature and quality of the desired behavior. If it could be interpreted as an ethereal type of behavior, she could begin to experiment with choices that hopefully would stimulate a like response.

For example, if it was a dreamlike nostalgia that infiltrated most of Amanda's behavior, particularly at those times when she speaks of her life in the South, the actress might work to re-create events and experiences, or objects related to those events, which might stimulate an inner and underlying quality of subtle nostalgic preoccupation. She could explore a variety of choices and choice approaches that would organically affect the way she moves and speaks. In fact, there is no end to the possible paths of exploration. The subtextual-obligation area is one of the more difficult areas to pin down. However, once it is clear to the actor, the process of approach is like any of the other areas of obligation.

HOW TO IDENTIFY THE OBLIGATIONS IN A PIECE OF MATERIAL

It should all be there in the material: all the information that tells the actor what the various responsibilities are. There is a fairly simple list of questions to follow in order to determine what the obligations are and if, indeed, a specific one exists in this piece of material.

WHAT THE AUTHOR SAYS ABOUT THE PLAY AND THE CHARACTERS

Usually right at the beginning of a play the playwright sets the time, the place, and the period. Throughout the piece, usually in italics, he supplies information about the play and his visions of the characters and their behavior.

He most often describes the characters from the way they look and think. Sometimes there is a short biography of some of the more important characters in the play. This enables an actor to understand the genesis of the character and some of the reasons he behaves as he does later in the play.

The playwright will very often describe the environment with such emotional content that the reader will actually have a visceral response to the time and the place without ever having been there.

On occasion, the writer will even tell you the theme of his play and which character states it or symbolizes the statement.

Writers expose themselves in their work and quite frequently identify with one character in the play. The personality and the emotional makeup of that character, as well as his living philosophy, very often mirror the writer. If the actor knows the playwright or knows a lot about him, he can gather needed information from that knowledge.

Example of an Author's Description of a Character:

He is rich and confident. He dresses with a knowledge of style and learned taste. He is aggressive, yet kind to those who are his subordinates. He knows what he wants and how to get it, as his station in life proves. There is, however, an almost imperceptible betrayal of this confidence when he is challenged by the people he respects. He is a self-made man who struggled to educate himself so he could escape his coal-miner heritage . . .

There is a whole book in that description! There is, for sure, more than that to go on, so the actor has very rich material on which to base his journey to the realization of the obligations.

WHAT THE OTHER CHARACTERS IN THE PLAY SAY ABOUT YOUR CHARACTER

From the dialogue the actor gets an enormous amount of information about his character. The other characters may talk to him or to each other about him and, in doing so, expose their perceptions about his emotional state, his psychological characteristics, his actions, and, sometimes, what they think motivates his behavior. They expose the way they feel about his character and what makes them feel that way—all of which gives the actor a clear view of the various obligations.

Examples:

"Joe, why are you always so quick to defend yourself? I was only trying to point something out to you!"

"You know, you are one of the most defensive people I have ever met!"

"Why is it that every time I try to talk to you a wall seems to go up?"

Dialogue like that makes it very clear that our character is defensive. Finding out why he is gives the actor the blueprint for the exploration of choices that might motivate that defensiveness.

"I love the way you relate to animals! I think you must love everything alive."

"You talk to your son with such understanding."

Here again, the lines are full of clues to the character.

WHAT THE CHARACTER SAYS ABOUT HIMSELF

In almost every piece of material, a character has a monologue which informs the audience about him or his life as a child, or his war experiences, and so on. In addition, every character expresses what is going on inside by the things he says in the play. It doesn't always have to relate to the character himself to let the reader know how he feels or essentially what kind of person he is.

Example:

"All my life I have been standing on the outside looking in . . . Those bastards born with a silver spoon in their mouths make me sick! I hate the way they look down on me . . . I had to work for everything I ever got! My mother used to make my Christmas gifts. I never got nothin' I didn't earn or take!"

It is obvious from that piece of dialogue that this character is seething with resentment and envy, filled with anger and hatred that he self-righteously justifies. It is certainly a key to his character.

Most material is rich with clues to the character—how he thinks, what he feels and why, things he exposes about his relationship to the other characters in the play. He also lets the actor know how the environment affects his life and behavior, as well as how the forces of the period he lives in operate.

THE ACTIONS AND INTERACTION OF THE CHARACTERS

This is what takes place in every scene—not only the dialogue but also the physical behavior.

Examples:

He explodes in a fury of rage, swinging his arms and moving like a wild animal through the living room. Like a tornado, he destroys everything in his path, and before stalking out of the room, he issues a scream like that of a wounded and dying animal.

When he laughs, his entire body cooperates; he jiggles with laughter, and his being seems to radiate sunlight.

They embrace with an energy that seems to come from the center of the earth. It is easy to see the depth of the love they have for each other.

As artillery shells explode all around, he crouches lower and lower, slithering along the ground like a worm looking for the opening in the ground he can disappear into. He seems to get smaller and smaller as he shrieks with each explosion.

Each description of action in the above scenes conjures up some kind of feeling or knowledge adding to the component parts of the character and the obligations of the piece.

Body language tells its own tale, and in the description of the action of the play any reference to physical attitude or body language is filled with pertinent insight into the character.

THE CHRONOLOGY OF OBLIGATIONS

This is the order in which the actor approaches the various obligations of a piece of material. Which obligation needs to be approached first is totally dependent on how the various obligations are interrelated and impact on each other.

If the relationship in a scene is so powerful that all the feelings and emotional responses are a result of who these people are to one another and how they are affected by one another, then the first responsibility of the actor is to work for the stimulus that makes the relationship as meaningful to him as it is to the character he is working on. All of the choices he makes related to any of the other obligations will be affected by the relationship elements. Therefore, it would be very wise to start with the relationship.

Example:

You are doing a religious film. The character is a blacksmith who comes into the presence of Jesus. The blacksmith has heard tales of this magnificent healer and teacher. It has been rumored that he, Jesus, is the Messiah! The blacksmith is a common man who has never experienced someone as holy or exalted, and he is rendered speechless in the presence of Jesus.

Before the actor could deal with any other element in that particular scene, he would most definitely have to confront the power of the relationship obligation. Once he made that real for himself, he could deal with the emotional obligations of the scene, as well as any other which might exist.

If the actor chose to work in another area, he would soon see what a strain it would be to find a choice in the emotional-obligation area that would have such an enormous impact on him. With a little experience using the work, it becomes deductive exploration of the text that leads to making the proper decision as to which obligation to address first.

In the film *Flight of the Phoenix,* a plane has crashed in the desert. The entire film is about battling the environment and surviving (fighting thirst, exposure, and hostile Arabs who kill some of the characters). There are, of course, relationships between the characters in the film, dynamics, and emotional exchanges. There is conflict, possibly even a theme somewhere intertwined in the action of the film. However, everything that happens is a direct result of the place, the environment, and the effect of that place on all the people in the film. The emotional life, the responses, and the interrelationships of all the people are influenced by how the place affects them. The personality elements of all the people are piqued by the impetus of thirst, exhaustion, dehydration, exposure, fear of death, and so on. These same people lounging in the luxury of a beautiful hotel on the French Riviera would most definitely not behave this way, nor would these facets of their characters ever rise to the surface. Without creating the realities of such a place, the actor would not have a meaningful enough foundation or impetus to reach the height of the emotional life of the character. Unless the actor can really experience the physical calamities of being exposed to the desert, he would be too "civilized" to behave in such a way.

The character obligation is often so pronounced and impacting that the actor must start there.

Example:

The character is volatile. He is very explosive; he is an angry man. It takes very little for him to become enraged, and when he does, he is very abusive. There is an underlying threat of violence.

These are very specific character descriptions, and if the actor had a temperament quite different from that of the character, he would be advised to start building those characteristics before attempting to work for choices in any other obligation area.

Very often the nature of the emotional life and expressions of a character in a play comes out of the superstructure of his personality. This volatile character is the way he is because of his psychological makeup. An actor approaching the character's eruptions on a scene-to-scene basis might be able to be volatile, explosive, and abusive; however, it would not come from a place of character justification and would therefore lack depth, dimension, and understanding.

The historic obligation would have an enormous impact on forming behavior patterns, character elements, personality, and the way a person relates to the world overall.

If a person grew up in the Middle Ages, in an environment where his life was in danger almost every moment of every day, in a time when the world was filled with ignorance and superstition, when an eclipse of the sun meant a demand for human sacrifice, when self-appointed "holy men" could take your life on a whim, fear would be a very strong and impelling force in his life! If the actor identified the strength of such an important historic obligation, he would know that it is the impact of that time that would totally form the character's personality and behavior. Therefore, logic points to beginning with the historic obligation before considering the individual scene responsibilities. For someone living with that constant insecurity and fear of death, every relationship would be influenced by suspicion. There would be a feeling of having always to be on guard. Every relationship choice, every emotional obligation that the actor would approach would be affected by the impact of the elements of the historic obligation.

In a sense, the chronology of obligations is like a preparation to act: there is a logical order in which certain forces act on each other. Choosing the right obligation first lays the groundwork for the next to become a reality.

The decision of which obligation to explore first is sometimes a matter of common sense, at other times trial and error. It depends largely on how much experience an actor has with the craft. After spending a lot of time following the various paths, the actor develops a sense about which comes first.

It isn't often that an actor has to deal with all seven obligations in a piece of material. If the piece is set in a contemporary period, the historic obligation doesn't exist. If the character in the piece is so like you that it could be you, then you need not concern yourself with a character obligation. Suppose there is no thematic line to follow through your character and no definable subtextual responsibility; then the only areas left would be time and place, relationship, and the various emotional obligations that exist in the play. These three obligations always exist in material, since the scene takes place somewhere and at some time, your character relates to other characters or at least talks about them, and, of course, he certainly experiences some kind of emotional life, no matter how subtle.

When reading the script, the actor almost always can determine the chronology of obligations, because it is fairly obvious. When it seems that the material can be approached from a variety of beginnings and that there isn't a necessary starting obligation, then I would suggest that a very good place to begin the creative process would be the time-and-place obligation. There are a number of logically good reasons for starting there: To begin with, creating a place at a certain time builds an environment for the actor that takes him off the stage, allows him to be affected or influenced by the place he has created, and also promotes the reality of the environment for an audience. The phenomenon of public privacy comes from an actor who has created an environment which absorbs his concentration and involvement to such a degree that he can feel alone, and at the same time, on an Eleventh Level of Consciousness, he knows he is on stage and in "public."

CHOICES

WHAT IS A CHOICE?

A choice is an object, a person, a place, or a thing! (I use the word "object" to describe odors, sounds, music, weather, the wind, heat, cold—anything that can be experienced or perceived through the senses.) *The choice is that which the actor works for in a scene to make himself feel what the author tells him the character feels.*

A choice is not a decision! If the actor decides to go in a certain direction or if he decides to use a certain object or chooses a particular choice approach, those are all decisions and are not to be confused with a choice, which is an object, a person, a place, or a thing.

Examples:

"I am working for a specific piece of music because that piece of music makes me feel nostalgic and sad. It makes me yearn for times past!"

"I am working to create a place because that place makes me feel the way I think the characters feel in the place they are in."

"I am attempting to create a ring that my father gave me for my high-school graduation, because I think the ring will make me remember and feel all the feelings that I had for my father and that period in my life."

"I get slightly depressed at dusk. That time of day has always made me feel contemplative and down, so I'm trying to work for that through the use of Sense Memory, so that I can stimulate that emotional life."

"I want to feel that uneasy feeling when I hear the wind howling outside, whistling through the eaves of the house, so I will work for a room in my house and the sound of a ferocious wind whipping around out there. If I succeed in creating the reality of that choice, hopefully I will experience the uneasiness I am obligated to."

The choice in all of the examples is the element that stimulates the desired response.

In the first example it was the *music*.

The second dealt with the *place*.

The *ring* was the choice in the third example.

In the fourth instance, it was the time of day—*dusk*.

The last example related to a choice of a *room* and *the sound of a forceful wind*.

The choice is the object you create and use that addresses the fulfillment of any of the seven major obligations in a piece of material.

The obligation in a play may be a character obligation of a very timid person, and the actor might decide to work to create the sense of an animal, a rabbit, in order to establish a foundation for an important character element. In this case, the choice is a rabbit! The way in which the actor creates the sense of the animal in relation to himself is through the use of a choice approach.

THE OBLIGATION: What the actor wants to feel, experience, or accomplish.

THE CHOICE: The object the actor picks, hoping that it will stimulate the experience and fulfill the obligation.

THE CHOICE APPROACH: The way in which the actor makes the choice real; the process for creating the choice; the approach to the choice.

Choices exist in many forms and in all sensory areas. There are an infinite number of choices that an actor may have experienced, and calling them forth is dependent on being in touch with the largest number possible. An actor should always be aware of new experiences, acquiring fresh choices for future use and reaching back into the memory banks for forgotten choices to be resurrected at any moment to stimulate an experience.

There are a number of good exercises that specifically deal with finding and remembering events and experiences pregnant with choices. I will discuss some of these techniques later in this section.

LIST OF CHOICES

An important person, your father, mother, any member of your family, your wife, husband, your kitchen, the smell and sound of bacon cooking on the kitchen stove, a photograph, a painting that moves you, your dog, any pet that you ever had, the beach, snowflakes dropping on a quiet winter night, your bed, the living room, a piece of jewelry, laughter, the sounds of someone in pain, a telephone ringing in another room, sitting in your car, the sound of a high-performance automobile shifting through the gears, a dog howling in the distance, the sound and smell of rain, the wind, a love letter or any other meaningful kind of letter, a statue, a gift, the National Anthem, an autograph book from high school, a stuffed animal, a model airplane, lightning and thunder, fireflies, the sounds of summer, winter, the ice-cream truck, church bells, a nightgown, weather conditions of any kind, a headache or any other physical ailment, a diary and its meaning to you, your first bicycle, the taste of a particular food, sweat, oil on your skin, a police officer, candy, the sights and sounds of a circus, times of day and night, rainbows, the smell of apple pie, sitting around a fire roasting marshmallows, freezing-cold weather, a movie, a favorite object, a funeral, uniforms, the smell of a doctor's office, the sound of a dentist's drill, a sink full of dirty dishes, a mouse scurrying across the floor, cockroaches fleeing into the cracks late at night, Christmas, the tree, Thanksgiving dinner, a coffin, the smell of sickness, a look in a person's eye, the ravages of age, a baby laughing, crying, playing, awards, diplomas . . .

The objects that exist and can affect the actor number in the hundreds of thousands. They appeal to every known human emotion and, if used properly, will stimulate physical, psychological, and emotional responses.

The smell of something can bring back an entire experience and stimulate an emotional state. We often, without being conscious of the component elements, suddenly remember a time from our past. We may even talk about it with someone near us, recalling the places and the people who were there at the time. We seem to take a "trip" into our past, fondly, and sometimes not too fondly, discussing the way things made us feel. This trip may have been stimulated by a familiar smell of pipe tobacco that our grandfather used to favor or passing a person on the street who reminds us vaguely of a close friend we haven't seen in years. The "kicker" can be almost anything; the "kicker" is the *choice*—the very stimuli that sent us on that trip. An actor essentially identifies the trip he wants to take in the scene and then picks a choice, hoping that the choice will take him on the same trip that the character in the play is on. Knowing how things affect you is extremely helpful in making the right choices when dealing with a piece of material. *An actor is an actor twenty-four hours a day!* He should be cataloguing, trying, using, and exploring choices all the time, so that when he needs the right one, he will have had recent experience in using something which just might work for the scene.

Knowing oneself is a great prerequisite to acting. Since feelings and impulses are ignited by stimuli, the actor must have knowledge of what kinds of stimuli do what to him. He must know what stimulates a feeling of guilt, happiness, anger, depression, lust, apathy, joy, confusion, curiosity, patriotism, violence, and so on.

MATERIAL EXAMPLES OF CHOICE USAGE

In the play *Lunchtime,* by Leonard Melfi, the leading character, Rex, has a monologue in which he tells the woman, Mavis, about his marriage. He tells her that he feels trapped and unseen by his wife and that the only reason he stays is because of his son, Little Rex.

Rex is an unhappy, bitter, and somewhat lost man. He refinishes furniture for a living and hates his work. He deals with the frustrations in his life by escaping into sexual liaisons with equally frustrated female clients.

The monologue is somewhat self-justifying, and there is also the reality that Rex wants to sleep with Mavis.

The actor approaching this scene has two major responsibilities:

1. To create a strong attraction and sexual desire for the actress playing Mavis

2. To stimulate a personal desperation and a feeling of being trapped in his own life, as well as the elements of being unfulfilled

The reason Rex tells Mavis about himself may very well be to appeal to her, getting her sympathy and understanding and persuading her to make love with him. That may be what impels him to do this monologue. If this is the truth, his desire for Mavis must be very strong and impelling. Therefore, the actor should start with that.

The actor's choices:

1. The actor might fulfill the first obligation element in the scene by relating to all the features that he finds attractive and sexually stimulating in the actress playing Mavis—intensifying to himself certain of her movements and behavior so that they become sensual and provocative to him, encouraging sexual fantasies about himself and

the actress, being familiar with his own sexual "risabilities," emphasizing certain areas of the actress' body.

The above suggestions deal strictly with what is available—the available stimulus: *the actress.*

If, for whatever reason, the actor cannot use the actress as his choice, he would have to opt for another woman in relation to her. In such a case, he would pick someone whom he finds very attractive sexually and who would make him want to seduce her. He would then work to create his choice in relation to the actress playing Mavis. He would do this through a choice-approach process called Endowments. The really important thing is that the actor be so strongly attracted and lustful that it motivates all the rest of his behavior.

2. For the second obligation element in the scene, the choice easily could be any of the parallels in the actor's life. Suppose he is working at a "regular" job that he hates (while waiting for acting jobs). He never has enough money to buy the things he sees others having. He feels he is getting older and going nowhere. He feels trapped in a rut of living that he is powerless to change.

All of these feelings are only a part of the actor's reality. On other levels he functions quite happily: he is pursuing a career, he has hopes of working and being successful, and so on. However, if he were to just concentrate on the negatives in his life, he could quickly feel all the things that Rex feels.

The actor would make the choice real for himself by doing a choice-approach process called Inner Monologue—silently talking to himself about all the things that make him feel desperate and like a loser. He does this process under the lines of the scenes and in between them.

There are an infinite number of choice possibilities for the above example; the two listed are examples of what choices are and how they might be activated.

Alma, in Tennessee Williams' *Summer and Smoke,* has a famous monologue to the doctor in which she tells him that she loves him and has loved him for a long time. It is a very moving monologue, full of emotion and caring, as well as the need to maintain her dignity. She has a variety of feelings here: she feels rejected by him, she wants to let him know how and what she feels and at the same time hold her ground. She is quite vulnerable and nervous.

These are some of the complex elements existing in Alma and this monologue. The actress selects a choice or choices in order to evoke, stimulate, and create the inner life that Alma is experiencing.

The responsibilities of the actress in this monologue are:

1. To stimulate a deep love and admiration for the other character, a love that has evolved from childhood
2. To feel a strong need to express this love and the history of it, as well as a need to maintain pride, integrity, and dignity

There is a lot at stake here for Alma, and so there must be for the actress playing the scene. A good choice would be a person in the actress' life who affords a parallel, possibly a first love that she has never quite recovered from. If she cannot find one person to fill the bill, she might use a conglomerate choice, which simply means a combination of several people in her life who, together, make her feel the way Alma feels.

The choice then becomes *the person or conglomerate people* she selects to use for the monologue.

To make the choice real the actress could use one of several choice approaches: She could create the choice (the person) sensorially or do an Imaginary Monologue with the choice. The Imaginary Monologue should be approached as an Inner Monologue while in the framework of the piece.

The elements that create the vulnerability and fear for Alma are that she might be rejected and hurt by the doctor's response and that she has certain proprieties she has nurtured all her life. The actress can approach these responsibilities by emphasizing responses and certain behavioral guidelines, in the performance, that she has selected to relate to and that indicate jeopardy for her. She can put her own pride and dignity on the line.

Once the obligation in the piece has been identified, the very next step is to find the choice that will produce the same, or a similar, inner life for the actor.

HYPOTHETICAL OBLIGATIONS AND POSSIBLE CHOICES

The obligation is to feel exalted and triumphant. The choice might be a piece of music that affects you that way or the re-creation of a curtain call complete with the thunderous applause.

The obligation is to feel sad and vulnerable. The choice could be a place that has made you feel that way, or a person, or an object such as a letter, a photograph of a deceased person whom you loved, etc.

The obligation might be sensuality, a character of enormous sensuality. The choice may involve doing a sensuality exercise, which means getting in touch with your own body on a sensual level, epidermally, with sensual movement, etc. An actor might stimulate sensuality by creating certain music or rhythmical beats like a drumbeat. The choice can also be the creation of a provocative member of the opposite sex undulating suggestively.

The obligation could be uproarious laughter. The choice exploration could involve various sensorially created visions of people doing funny things, scenes from movies, a hilarious story re-created. The actor could exaggerate and distort, in a humorous way, the available environment by having the people behave in fantastic ways; he could accomplish this through the use of the senses or through suggestion or through a choice-approach process called Believability.

Wherever there is an impulse, a thought, or a feeling, there exists a choice that will stimulate it.

HOW TO USE A CHOICE

Before you can explore a choice to see where it takes you, a selection must be made. Picking a choice in the right area can save the actor a great deal of time and frustration. Making a proper selection depends on two things: first, clearly identifying the obligation—what it is that you want the choice to do specifically—and, second, having a good idea of what kinds of choices take you where. Both those realities depend on some kind of experience with the work. However, even in the beginning the actor can take some "Inventories" to focus more clearly on the nature of the objects that might elicit the desired responses.

The bedroom scene between Biff and Happy in Arthur Miller's *Death of a Salesman* has a number of obligations for both characters. Let's list a few and pick a number of possible choices as examples for the scene.

Biff has just returned home after a long absence, and he and Happy are sleeping in the same bedroom they shared as boys. A lot has happened in the interim. Biff has been a wanderer and itinerant worker for minimum wages, while Happy has a responsible job as an assistant buyer in some department store. Happy has always looked up to Biff, has always sought Biff's approval. Biff experiences the unrest and conflict that drove him away, and every time he returns, he encounters his father's disapproval of his lifestyle and evident lack of success. He carries an anger and disappointment in his father so deep as to have been the catalyst in causing his self-sabotage. It is an unresolved private conflict between Willy and Biff, and it lurks just beneath the surface whenever they relate. In the scene, Biff and Happy nostalgically recall the old days growing up in the house, things they did, women they shared, and so on. This leads to an exposure of what they are doing with their respective lives now and how they feel about themselves and each other.

This description must now be translated into obligations, the various obligations need to be clarified, and a chronology must be decided upon by the actor. Then the actor must begin the process of selecting choices for the scene. In the rehearsal process, both actors explore and experiment with the choices in whatever order they have decided to employ them. They say the words of the scene, being irreverent to the logic until they learn where the choices will take them.

Example Using Biff:

He is restless and disturbed throughout the scene; being here again stimulates a lot of feelings that distance quells. He feels that old resentment for Willy. Being home again makes him feel like a failure and a disappointment to his father and his mother. He feels that he has been wasting his life. There is an element of nostalgia, and he loves his brother, even though it's hard to find a common ground to relate to Happy. He feels that Happy is superficial and has distorted values. Biff wants different things from those his father tried to foist on him while he was growing up, and because he truly loves Willy and wants to be loved by him and get his approval, he doesn't even accept his own judgment of what makes him happy.

The actor playing Biff, having clearly identified the responsibilities to the scene, could:

1. Create a place from his own living experience that has a number of the same elements as the scene.
2. Work for a choice related to the actor playing Happy, a choice that makes him experience feelings for that actor similar to those Biff has for Happy. He could use any available realities in the other actor and/or work for a person, possibly his own brother, in relation to the actor playing Happy.
3. Work for a choice, possibly stimulated by the place he is already creating, that arouses the inner conflict Biff experiences. Let's imagine the actor has had a conflict with his father, which to this moment is unresolved. They both have swept it under the carpet and function in spite of it. The actor could re-create his own father and selectively emphasize the behavioral elements of the conflict they have, and hopefully he would rekindle the flame of conflict and the need he has for his real father.
4. Deal with his own feelings of failure and confusion by doing a "litany of woes" related to the selectively emphasized areas of his own lack of success as an actor, in life, in love situations, with his own family, and so on.
5. Deal with the time of night, since it is very late. The hour would have an effect on how the characters relate to each other.

6. Deal with a facet of his relationship with his own father that piques the same kind of ambivalence that exists in the play. He could, for example, work to create his father saying things that would ignite that kind of ambivalence.

With the six possible choice areas suggested here, the actor would have to decide in which order he could work most expeditiously. He might even discover other choices spawned by these.

Again, the six possible choices are:

1. A place
2. Available stimulus in relation to the actor playing Happy, or another person such as his own brother or a friend, created by endowing the other actor with that person
3. His own father, with Selective Emphasis; the place itself as an environment where the actor has had trauma and inner conflict as well as unresolved conflict with others
4. "Litany of woes" about his own lack of success and unhappiness, also selectively emphasized
5. Time of night
6. The sound of his father carrying on and saying things that would upset him; possibly exaggerated and distorted expressions

The elements of nostalgia could be dealt with by either bringing personally meaningful objects to the theater or creating things that would stimulate nostalgic feelings.

Often a variety of obligations such as in the *Death of a Salesman* example can be fulfilled with a single choice.

Suppose the actor playing Biff had experienced most of the realities Biff had. All the years of grade school and all the way through high school the actor lived in one place, and in this place he was exposed to the conflicts, pressures, and demands that Biff faced as a young man. There was conflict with his father, even though it did not have the same origin or reasons. There were the obvious and subtle pressures to be something, to accomplish, to want the things his family wanted for him, etc. This same actor was an athlete in school, as was Biff, and he had sibling relationships that could fit, and so on. It isn't often that the parallels are so close, but often there are similarities that, with very little adjustments, can work as choices.

Suppose that every time this actor went home to visit, he experienced many of the old conflicts and feelings. If he didn't protect himself from experiencing them, he would probably feel and behave much the way Biff does in the scene. Therefore, the choice would be to create that house, specific parts of it, including the people present and selecting the specific events that would most closely mirror the scene. The choice then would be *a place at a specific time and an experience that occurred in that place and time!*

The choice approach in this case would be Affective Memory.

The actor playing Biff, through the entire production, would have to explore many choices in all the obligation areas that are pertinent to his character in the play.

The spectrum of choices is multivarious. The perimeter of possibilities is as wide as the imagination. There are choices which you use over and over because you know that they are meaningful and work all the time. There are "way out" choices that you experiment with in rehearsal that might make it all the way to performance. There are also areas of uncharted territory which you may never have explored.

Once, a very long time ago, I visited a class that was Method oriented, where one very pretty and talented actress was working for the sense that her eyelashes were beautiful butterfly wings; another actress was trying to create a sense of being molten lava moving down the side of a mountain. The second actress was doing Medea. Now, both of those choices are definitely imaginative! The concept of molten lava for Medea seems not only imaginative, but accurate. Such choices are exciting in concept, but if they are not made real, they remain an intellectual concept and do not promote an organic state on the stage. If both actresses were able, through a craft process, to really stimulate the authentic sense of those choices through their own physical instruments, those would be sensational choices!

Many years ago, when I was studying acting, I was doing a scene in class from *Dark of the Moon*. I was playing the Witchboy. The scene we were working on was at the end of the play when Barbara Allen dies and the witches, in the form of eagles, are coming to reclaim the Witchboy and make him a witch again instead of the mortal that he has become. The obligations are enormous in size and scope! He(the character) is anguished at learning that Barbara Allen cheated on him, which is why she must die and he must return to the life of a witch. He feels ripped apart by hearing "the flapping of eagles' wings," signifying their coming for him. He is grief-stricken as Barbara Allen dies in his arms, and terrified of what is coming. There is certainly a very theatrical mixture of emotional obligations.

A number of years before working in that class on the scene, I'd had a very unsettling, and what I considered to be a supernatural, experience; it was so frightening and upsetting that I didn't speak of it for many years. My aunt was dying in the hospital, and I was visiting her. She was conscious but sedated. As we spoke, I held her hand. Her daughter, who was also in the room at the time, was suddenly called away for some reason. Shortly after she left, I became conscious of a sudden chill in the room. The light also changed. It was almost as if the sun had gone behind a cloud, but there wasn't any sun! The shades were drawn, and the lights were on. Nevertheless, the room grew dim. I felt a presence. An undeniable presence had come into that space. My aunt sat bolt upright with her eyes wide open and said, "No, I won't go!" She clenched my hand with an incredible strength that no dying person ever had. At that moment I knew that the Angel of Death was there! I knew it; I felt it! I was convinced of it! Never have I known such helpless terror. I was afraid for my aunt and for myself. I didn't know what to do, and in that moment I also knew that I could do nothing. A moment later the room was filled with people: her daughter, doctors, nurses, orderlies. The doctor examined my aunt and later said that she had come very close to death in those short moments when we were alone. To this very day, I still get a cold and eerie feeling when I think about it or talk of it.

I used that as a choice for the final scene in *Dark of the Moon*. I worked for that room. I created the odors, the visual elements, my aunt, the coldness, the power of that presence I felt that day so many years ago, and I did the scene! The impact of that choice was so enormous and the emotional results so incredible, I didn't remember what had happened during the scene. I experienced almost everything the playwright said the Witchboy experienced and maybe something more. I do know that the choice was so powerful that I seemed to cross that very important line into what I now call an Ultimate Consciousness experience. That is when the actor consciously trips into the unconscious and there is an uninterrupted flow of electrifying life on the stage.

I don't know how many choices like that any of us has; however, I do know there are more than one or two. It is the artist's responsibility to dig deeply and put himself in "harm's way," so to speak. When an actor crosses into never-never land, there is nothing like it! That is when we realize why we need to act. That is when it all comes into focus. There isn't a feeling in the world quite like it.

FINDING CHOICES

There are a number of ways to locate choices. There are various inventories the actor can do that will isolate certain areas and narrow down the number of possibilities. You can chart choices: keep a journal of every scene, film, and play that you do, complete with a chart of obligations/choices/choice approaches you have tried, allowing for a column that reminds you of the results of the choices you tried in each scene.

At the present time, I have a student in my class who keeps a card catalogue of choices, separated into the various emotional categories. When he gets stuck for a choice, he goes to his card file. Some actors I know separate their repertoire of choices into periods in their lives. Other actors I have worked with use the same twenty choices over and over again.

DAILY INVENTORIES

An actor should always be working! Besides the daily exercise work with Sense Memory, scenes and monologues, and working on animals, the actor must be "out in the field" observing and perceiving human behavior. He must become familiar with how people behave and why they respond as they do. He should be extremely aware of the impact of stimuli on himself. During the course of one day, we have thousands of stimuli encounters; we are affected in thousands of ways each hour. Some of our responses are imperceptibly subtle, while others are large and explosive. If we train ourselves to become aware of why and how we function, we can collect new experiences and new choices every day. It cannot be approached generally. The process of Inventory must be very specific for it to be of value. A simple encounter with a pretty woman at the cash register in a restaurant can be isolated, inventoried, and catalogued for future use.

Example:

The experience: *I looked at her. I found her attractive. Looking at her made me feel good—I felt warm and a little embarrassed when she returned my look.*

Inventory (after the experience): *What was it that made me notice her? Her coloring: her eyes were a pale blue and seemed to be so deep. I liked the color of her hair and the way it was shaped. Her nose was perfect. The size, shape, and color of her mouth were arresting . . .*

As the actor takes the Inventory of the stimulus and is totally aware of how he was affected by it, he can be re-creating the object (person) sensorially at the same time, since that process will set it in the sense, as well as the mental, memory.

Example:

The experience: *I didn't like the way he spoke to me. I simply asked a question about the special of the day, and he responded rudely! . . .*

Inventory (after the experience): *How did the incident make me feel? . . . At first I was taken aback by his response, then I became angry. After that, I wanted to confront him about his attitude and response to me . . . I felt myself flush and get warm, and then I noticed that my heartbeat was stronger and faster . . . I clenched my fists . . .*

What were the stimuli elements in that experience? How did he look? How tall was he? What was his physical attitude? the expression on his face? . . . What did I see in his eyes? . . . What did his mouth look like? . . . How close to, or far from, me was he when he said what he said? What did his voice sound like? What were his first words, and what did they sound like? . . . What was the quality in his voice that told me he was rude? . . . How did his mouth move and form the words that he said? . . . How long did the whole exchange take? . . .

The Inventory can go on for as long as you feel it is necessary to solidly own the experience for future use. The responses to the Inventory questions should be both intellectual and sensorial.

An actor can catalogue a minimum of a dozen experiences a day, and sometimes each experience contains more than one usable choice. The process need not call attention to itself. As a matter of fact, no one but the actor himself should know that he is doing it.

CHOICE HUNT

This is an involvement that can be done particularly when you are alone, before retiring at night or at any time when you can find the quiet and solitude that will allow you to concentrate.

Do the exercise lying down on your back with your eyes closed. Go back in time to meaningful and emotional events: graduations, holidays, weddings, picnics, family dinners, funerals, birthdays, parties, celebrations of all kinds—in fact, any event that you can easily recall. Re-create the experience as totally as you can, first remembering it and then making it a sensory experience.

Ask questions about weather, time of year, day, month, temperature, light sources, sounds, smells, people, how they were dressed, what they said, how they behaved, how you were dressed, how you felt, and so on. Respond to your exploration by actually attempting to smell, taste, see, and feel all the elements of the event. Take a sensory and emotional "trip" on the experience. When you have exhausted that particular memorable experience, ask yourself what interesting thing may have occurred just before or right after it. As you remember each new event, take the same kind of "trip" on all of them. The advantage of approaching the Choice Hunt in this manner is that the experiences that you remember may spark the recall of others which happened around that period of time. It is as if you were opening the memory banks in a certain time frame; and, as you opened them, a cornucopia of experience poured out all over you.

The value of doing Choice Hunts is that you acquire more choices, and as you repeat the exercise, the memory responds much like a muscle: it begins to release its secrets, and before you know it, you are remembering things all the time, even when you are not doing the exercise.

While you are doing the Choice Hunt, encourage the expression of all emotional impulses stimulated by re-creating the experience. A surprising amount of impulses and feelings will be generated by the exercise.

TASK INVENTORY

Task Inventory is a process through which you find the right choices to use in a scene. I invented it in a moment of great desperation. Finding the right choice is sometimes an exasperating chore, and many times an actor must experiment with a variety of different ones in order to select the one that works in the scene. When all else fails and you can't think of a choice, and you are not even sure that you ever felt that way before, *you do Task Inventory.* When you have become experienced with the process, it can be done quickly. If you were in front of the camera and really against the wall for a choice, you could do this exercise even with the limited time an actor has in films.

Task Inventory is a marvelous process that eliminates confusion and the inability to locate a choice. It instills confidence through the various parts of the technique:

1. Identify the *obligation,* making it *very clear* to yourself.
2. Restate the obligation, putting it into language that describes it completely.
3. Ask yourself if you have ever felt that way before. When?
4. Go back to that time in your memory, and attempt to recall as much of the experience as possible.
5. Ask yourself what it was about that experience that made you feel that way.
6. Having completed the above, ask yourself whether there was another time when you experienced the same or a similar kind of response.
7. Again, attempt to recall, through memory, the entire experience.
8. Determine what the common denominator is between the two experiences and how they are similar or dissimilar. (A common denominator would relate to any parallels between the two experiences. Suppose that the obligation was to experience a certain kind of hostile conflict involving a confrontation with another person; the common denominator then would be the confrontation or the argument.)
9. Determine the choice. (Weigh the impact of both experiences, and choose one.)

10. Explore the translation of that choice. (Put the choice into an applicable and functional approach, deciding exactly how you are going to make the choice real for yourself. This would be the choice approach.)

Having accomplished all these steps, you would be ready to start working with the choice through the use of a choice approach, and, hopefully, it would all lead to the fulfillment of the obligation.

There is one final step in the Task Inventory process. This is the step I call "the Fail-Safe Device"—the part of the exercise that makes it *foolproof!*

You resort to this step when all else fails, when you cannot think of an experience, when you cannot even remember feeling that way. You have exhausted all recollections and have come up empty.

11. Ask yourself, *What would make me feel that way* if it existed in this place right now? How can I create it?

The entire world is open to the actor—anything that his imagination can supply, the world of reality and fantasy.

(There is an important footnote here. Before embarking on the Task Inventory journey, the actor should ask a very important question: Is there anything in the existing environment that will make me feel the way I want to?)

An example I frequently use to make Task Inventory clear is *to state the obligation as an overwhelming feeling of elation, a feeling of fulfillment.* I recall two separate experiences that produced that kind of elation in me:

Many years ago I was doing a Showcase evening at a small theater in Hollywood. I was playing Coney in *Home of the Brave.* When we finished the scene and I was walking off the stage, an older man in the audience grabbed my arm firmly, looked right into my eyes, and said, "Brilliant! Brilliant!" I smiled, nodded a thank-you, and walked off the stage. Just as I reached the backstage area I realized who that man was: it was Joseph Schildkraut, an actor I had grown up admiring, a marvelous old character actor who had given me many hours of pleasure. This was a man who had started on the stage and had done hundreds of films. To be told that I was brilliant by an accomplished actor like him made me feel as though I had just been given an Academy Award. I was elated. I felt a sense of accomplishment that was enormous. Certainly this experience qualifies as a possible choice, dealing with the stated obligation.

The second experience took place many years later. (I was only twenty-one when the first experience took place, and I was in my thirties at this time.) I had just completed an audition for a running role on *The Phil Silvers Show.* When I arrived home I received a call from Evelyn Silvers, telling me that I had the part and that they were extremely impressed with my audition. I was elated, speechless. It was like a dream come true!

The common denominator in the two experiences was that *something was said to me about me.* The next step in the process would be making a choice between the two experiences. Which one had the most impact in relation to the obligation? Which of the two produced more of the specific elements I want to experience in the scene?

My instincts tell me that the first experience is a better selection because, on a really deep level, it seemed to be more validating of my talent than the second experience; also because the emotional response produced by the first seemed to have the quality of elation that I want to feel.

Understanding that the common denominator was something told to me, something I heard, makes it easier to identify the translation into choice-approach terms.

For example, let us say I had decided on the second of the two experiences. The common denominator points to the telephone conversation as the impetus for stimulating the desired emotional life. The choice-approach translation would be to sensorially create the environment: the telephone itself, the conversation, the sound of Evelyn Silvers' voice, the words, how they sounded, and so on—in other words, re-create the entire experience through an Affective Memory choice approach.

An alternative choice approach, and a much shorter process, would be to use Evocative Words relating to the experience to see if that would have as impacting a result.

Having made the decision to use the first experience as the choice, I would specify the *choice* as being *Mr. Schildkraut* saying to me what he said.

In order to be affected on as deep a level as I was then, I would essentially have to re-create the entire experience, which means an Affective Memory approach, creating the time, the place, the other people in the scene, how they looked, sounded, how they were dressed, myself, how I was dressed, the sounds in the room—everything leading up to the *moment* that made up the impacting element of the experience. Of course, Affective Memory is an approach that is totally dependent on a sensory process. The actor asks the sensory questions related to the elements of that time on a here-and-now basis—e.g., *What color are the walls? What do I hear? How far away is he sitting?* . . .

There are simpler alternatives than Affective Memory; however, they might not stimulate such a dimensional and rich reality as going back to the original time could produce.

For instance, I could have a Fantasy Imaginary Monologue with Mr.

Schildkraut; or I could do an Inner Monologue, relating the entire event to myself and possibly restimulating those feelings. Experimentation is a large part of the creative process and is to be heartily encouraged. I, however, would favor going all the way, taking the time to explore the Affective Memory choice approach.

The Task Inventory process is a simple ten-point exercise. If you follow the directions of the exercise, it will certainly help you locate the right choices for the material. If the ten steps fail to lead to choices, you have the Fail-Safe Device.

The process will work in relation to any kind of material. If you cannot find a common denominator, or even a slight parallel between the experiences, just identify the element in the experience that stimulates the organic response that you are after. Practice Task Inventory even when you don't actually need it, so that you can become facile with it. Because when you *do* need it, you REALLY NEED IT!

Quite frequently, an actor I am working with will tell me that his choice was an experience, and I will say, "The whole thing?" Usually that gets a laugh. What I mean is that the only way an entire experience can be a choice is if the actor creates all the component parts of the experience. That means a complete Affective Memory exploration.

If you pick an event or an experience because you felt and behaved in a particular way and that is what you want for the scene, then you have the opportunity to break the experience down into its components. Suppose that the experience was your college graduation, on the sunny lawn of some impressive university. It was hot, and you wore cap and gown. Your family was there and some of your very close friends too. The part of the experience that made you feel what you want to feel for the scene was when your father came to you with tears in his eyes, put his arms around you, and told you that he was proud of you.

It is very likely that if you decided to work for your father doing and saying those things, you might experience a similar response. So, instead of a complex experience, you now have a single choice—your father. That is much simpler to create than an entire experience. If what you are looking for is part of an event, see if you can't isolate one single choice element.

CHOICE APPROACHES

CHOICE APPROACHES
AND CRAFT TECHNIQUES

Choice approaches are the tools an actor uses to create the choice he has selected. They are the way an actor "approaches" the choice, the functional and practical ways he works on the stage. In a sense, both the obligation and choice areas are basically intellectual decision and identification areas, while choice approaches are the tools the actor actually uses when he is acting: the "pick and shovel" of the job.

At the present time there are twenty-two choice approaches and craft techniques. When I started teaching, about twenty-five years ago, I had only four or five. The others have been developed over the years with the help and cooperation of all the actors I have taught. The value of having such a large number is in the alternate possibilities that so many afford an actor in his work. In addition to that, some choice approaches work in certain material situations far better than others. Knowing how, why, and when to select and use a specific choice approach depends on how much experience the actor has with the craft.

A craft technique is a choice approach that can be used in conjunction with other choice approaches. Such is the case with Affective Memory. In order for Affective Memory to work, it must be approached through the use of Sense Memory, which is its own choice approach as well as a craft technique. All of this will become very clear when we get into the description of the individual approaches.

When an actor is on the stage acting, he hopefully is working with his craft. That craft is the work he is doing with the specific choice approach he is involved with. That is what the actor does besides memorize lines. The goal of this involvement is to make a choice real through the use of the choice approach so that he can fulfill his responsibilities to the material—the obligations. The nature of the actor's involvement on the stage depends totally on the mechanics of the specific choice approach.

Each approach has its own mechanics in terms of process. If the actor was using Sense Memory as his approach in a scene (let's say that he was working to create a specific place), he then would be involved in the process of asking sensory questions and responding to those specific questions with the sense he is asking the questions of. If he was doing an Inner Monologue, he would be saying things to himself under and in between the lines of the play. If he was using Available Stimulus, he would be relating to the specific object or person on the stage whom he was using as the choice. Doing Evocative Words would mean that his working process would be to say (to himself, silently) words and short phrases that related to some experience he was using, hoping to create an emotional response for the scene. Whatever the choice approach might be, the actor should be involved in the specific demands of that process in order to promote the reality and impact of the choice!

EXAMPLES OF OBLIGATIONS, CHOICES, AND CHOICE APPROACHES

Just for the sake of clarity, I would like to redefine the three major categories and how they relate to each other.

OBLIGATION	CHOICE	CHOICE APPROACH
A feeling of love and pride toward someone you love	Your child	Endowments: Work sensorially to endow the other actor with your child's features and behavior
Hurt and anger, as well as the feeling of not being "seen" or respected	A person in your life with whom you have such a relationship	Imaginary Monologue: Talk to the other actor as if he were your choice
Intense attraction and sexual interest; a strong need for the other character	The actress you are working with in the play	Available Stimulus, possibly with the use of Selective Emphasis
Nostalgia, reminiscing about the old days	A place where you spent time and about which you have good memories	Sense Memory, recreating the place sensorially

That should give you some idea of the connection between the obligation, the choice, and the choice approach.

Everything we do in life has a system, a "how." If you know the system, if you know how to do whatever it is you want to do, then you *can* do it; and if you don't know how, you just can't!

THE CHOICE APPROACHES

1. SENSE MEMORY

It is not an accident that this choice approach heads the list. Sense Memory is a foundation approach, which means that it is an integral part of many of the other choice approaches.

Besides being a profoundly important tool in the creation of reality on the stage, it is instrumentally tied into the actor's "risability" and affectability. The ability to perceive and respond is a sensory process.

The senses have their own memory of experiencing stimuli. It is not an intellectual process; it is a *response* process! The senses can be trained to respond to objects that are not really there as if they really were there. If an actor is willing to put in the time every day practicing Sense Memory exercises, he will ultimately accomplish the ability to create objects that are not really there at the moment. Furthermore, he will be able to create these objects so that he can see them, feel them, smell them, hear them, and taste them *for real!* I know what you are thinking as you read this, if you are not already involved in the use of Sense Memory: You are saying to yourself, Oh, come on, now, *really see them?* The answer is Yes—really! Not at first, of course, but in time.

Sense Memory as a choice approach is an explorative process, which uses all five senses whenever possible. The actor attempts, through his sense memory, to create an object, person, place, or thing that he feels would affect him in a specific way, in order to fulfill his responsibility to the material. The process starts with the first sensory question which is directed to a specific part of one of the senses.

The purpose of asking questions that are responded to by each individual sense is to make an "imaginary object" real. If the choice you have decided to use in a scene is a person—your girlfriend, your mother, or anyone who is meaningful to you—making that person real, creating his or her presence so that he or she exists on the stage for you, is why you do Sense Memory. The actor uses Sense Memory to create all kinds of things, not just people. Sense Memory can be used to create a place, a time of day, weather conditions, the wind blowing through your hair, cold, warmth, the way a certain piece of clothing caresses your body, and so on. In fact, Sense Memory has very few limitations as to the kinds of stimuli that the actor can create. The sensory process is a very specific involvement. After the actor decides on the choice he wants to create, he starts asking very specific questions related to that choice.

Example:

Let us say that this actor wanted to create a place. He would then start asking sensory questions in one of his five sense areas:

What is the color of the walls? (That is a visual question, to be responded to by the visual sense, what the actor sees.)

Are there any variations in the color I see on the walls? (Again, he would attempt to visually respond to that question.)

Are there any contrasting colors? (The actor attempts to create the other colors that contrast with the original overall color he re-creates through Sense Memory.)

How do the other colors blend and contrast with the overall color? (The actor answers through the sense.)

How does the light in this room affect the color? (He relates totally through the visual sense to the impact of the light and its effect on the walls and the color.)

Where is the color the deepest? . . . How many different shades of the major color can I see? . . . On which part of the walls do I see any variations in color?

Are there any faded spots? . . . Where? . . . How do they differ from the other places I see? . . . What seems to be the major primary color? . . . How does the color of these walls affect me?

The actor can stay with the color as long as is necessary to begin getting visual responses. He can ask as many as fifty or more sensory questions in that area alone, or he may leave that and come back to it later in the exploration.

How high are the walls? (He attempts to actually see the height.)

At the point where the walls meet the ceiling, what do I see? (He tries to answer that question visually, attempting to sensorially remember how the ceiling and the walls meet.)

What is the texture of the walls? (That too is a visual question to be responded to by the eyes of the actor.)

What would it feel like to touch the walls? (Here the actor departs from the visual and is going to the tactile sense. He may walk over to the imaginary wall and feel the texture, or he may just "sensorially speculate" on how the wall might feel to his touch.)

As I move my hand across the surface of the wall, what do I feel? (The actor is specifically concentrating in the hand and what he feels as he moves across the imaginary field.)

How does the texture differ from place to place? . . . Where in my hand and fingers do I feel the most? (All of the responses are totally in the tactile area!)

Do I feel any irregularities in the surface? . . . What do they feel like? . . . If I were to press my fingers into the wall, how much resistance would I experience? . . . What muscles in my hand must I flex to apply that pressure? . . . Where do I feel the tension the most? . . . Is there any give in the object, the surface of the wall?

Do I detect an odor in the room? . . . from the walls themselves? (At this point the actor is involving a third sense, the olfactory, the smell. All responses take place in the actor's nose!)

What does that smell like? . . . How many different odors do I detect? (If the actor asks several questions as part of one, it is important to respond sensorially to each one and, in effect, answer each one.)

Where do the odors come from? (He may move around the stage, attempting to identify the origins of the various odors.)

Which is the strongest odor? . . . the most identifiable? . . . How do the various odors blend with each other? . . . Where in my nose do I smell these odors? . . . What do they remind me of? . . . Is there a particular odor or smell indigenous to this place? . . . What is that odor? . . . Where is it coming from? . . . If I closed my eyes and smelled the fragrance, would it remind me of this place?

At this point the actor might return to a group of visual questions:

What do I see hanging on the wall in front of me? (Again his responses would be visual; however, he would not exclude any of the other sensory responses he has already created. That is to say, if he still had a sense of the odors in the room, he would encourage those responses to sustain themselves.)

How large is the object hanging on the wall? . . . How wide is it? . . . What do the edges look like? . . . What are the major colors in the piece? . . . What is the shape of the objects in the painting? . . . Just below the object what do I see? . . . How close to the wall is it standing? . . . What is the shape of that object? . . . How wide is it? . . . How deep? . . . What does it seem to be made of? . . . What is its color? . . . texture? . . . If I were to touch it, what would it feel like? . . . How does the texture of this object differ from the texture of the wall? . . . How many different objects do I see on that wall? . . . Where are they? (All of these sensory questions are answered very directly and specifically in that part of each sense that the question is directed to.)

Are there any sounds in this place? (The actor has brought in a fourth sense in his exploration of the place.)

What do I hear? (Here the actor concentrates on his ears, attempting to actually hear the sounds he is relating to.)

Where is that sound coming from? . . . What does it sound like—the actual sound experience as I hear it? . . . What are the component parts of that sound? How many different sounds is it made up of? . . . How many can I hear? . . . What are the most obvious sounds in this place? . . . What are the more subtle sounds? . . . and where do they come from? . . . Are there any sounds coming from outside this place? . . . From where? . . . What do they sound like? . . . How do they interfere or blend with the other sounds I hear? . . . Are there any sounds I hear that are indigenous to this place? . . . What are they? . . . What are they made up of? . . . and what objects in this place cause those unique sounds?

If, at any point, the actor can logically involve the fifth sense, the gustatory—taste—then he should. But if it would not logically fit into the exploration, he could proceed with the other four:

As I move around this room, how do the sounds vary? . . . What do I hear in this area? . . . With which ear am I hearing that sound? . . . What is its origin? . . . How does it make me feel? . . . What do these sounds remind me of individually? collectively? . . . Do I associate other sensory responses with the sounds?

At any point in the sensory-exploration process, the actor can elect to go back and forth between the senses:

As I touch the object what do I feel? . . . What does the shape feel like as I run my fingers over the top of it? . . . What is the texture? . . . In which part of my hand do I perceive the texture most? . . . What are the variations in the texture? (Returning to the visual.) *What is the design of the fabric? . . . What is the shape of the objects imprinted on the fabric? . . . How many objects do I see? . . . What do they look like? . . . How are they related to each other? . . . What are the various colors of each of the objects imprinted on the fabric?* (The olfactory.) *What does the object smell like? . . . As I move my nose along the rim or the top of the object, is there more than one odor? . . . What do I detect in my nose? . . . How many different olfactory sensations do I experience? . . . If I were to taste the fabric, what might it taste like?* (Here the actor could actually taste the fabric or speculate on its taste.)

Please remember that all of the responses to the sensory questions take place in the sense that the questions are specifically aimed at. If the actor answers any of the questions with an intellectual answer or with words, he is not doing Sense Memory. For example, if he asks what color the object is and then says, "Blue," he is *not doing Sense Memory!* The color should be seen, not described!

In the above example of working to create a place through the use of the Sense Memory choice approach, the actor can ask as many questions as is necessary in order to stimulate the reality. The success of the process in this case is really getting a sense of BEING THERE!

THE OBLIGATION:	To feel anxious and on edge, with a feeling of not wanting to be here.
THE CHOICE:	The place the actor has chosen to re-create because he actually feels that way in this place!
THE CHOICE APPROACH:	Sense Memory.

USING THE APPROACH

If this was the process the actor was using for a specific scene, he would work to create the place while he was saying the words of the piece. He might, of course, begin much earlier, even before the play started. When I was doing summer stock many years ago, I would come to the theater as much as two hours before curtain time and walk around the stage, attempting to create the desired environment for myself. The process of asking questions and responding sensorially actually goes on while the scene is in progress—in between the lines, while the other actor is speaking, etc. You still hear the other actor and are affected by him, but you are also doing the process.

THE SCENE:

It takes place in a house that the two characters lived in while they were married. They are now divorced and have been living apart for a while. He comes here to discuss settling their affairs before leaving for Europe. All the while, he is reminded of uncomfortable things by the environment. It is clear that he would like to finish the business quickly and depart.

Because the environment in the scene has such a strong impact on the character, the actor might decide to find some parallel in his own life. So he chooses a place as a choice, a place that brings back uncomfortable memories. He attempts to re-create the place through the use of Sense Memory.

SHE: (Also quite ill at ease.) So how have you been?

HE: OK, I suppose. I've been real busy with my work.

SHE: Well, it's kind of strange being here in this place together again, isn't it?

HE: (Working with the choice and relating to her: *How far away is the table? How high does it stand off the floor? What kind of wood is it?*) Yes, it is strange. Listen, Laura, I have a lot to do before Tuesday, so let's talk about settling our affairs, OK? (Continuing to relate to her and asking sensory questions.)

SHE: Fine! Where shall we start?

HE: *(What sounds do I hear? . . . What are they specifically? . . . Where are they coming from?)* What do you want? I mean, what would make you happy?

SHE: Oh, now, don't ask me what would make me happy! You didn't seem to want to know that all the years we were married!

HE: (Responding to her and dealing with any possible choice he may have in relation to her, he continues to ask the sensory questions and allows the life to express itself in the scene.) I didn't come here to argue with you. I've had quite enough of that already! *(What do I smell? . . . What is that particular odor?)*

SHE: Yes, I think you're right—going over old ground won't accomplish anything except to upset us both. I want the house; you can have anything you want in it . . . Your paintings—I wouldn't lay claim to those. I know how much they mean to you!

HE: (Responding in the moment, allowing everything he feels to irreverently become part of the life on the stage: *What does the chair I'm sitting in feel like? . . . How far up my back do I feel it? . . . What is the texture of the fabric? . . . How does it wrap around my body? . . .* The actor responds to all of these sensory questions and hopefully the place becomes a greater reality, stimulating the desired emotional life for the scene.) Thank you, I appreciate that! OK, you can have the house. I think your shop is yours, and my business is mine. Is that fair?

SHE: (Hesitating.) Yes, that seems fair. . . You know, I'm still in love with you, Jack!

HE: Oh God, Laura, I think we ought to let sleeping dogs lie. (At this point the actor might be functioning quite well in relation to the environment and might choose to concentrate on her.)

Sense Memory as a choice approach is a process of sensorially creating objects through the asking of sensory questions and responding with the corresponding sense. This is done for the purpose of creating an object that doesn't really exist on the stage, in the hope that through this choice approach it can become real enough to produce the kind of life the actor obligates himself to in the scene. The number and kinds of questions the actor asks are totally dependent on what he needs to stimulate the reality for himself. He may have to do the process for the entire length of the scene, or he may very quickly accomplish his goal in the early part of it.

The mechanics of the process have some variables, and those are dependent on the individual actor. If the actor has difficulty asking the sensory questions in between his own lines, he may have to do the process while listening to the other actor before the scene or both before and during the action of the scene. The actor, through experience with the craft, will soon learn what works best for him.

It is important to know that while the actor is involved with the process of using the sensory choice approach, he allows all the impulses he is experiencing to express themselves through his behavior, moment to moment. The life flows from one impulse into the next, and there is an unbroken stream of expression—the expression of his here-and-now reality. He must do the process and allow, permit, accept, and include all of his impulses—irreverently!

As I stated earlier, Sense Memory is also a craft technique and is used in conjunction with other choice approaches. When discussing these other approaches, I will make it quite clear how Sense Memory would be specifically employed.

For a deeper understanding of Sense Memory, I encourage you to look at my first book, *No Acting Please*. The entire third chapter is devoted to Sense Memory and would be a great supplement to your research and understanding of this incredible technique.

2. AVAILABLE STIMULUS

This is also a marvelous choice approach. It should be your first consideration when you are preparing to work, since it is the most "available" if it exists. Available Stimulus is one of the easiest choice approaches to use. What it means is relating to anything that actually exists in the environment. It is really there! Once the actor identifies the responsibility, the obligation of the material, he can ask himself if there is anything there in the place that would affect him the way he wants to be affected.

It could be almost anything there: the other person or people, the place itself, a sound, an odor, the energy of the environment, an object in the room, a photograph on the table, the way someone is dressed, and so on. Available Stimulus could be how you feel at this moment. If the emotional life is such that it parallels the demands of the material, then it is a viable choice and a good choice approach.

Example:

Let's say that you are doing a scene with another actor and your obligation is to like and admire the other person. The play tells you that these two characters have been friends for a long time, all through grade school and beyond. They have great mutual caring and respect for each other and freely express all of these emotions throughout the scene. The reality is that you feel a lot of the same things for the actor you are working with, and, with a little Selective Emphasis, you could feel all of the things dictated by the script.

So, in order to approach the scene organically, you would use the available realities and encourage the life to come from there.

THE OBLIGATION: To like and admire the other character and to enjoy being with him.

THE CHOICE: The other actor.

THE CHOICE APPROACH: Available Stimulus.

Again, Available Stimulus is something that is really there. It does not have to be created. It may exist in a variety of objects and in many forms, but indeed it exists.

There are a number of ways the actor could approach this choice approach mechanically:

If it is something that you can see, you would just look at it, relate to it. The same holds true for hearing, smelling, tasting, and feeling. If you wanted to be chilled in the scene and you were really feeling cold, you would simply allow yourself to concentrate on feeling cold and be affected by it. Quite often, all you have to do in this category is just simply relate to the existence of whatever the object is that affects you.

USING SELECTIVE EMPHASIS AND SELECTIVE ISOLATION IN RELATION TO AVAILABLE STIMULUS

Very often it is only a *part* of an object or an element that affects you, while the whole of the object has quite a different impact on you. For example, you are in a room that doesn't seem to have any significant meaning, but in one corner you see a beat-up old rocking chair that instantly reminds you of your grandfather whom you loved deeply. Just relating to that object in the room makes you vulnerable and nostalgic for all of those beautiful growing-up years, listening to his stories and being rocked gently back and forth while you savored the delicious odor of his pipe.

That is an example of Selective Isolation—taking one part of the room or one object in it and relating only to that one part or object for the purpose of stimulating the desired life.

You might selectively emphasize all the dirty spots on the carpet and the dust and cobwebs in a room to feel a certain way, when as a whole the place doesn't repel you. You could selectively isolate the eyes of the other actor because her eyes mean a special thing to you. You could further selectively emphasize the joy and life in those eyes to stimulate certain feelings.

Selective Isolation and Selective Emphasis are craft techniques that are used in relation to other choice approaches. As I discuss those other approaches, it will become very clear how the techniques are used in each case.

USING INNER MONOLOGUES IN RELATION TO AVAILABLE STIMULUS

There are times when the actor must stimulate a running stream of thought on an inner level in order to use Available Stimulus. This is when the actor has a certain emotional point of view in relation to the other actor but must "tell himself" about his feelings in order to stimulate their impact. Let's imagine that you don't like the other actor. It doesn't have much to do with the way he looks or sounds, but more specifically with actions you have witnessed. You could do an Inner Monologue, talking to yourself about those actions.

Inner Monologue: You are a real shit. The way you spoke to that fright-ened little girl! You know she is just beginning her career, and you played big man with her, humiliating her and making her feel stupid!

If the actor uses this Available Stimulus choice approach in this way, he is stimulating the desired emotional point of view while at the same time saying the words of the scene. He can vary the Inner Monologue in any way he feels would profit him.

The actor can also use Inner Monologues in relation to Available Stimulus by talking to himself about how he feels, here and now. If the realities match, he can use his own moment-to-moment realities to fulfill the material, and all he has to do is a running Inner Monologue relating to his impulses.

THE OBLIGATION:	Irritability and impatience with the other character, and a feeling of intolerance.
THE CHOICE:	The specific feelings that parallel the obligation.
THE CHOICE APPROACH:	Available Stimulus (aided by an Inner Monologue).

Example:

Inner Monologue: God, I feel that if I have to listen to this stupid moron spout his ignorance for one more minute, I'll explode! Everything about him turns me off! He really irritates me, and all these fools running around here trying to look important make me want to vomit!

The Inner Monologue stimulates the feelings of your character in the scene, and if you say the words of the scene while backing it up with Available-Stimulus Inner Monologues, you are constantly supplying impetus for the material.

USING THE APPROACH

After identifying obligations of the material, the actor can inventory and explore the various realities of place and people involved and decide whether or not there is anything in the environment that he can use to approach the demands of the piece. It is important that the actor take the time and explore the existing environment in depth, since it is easy to miss some excellent possibilities by just "sweeping" the area and opting for another choice approach. Explore the entire environment, using stream-of-consciousness-type narrative to assure you of greater success in finding available stimuli.

Know what you want to experience, how you want to be affected, how you want to feel in relation to the other people in the scene. Understand what your relationship is to everyone in the play and what your responsibilities are.

Deal with one obligation at a time.

Example:

Is there anything on this stage or in this place that will stimulate the impulses I want to experience?

How am I affected by the whole place?

As I scan the place, the entire environment, do I see anything that affects or changes my emotional point of view? . . . If so, what? . . . How does that corner of the room affect me? . . . How does that object affect me? . . . What does it mean to me?

Are there any sounds or odors that mean anything to me? . . . If I were to isolate and emphasize some of the sounds I hear, would that make a difference in the way I feel in this place?

What about the furnishings? . . . the colors? . . . the way everything is arranged?

How does the light in this room make me feel?

What about the individual people? . . . How do I feel about them collectively? . . . individually?

If I were to consider the component parts of each person, how might I be affected? . . . What do I feel about him? . . . overall? . . . the way he stands? . . . his essence? . . . the sound of his voice? . . . In the play I am supposed to admire him and look to him for advice. Is there anything about him that stimulates those feelings? . . . What is it? . . . How can I use it as an Available Stimulus choice approach? . . . She is supposed to be my girlfriend; I am obligated to be very turned on by her, unable to keep my hands away from her. What is it about the actress that I find that attractive? . . . What do I like well enough about her to really consider her a lover? . . . Is it physical? . . . If so, what elements? . . . What is it about her personality that makes me want to go to her, be with her, and how do those elements manifest themselves?

What are my existing prejudices related to the place, the director, or the other people?

If I were to isolate or emphasize any of my own feelings, how would I use them?

As things happen in rehearsal which I identify as real things that make me feel as the character does, I will use them in the moment, and beyond the moment if they leave a lasting impression.

Is there anything I feel about this play that fits the character's emotional fabric?

Do I have a relationship to the statement of the play? . . . Does what the playwright says mean something to me? . . . Does it stimulate an emotional response? Can I use it to promote the reality of my character? . . . Do any of the lines or words that I say mean anything to me? . . . How can I use their impact to stimulate the desired life?

Does anything in the play, the actors, or the place remind me of anything in my life that, if I isolated, emphasized, or magnified it, might be a usable impetus to promote the behavior I am after?

You can add to the above checklist as you work with Available Stimulus. It is, however, an example of the specifics with which you should approach an Available Stimulus choice-approach *exploration!*

Sometimes, a specific element or part of an object that you decide to use as a choice will need some adjustment or translation or a little Creative Manipulation so that you can use it in a scene. All that this means is: focus the element so that it will affect you in the manner in which you want to be affected. *(I love that little twinkle in her eyes: that excites me.* The adjustment: *That twinkle is for me! Every time she looks at me, she lights up and twinkles!)* That's just a simple example of using a Believability adjustment in relation to an already existing reality. *(Her eyes really do twinkle. Now they twinkle for me, and it makes me feel special, the way the character does.)*

THE SCENE:

A man and a woman, married for some time, with two children who are sleeping in the other room, are in the midst of one of their usual arguments: she, nagging and carping at him because he doesn't earn enough money; he frustrated, angry, and defensive. He allows her to browbeat him because on some internal level he feels inadequate.

HIS OBLIGATIONS: Frustration with her, the relationship, and the circumstances. He feels angry and defensive, also helpless and inadequate. She frustrates him. There may be some remnant of love left, but it is obscured by his anger and his dislike of her.

The obligations of the piece could be approached in a variety of ways, using an almost endless list of choice possibilities and any number of choice approaches. However, as an example of using Available Stimulus as a choice approach, that is the way we will break it down.

THE CHOICE: 1. The actress playing his wife.
2. Selectively emphasized things that he feels about himself.

THE CHOICE APPROACH: Available Stimulus.

MECHANICS OF THE APPROACH

Dealing with the frustration with his wife, the actor can use Available Stimulus related to how the actress frustrates and angers him—e.g.: *I hate the screeching of her high-pitched voice . . . It drives me crazy! . . . She stops on every line and asks the director for a definition of meaning . . . I would like to strangle her! . . . She is in reality very critical, and I feel her criticism of me constantly . . . She doesn't listen. She doesn't listen to me, and that makes me feel discounted! . . . I know she is thinking of her next line, but she is selfish and self-involved! . . . I did like her at first! I was even attracted to her, but she frustrates me so much I don't even see her as a woman anymore.*

Most of the above responses come from what the actor sees, hears, and experiences from relating to the actress.

All that needs to be done in implementing the choice approach is to relate to those realities and select the proper moments in the scene to promote the specific feelings of the character. The process of using the right element at the proper moment is a technique called Creative Manipulation, which will be discussed in detail when I get to that specific craft technique.

For the part of his obligation that deals with his insecurity and feelings of inadequacy, the actor would selectively emphasize his own feelings in that area. He is an actor, so suppose work is scarce and he feels that he has failed as an actor on a certain level: he feels that he has not achieved what he thought he might have by now, possibly because he hasn't done enough to promote his career. He hasn't because he is frightened and insecure about his talent. Those elements are all true to some degree or other. So the actor in this play decides to use the available realities about himself to fulfill the obligation of insecurity and inadequacy.

By using an Inner Monologue in tandem with Available Stimulus, he can "talk to himself" about his feelings of failure and fear.

Inner Monologue (using Selective Emphasis): *I'm doing this play for no money! . . . Most of my acting life I have worked for nothing! . . . I am better than this . . . or am I? I'm here, right? Some of the things she is saying to me really fit . . . I don't get off my ass . . . I do procrastinate! . . . I wait for the telephone to ring, and get depressed when it doesn't . . . but I don't go out there and find work . . . I know I'm talented, but when I do get work, I'm scared to death—scared of failing, tense, uncomfortable . . . It isn't fun! . . . I even care what this bitch thinks about me as an actor! . . . It's agony . . . I want this life, but I'm not sure it is anything more than a dream . . . I'm terrified of being sixty years old and still doing small* *plays for no money...Oh God!...I feel helpless!...She is the most insensitive person I have ever met!...She knows she is hurting me and won't stop. I hate her!...The fucking director isn't any better...He isn't satisfied with anything, and when he might be, he doesn't say anything at all...I don't think he likes what I'm doing...I hope he won't replace me; I just couldn't handle that!*

The Inner Monologue can go on for however long it is necessary to create the inner life of the character. The actor can selectively emphasize the most impelling realities and manipulate that Inner Monologue to "fit" the scene. Both the actress and his Inner Monologue are focused on while he is doing the scene. He says the lines and expresses what he feels through them.

It is during the rehearsal period that actors have the opportunity to explore and experiment with the choices and approaches in order to set the choice and refine the mechanics of application. An actor who doesn't use the rehearsal time properly, either because he doesn't know what to do or because he is lazy, ends up with a "polished reading" and not a creative performance.

3. SENSORY SUGGESTION

This is a choice approach that combines suggestion and Sense Memory. It is not a "shortcut" to Sense Memory, nor does it take the place of that process. It has primarily been designed to be used when a full sensory exploration is not possible. The reason there is such a variety of choice approaches is that some work better than others in certain material circumstances. It is like choosing the right tool for the job. Just as a carpenter would not use a hammer to cut a two-by-four in half, an actor wouldn't use a choice approach that didn't do the job.

There are many reasons an actor might decide to use Sensory Suggestion in preference to other approaches. One might be to make a quick transition from one emotional state to another. Another logical reason could be to "trick" himself emotionally so as to fulfill the obligation, while at the same time keeping the level of unpredictability high.

It is a simple choice approach to use, since it combines suggestion with sensory questions as a backup. The Sense Memory part of the technique is to hopefully support the suggestions with a level of organic reality. If the actor attempts to create the object, as well as suggest its existence and actions, he has a better chance of being authentically affected by the choice. The sensory element in the approach also helps to prevent the suggestive elements from being cerebral and from encouraging the actor to lead himself and to facilitate emotional responses.

Example:

He's standing in the doorway . . . He looks crazed! . . . What do I see in his eyes? (Answer the question sensorially.) *What do I see in his face?* (Respond sensorially.) *He's angry . . . enraged . . . He's moving toward me . . . What is it in his movement that tells me he is violent?* (Sensory response.) *What is the color of his face?* (Sensory response.) *How tall is he?* (Sensory response.) *He is taking a gun out of his pocket! . . . What does that gun look like?* (Sensory.) *Can I see the opening of the barrel?* (Sensory.) *What is the expression on his face?* (Sensory.) *How is he moving toward me?* (Sensory.) *He is lifting the gun and pointing it at me! He looks even more violent! What do I see in his stance?* (Sensory.) *In his face?* (Sensory.) *What does his mouth look like?* (Sensory.) *He has stopped looking at me . . . He looks as though he wants to say something . . . What do I see now?* (Sensory.) *How has his manner changed?* (Sensory.) *What is the attitude of his body?* (Sensory.) *What is his mouth doing as he starts to speak?* (Sensory.) *He is saying that he is going to kill me. What is the first sound I hear?* (Sensory.)

In order to establish the above reality, just using Sense Memory would take ten times the amount of time, and in some material instances you just don't have that kind of time to react or to stimulate the desired emotional responses. The technique can be used in relation to an imaginary stimulus as well as a real stimulus. The entire above example of the man in the doorway with the gun could be created as an imaginary stimulus in order to produce a specific emotional response. If there was an actor with a gun in his hand and he looked angry and as if he were going to kill you, you would have no need to make those suggestions or ask those sensory questions.

When using Sensory Suggestion related to another real actor, you might suggest attitudes and behaviors that do not exist at the moment and attempt to support your suggestions by using Sense Memory in an Endowment way.

Sensory Endowments is one of the twenty-two choice approaches, so there will be an in-depth exploration of it later in this section.

Example:

She's sitting in the chair, and I can see that she's angry, hurt, and sad . . . How much of the chair does she occupy? (Sensory response.) *How high is her head over the back of the chair?* (Sensory response.) *What do I see in her eyes?* (Sensory.) *I see that she is crying. There are tears pouring down her face . . . What color is her hair? . . . How long is it? . . . What sounds do I hear from her?* (Sensory responses.) *She's sobbing . . . What does it sound like?* (Sensory.) *Her head has dropped forward, and I can see only the top of her head. The sobbing seems to be coming from a much deeper place. What tells me that?* (Sensory.)

Both of these examples of how to do Sensory Suggestion are related to an imaginary choice. The actor would do this kind of thing in order to stimulate a specific emotional state, to deal with and fulfill an obligation of some kind.

If the actor was working with another actor in a scene and wanted to create a relationship between the two of them that did not in reality exist, he might use Sensory Suggestion to change the behavior of the other actor.

Example:

(The obligation is to feel love and affection for the other character while discussing your future together.)

I see love in her eyes . . . How does that look? (Sensory response.) *She's smiling at me . . . Her whole mouth radiates the love she feels for me. What happens to her mouth when she smiles? . . . How does the love manifest itself in her face?* (Sensory.) *I see a softness . . . What tells me that?* (Sensory.) *What do I hear in her voice when she speaks to me?* (Sensory.) *Her whole body seems to reach for me . . . Where do I see that? . . . What are her arms doing as she gets closer?* (Sensory.)

This technique can continue for however long it needs to in order to make the actor feel the things he wants to in the scene.

I hear the wind howling . . . the shutters banging . . . What does that sound like? . . . Where is it coming from? (Sensory response.) *The rain is pounding against the window, and the storm has blown down the wires . . . It's dark in here! . . . How much can I see of the room by whatever light is filtering in?* (Sensory.) *Can I hear the rain hitting the roof . . . the windows?* (Sensory.) *I hear strange sounds coming from the porch outside—almost as if there is someone there! . . . What do those sounds sound like? . . . Distance? . . . Direction? . . . What do the lightning flashes do in the room?* (Sensory.) *I'm afraid . . . I can hardly make out the objects in the room, and the shadows are doing funny things on the walls . . . What do those shadows look like? . . . Can I make out the shapes?* (Sensory.) *I feel an eerie creeping feeling up my spine . . . What does that feel like in my back? . . . Where does that feeling start? How far up my spine does it climb?* (Sensory.)

If this actor was trying to scare the hell out of himself, I think he would be well on his way to doing just that. Sensory Suggestion is a very usable choice approach, particularly when it's just right for the circumstance.

USING THE APPROACH

Let's use the requiem from the play *Death of a Salesman*. Linda, Willy's wife, is at his grave side, alone, talking to him (a kind of Coffin Monologue). She is telling him that she made the last payment on the house today and asking him why he killed himself. She tells him that she just can't cry, even though it is obvious to the audience that her heart is breaking.

Again, there are a great number of choice and approach possibilities for this piece. Using this one, the actress might suggest that someone she loves very much is dead and in the ground. She could work for a person whom she can see in the coffin and support that sensorially, or she might create a cemetery and work for the grave. In either case, the choice of the person should have some parallel to Linda and Willy's relationship.

Example:

I can see only the upper part of his body in the casket! . . . His face is so white and lifeless . . . What is the color of his skin? (Sensory.) *How do I know he is dead? . . . If I were to touch his face what would it feel like? . . . Texture? . . . Temperature?* (Sensory.) *He looks so peaceful—for the first time in a long time . . . How is his body placed? . . . Where did they use makeup on him?* (Sensory.) *You died too soon . . . I told him he was killing himself . . . Has his face changed in death? . . . How are his features different?* (Sensory.)

Dialogue (not verbatim): "Well, Willy, I came to say good-bye." *(He's lying there very still . . . His flesh looks so translucent.)* ". . . I wanted to be alone with you, Willy . . . I'm sorry that I can't cry." *(How are his hands folded? . . . What is the color of the hands? . . . How many fingers do I see?)* "I made the last payment on the house today?" *(He has that ring I gave him on his finger . . . What kind of stone does it have? . . . What is the shape of the stone? . . . the color of the metal? . . .)* "We're free and clear now, Willy, free and clear." *(They're going to come soon and take him away for burial . . . Do I see any lines in his face? . . . Is there any evidence of the pain that he suffered? . . . Where do I see that?)* "Oh, why—Willy, why did you do it? What made you do it, Willy?" *(He's dead, he can't hear me! . . . I hear them coming for him.)* "Good-bye, Willy, good-bye, my darling . . ."

The audience sees an actress on stage—on a bare stage. They do not see what the actress has created. They hear the written words, and they experience the inner organic emotional life of the actress. They don't know what she is working for, and they shouldn't!

THE OBLIGATION:	Grief, remorse, and a feeling of confused helplessness over his suicide.
THE CHOICE:	A real person in the actress' life, a person, either alive or deceased, in relation to whom a parallel can be drawn.
THE CHOICE APPROACH:	Sensory Suggestion.

4. EVOCATIVE WORDS

This relates to experiences you have had in your life or certain belief structures you entertain. This choice approach, like many of the others, works extremely well in specific material circumstances. When an actor is searching for choices and approaches, he first attempts to find the proper choice. To make that choice work best, he needs a choice approach that fits into the material. The choice approach should not be intrusive or create an obstacle to the rhythm and flow of a particular scene. If, for example, the actor is playing a character who has a great many lines and speaks quite rapidly, going from thought to thought with lightning speed, he could not use a sensory choice very well because it would interfere with his behavioral obligation to the scene.

Selecting the right choice approach is therefore crucial to the success of the actor dealing with a piece of material. The expertise in making the right decisions about which choice and approach to use comes from exploration, experimentation, and experience. Trying an approach that doesn't work is every bit as profitable as finding the right one, since we learn as much from failing as we do from succeeding.

Evocative Words is the process of saying words or short phrases to yourself related to an experience that you have had, for the purpose of restimulating the emotional life of that particular experience. Suppose the actor identifies the emotional obligation of a scene in a play or a film. He understands very clearly what he would like to experience and recalls a specific situation in which he felt very much the same kind of emotional life as exists in the character in this piece. Re-creating the entire experience through Affective Memory, or even parts of it through the use of Sense Memory, would take too long and get quite complicated in light of the time he has to work. So he might decide to try Evocative Words.

Example:

Late afternoon . . . sitting in my house . . . looking at the city . . . getting dark . . . Depressed . . . don't like this time of day . . . Waiting for her to call . . . Telephone sitting there . . . black telephone . . . making no sounds . . . Tired . . . depressed . . . lonely . . . Why doesn't she call? . . . The sun is going down . . . city is getting gray . . . dark . . . Feel

*all alone . . . There are no lights on in the house . . . darkness . . . Starting
to rain . . . hate rain . . .*

The Evocative Words technique can be done out loud as a preparation
for a scene or with the help of an Inner Monologue craft technique. This
example might have been used to stimulate loneliness or depression or an
intense feeling in relation to the absence of another person. If those were
the qualities of emotional life that the actor wanted to pique, that would
have been a good choice.

THE OBLIGATION: Loneliness, depression, the hurt and
desperation over another person's
absence.

THE CHOICE: That specific experience from the actor's
own personal life.

THE CHOICE APPROACH: Evocative Words (executed through the
use of an Inner Monologue).

If the actor uses the approach either audibly, semiaudibly, or silently as
an Inner Monologue, he should stimulate some or all of the feelings that
existed at the time of the experience. The success of the technique is
largely dependent on his picking the right cluster of words and phrases that
will appeal to his emotional fabric. If he runs through the experience a
number of times, he is sure to find the most appealing and impelling
phrases and words.

USING THE APPROACH

In the following hypothetical piece of material, the character is very
much affected by the place. She is standing, looking out to sea and expressing the joys of being in an island paradise. She is telling the other
person, lying on the sand sunbathing, that she has spent her entire life
dreaming of being in a place like this and how unreal ordinary life seems
in such surroundings. It is obvious just watching her that she is absorbing
the beauty of this environment through every pore of her skin.

The actress might pull such a place and such an experience from her
own life, electing to re-create the experience through Evocative Words
rather than sensorially creating the environment.

*The Evocative-Words Inner Monologue: It's incredible . . . the
smells . . . the surf . . . I love the sounds . . . the sun . . . going
down . . . that's breathtaking . . . Carmel . . . I love it . . . the rocks . . . the
sea gulls . . . Standing in front of Robinson Jeffers' house, I feel
whole . . . The wind . . . blowing in my hair . . . seaweed . . . the
sunset . . . This place makes me feel as I feel nowhere else on earth . . . the*

spirit . . . the feeling . . . the beauty . . .

I pulled that from one of my own personal experiences, which could be a perfect choice for the hypothetical piece of material described. When I say those words and phrases, I feel a sense of that place. As the feelings that I had at that time return, fortunately I can feast on that incredible experience again and again.

As is true with all of the choice approaches, this can be used in conjunction with any of the others. If, for instance, the actress wanted to create a place through the use of Sense Memory and then do Evocative Words under her dialogue, that might be a great collaboration between the two choice approaches. The actor should always do what is needed and what is most expedient. He should avoid making extra work for himself, since nothing is accomplished that way except to complicate things. All of the choice approaches are tools; they are a means to an end and should be used as such.

USING EVOCATIVE WORDS
RELATED TO A BELIEF STRUCTURE

The use of this approach is not limited to just events or experiences. We all have things we feel very strongly about: beliefs, codes, morality, a sense of right, a sense of life, loves, things we hate, etc. These ideals and beliefs are impacting and impelling choices that can be used to fulfill the various obligations of material. The actor can say words or short phrases related to any of these belief structures and hopefully ignite the responses promoted by them. An example I frequently mention in my classes to demonstrate the use of a belief structure is related to the enormous anger, revulsion, and horror I feel about Fascism and the Nazis. Whenever I need to reach an extreme mixture of emotions of this nature, I do an Evocative Words approach.

Example:

I hate force . . . prejudice . . . I hate people who discriminate against others . . . I hate Fascism . . . Nazis . . . Neo-Nazis . . . the Klan . . . Hitler . . . hatred . . . white robes . . . burning crosses . . . Ku Klux Klan . . . the S.S. . . . the Brown Shirts . . . killing . . . genocide . . . cyanide showers . . . poor people . . . innocents . . . the death of children . . . the death camps . . . Jews . . . Auschwitz . . . the Third Reich . . . the ovens . . . extermination of six million Jews . . . my God! . . .

That makes me not only murderously furious but also sad, helpless, incredulous that man could do that to man. If I want to create a similar inner emotional life in a scene, all I have to do is that kind of Evocative Words choice approach.

THE OBLIGATION:	To feel anger, fury, intense sadness, help-lessness, and incredulity.
THE CHOICE:	The belief structure related to Fascism and the Holocaust.
THE CHOICE APPROACH:	Evocative Words (Inner Monologue).

All of the choice approaches can be used to deal with any of the seven major obligation areas. Evocative Words might be used to deal with a character-element obligation. The actor could accomplish this by using the approach to constantly influence his own personality in such a way as to "become" totally that facet of himself throughout the entire play. If the character, for example, was a hostile, explosive person, the actor might choose a belief structure that made him feel that way. By constantly re-investing in an Inner Monologue and promoting a specific belief structure, he would consistently fuel the fires of his hostility, anger, and explosiveness.

USING EVOCATIVE WORDS
RELATED TO ANYTHING YOU FEEL

The approach need not be limited to either of the two areas already mentioned. It can be adjusted to become its own craft technique. If the actor decides that what he feels at any moment in a scene might be sustained or might promote the desired emotional state, he could start an Evocative-Words Inner Monologue related to the other actor and to any impulses he might want to promote through the use of this approach.

In the midst of a two-person scene, he might choose to stimulate an attraction for the actress he is working with, because that is one of the obligations in the scene.

Example:
THE SCENE:
(At a notions counter in an exclusive drugstore.)

HE: That smells wonderful! What is it? (Evocative-Words Inner Mono-logue: *She's beautiful . . . skin lovely . . . soft . . . beautiful hair, like to touch . . . Wonder what she feels like . . . lips . . . nice . . . oooh . . . teeth . . . yes . . . definitely yes.*)

SHE: It's Bal à Versailles.

HE: Is it what you wear? (*Voice . . . great . . . love the way she sounds . . . looks . . .*)

SHE: Oh, no! I can't afford it, but—you won't tell anybody?—I work down the street, and two or three times a week I come on my lunch hour and put some on from the sample on the counter. Do you think that's stealing?

HE: *(Love the crinkle . . . separation in her teeth . . . adorable . . . I think I'm in love.)* Well, if that's stealing, it's for a good cause.

You can use Evocative Words in almost any framework. Use it to internally verbalize your inner feelings, creatively manipulate a thought process, do a running commentary on how you feel about the other actors in the scene, and so on.

5. BELIEVABILITY

This is one of the most enjoyable in the group of choice approaches. This choice approach can be done alone; however, it is a very important tool when used by two people in a scene. Both actors, knowing what the demands of a specific piece of material are, can identify the obligations and the conflict elements and decide to structure a Believability together. The approach is a mixture of some truth and a lot of untruth, starting with the threads of reality and adding elements to promote the relationship in the scene. Both actors can prepare to do a scene together by first doing a Believability approach and then carrying the life stimulated by the Believability right into the behavior of the scene. If they find a need to continue the Believability process into the scene itself, they can do it as an Inner Monologue, which takes only a minor adjustment.

Let's take an example play like *'night Mother* in which a daughter, just ten minutes into the play, informs her mother that she has decided to kill herself. She has reached the decision rationally and feels that there isn't any reason to go on with her life and that all she wants is peace and not to have to wake up anymore. From that point on, the mother attempts to dissuade the daughter from suicide.

Two actresses approaching the realities of this material might use a Believability choice approach at the beginning of each rehearsal or before each performance. The Believability could very easily be carried into the scenes of the play.

Example:

DAUGHTER: (Personal reality parallel to the circumstances of the play.) You know, I'm really tired of my life! I think about suicide a lot!

MOTHER: Come on, now, you're a little depressed and that's just your mood talking.

DAUGHTER: No, it's not! I mean it. I am really sick and tired of the struggle—of getting up every day to the same old *nothing!* My routine! What have I got in my life, Susan? I'm thirty-seven years old . . . I live in a cheap apartment that I hate going home to. . . My car is falling apart, I never have any money, I'm sick of lying to collection agencies about the check being in the mail . . . I have been pursuing an acting career for fifteen years, and where the hell am I? I don't even have an agent, for God's sake!

MOTHER: You think that you're alone? There are a lot of people in exactly the same place. They go on; they still have hope.

DAUGHTER: I don't care about those people! I can only think of me. What do I have to hope for—more of the same?

MOTHER: You're feeling sorry for yourself, Barbara, and that's OK, but you have a lot to look forward to. You're a good actress; you're attractive—

DAUGHTER: Don't give me that shit! Why don't you level with me? You're supposed to be my friend. Don't try to make me feel better! I can't think of one good thing in my life.

MOTHER: I *am* your friend, and I really care about you! I'm not just going to sit here and listen to you negate everything that you are! Why don't you talk to me about your feelings more often? Why don't you call me instead of letting everything mount up and wipe you out? Talk to me about things!

DAUGHTER: That's really funny, Susan. The night that Jerry left, I called you. I was in a real bad way, but you were on the run—some important appointment, wasn't it? You didn't have time to talk to me.

MOTHER: Now, wait just a minute! I called you back later that evening, and you didn't want to talk. I spent a half hour on the phone trying to coax you to talk to me, but you didn't. I have been there for you. For a long time I have been a good friend to you, and the way you talk—even that means nothing to you!

DAUGHTER: Isn't it funny how we all think of ourselves? I am bleeding inside, and you're defending your friendship to me. This doesn't have anything to do with you, Susan—do you understand? I would just like to be able to stop . . . stop . . . waking up in the morning and looking at that rotten ceiling . . . and thinking why I should get out of bed.

MOTHER: I'm sorry, Barbara; I was being selfish. I can see what you're feeling. Look, let me do something. What can I do? I—

DAUGHTER: Thanks, Susan, there isn't anything anyone can do. Can you take back my mistakes? I have an almost grown-up son I hardly know. Can you help me to go back and keep him instead of dumping him on his father? Can you do that, Susan?

MOTHER: You have to stop beating yourself, Barbara. That was a decision you made for his good. It wasn't a selfish thing you did. You didn't have any money. You were traveling around in a show. What could you have done with him?

DAUGHTER: I could have stayed home and been a mother!

The example is an improvisation between two actresses using Believability to stimulate the relationship elements and the emotional life that exist between the mother and the daughter in the play. The actresses, Susan and Barbara, started with truth (some of that truth may have been selectively emphasized, but it was nonetheless the truth)—real things that exist in their own lives and in their relationship to each other. Then they added other elements that are not the truth, weaving them into an improvised framework that hopefully becomes total reality for them. If indeed that does happen, the relationship obligation and a great deal of what is happening in the play emotionally are created between the two actresses.

The truth in the improvisation is that the actresses do have a friendship with each other, and they do really care about each other. Barbara does feel depressed quite frequently; she feels that she hasn't accomplished enough as an actress. She is really thirty-seven years old and does, in truth, have some anxiety about getting older. She works at other jobs to support herself, jobs she isn't crazy about, and there are some financial concerns. She recently ended a relationship with someone and has been down about that. She does have a son who did live with his father for several years but is now back with her. Susan is older than Barbara and does feel responsible for her in many ways. She often feels very frustrated with Barbara because she feels that Barbara doesn't listen and insulates herself. Barbara does talk about giving it all up, moving away.

These are the basic elements of reality, and I will say that there are quite a number of real parallels to the play. There is not, however, enough truth to fulfill the obligations of the scene. Therefore, all the other elements and things spoken about in the improvisation were untrue. These were the Believability additions that make the process work.

The untruth in the improvisation is that Barbara hasn't really been talking about suicide, even though she does tire of the life struggle. She is productive, pursuing work, and does have an agent. Her financial problems are not nearly as severe as she stated in the improvisation. She has a nice apartment and a pretty good car. *She* ended the relationship with the man she was involved with; he did not leave her. She has a really nice relationship with her son now. Barbara didn't call Susan, and Susan didn't tell her she had to run and couldn't talk to her. There are some really good things in Barbara's life that she chose not to relate to in the improvisation.

The Believability approach is designed to create a fabric of total reality. If the actors deftly mix the truth with the untruth, pretty soon these become indistinguishable. It is important to selectively emphasize both the truth and the untruth in order to structure the circumstances so that they will promote the desired results.

If, after the actors start the dialogue, they need to support the created realities, they can continue the Believability through the use of an Inner Monologue.

Example:

BARBARA: *It's easy for her to give advice . . . What does she know about being a mother? She hasn't even been married . . . I'm sick of defending myself to anyone.*

SUSAN: *She talks of being selfish. She is being selfish right now . . . feeling sorry for herself . . . and complaining about things that I have had to go through too. What about me? Why is she always talking about herself?*

This kind of Inner Monologue under the dialogue continues to feed the emotional life of the piece. The actresses can creatively manipulate what they say to themselves in order to stimulate the proper emotional point of view.

THE OBLIGATION:	A deep despondency, a complete loss of hope, a resolution to *stop* existing, a need to end all disappointment and pain.
THE CHOICE:	The subjects of conversation; the realities and the untruths that the actress chooses to relate to; the elements in her life that promote the emotional life leading to the fulfillment of the obligation.
THE CHOICE APPROACH:	Believability.

The obligation, of course, would be different for the mother, since she would have to deal with the intense need to stop her daughter from suicide. However, the choice and the choice approach would be the same.

Please understand that, in addition to the one listed above, there are many more obligations to the play: the relationship obligation between the two, the relationship to the husband and father, to her son and her brother. Also there are the time-and-place obligation, the character obligations, and so on. Each of the obligation responsibilities would have to be dealt with through the craft, choices and choice approaches.

Believability can be used as a preparation for getting into a specific BEING state for a scene. You can do it by yourself, without the knowledge of the other actor, and it can be structured to serve any purpose you decide to use it for.

Let us suppose that an actor in a scene is obligated to feel love and admiration for the other character. In addition to that, he is confident that she also loves and respects him.

THE SCENE:

(Sitting on the sofa sipping wine. The lights are low, and the background music is mellow. A perfect setting for a proposal of marriage.)

HE: (Doing a Believability to himself: *I like the way she looks at me! She is always intent when she listens to what I have to say...I see a great deal of attraction toward me! I can see that she thinks I'm a terrific actor. She has said as much. She wanted to kiss me yesterday, just before we started rehearsing ... Other people have told me about the wonderful things she has said about me! ... I love the way she looks...I would love to hold her in my arms and make love to her... When I have caressed her, she has had a cute way of moaning with pleasure.*) I love you. You know that, don't you?

SHE: I love you too!

HE: (*It's true—I think she really does. I remember the day in rehearsal when she changed, when she actually fell in love with me. I saw it!*) I have been thinking that maybe...we...might spend a little more time together. (*I think if I asked her to spend the night with me she would jump at it. Maybe I will!*) What I mean is a *lot* of time, you know—forever!

SHE: What are you saying, Joe?

HE: I'm asking you if you would like to marry me!

SHE: Yes!

HE: (*I knew it! She jumped at the question! This woman is crazy about me!*) Yes? Just yes?

SHE: Well, if you like, I'll hesitate, play it cool, and tell you that this is so sudden that I wasn't prepared for it! But the truth is that I have been manipulating you to propose to me for months.

(They laugh, and embrace passionately.)

In this example the actor used Believability privately. He did the process as an Inner Monologue, and the actress need not have known what his approach was. Of course, at any time he could have shared it with her if he had chosen to. When two actors use Believability together, they can structure it any way they want to—any way that will promote stimulation of the realities they are trying to create.

In this scene example, the realities were:

1. The actress does like him.
2. She is somewhat attentive.
3. She expresses warmth and affection.
4. She has told him that he is a good actor.
5. They have embraced each other—a *friendly* embrace.
6. He would like to hold her and make love to her.

The *untrue* elements were:

1. She has not really shown a great deal of attraction toward him.
2. She said he was a good actor, not a terrific one.
3. She never indicated that she wanted to kiss him.
4. She has never moaned when he held her.
5. There wasn't a day when she fell in love with him.

The mixture of the realities with the unrealities can create a web of truth for the actor that promotes his total belief in the circumstance.

THE OBLIGATION:	To feel love and attraction. To believe that she is crazy about him and wants him desperately.
THE CHOICE:	The specific realities he was relating to himself, as well as the untrue things he intertwined through the Inner Monologue.
THE CHOICE APPROACH:	Believability, with the use of an Inner Monologue craft technique.

TRICK BELIEVABILITY

This is a process that is applied improvisationally, without the knowledge of the other actor. Both actors, having read the material, know what the obligations and responsibilities are. Knowing where he wants to go, one actor can creatively manipulate an improvisation in order to stimulate a certain relationship and emotional life for the scene.

If the scene called for irritation and a lack of tolerance between the two characters as well as an ongoing relationship conflict, the actor might start talking to the actress without even letting her know that he has begun to work; herein lies the *trick* of the approach:

ACTOR: You know, Cindy, I resent sitting around waiting for you to finally get to rehearsal. You're always late! . . . And I think that's rude and inconsiderate!

ACTRESS: Hey! I'm not always late, and you know my car wouldn't start today and that's why I was late . . . And speaking of resenting, I resent your attitude toward me. Who the hell elected *you* director?

ACTOR: I don't have to be the director to tell you that I don't like sitting around while you take interminable amounts of time looking for your script in that shopping cart you carry around with you!

ACTRESS: That's total bullshit! Are you trying to make me angry? Because if you are, you're succeeding!

ACTOR: Look, we have to work together, so I'm trying to make the best of a bad situation. Just do your job with some semblance of professionalism!

ACTRESS: Oh, go to hell, Ray! You're angry at me because you can't get your own act together in this play. Isn't that it?

The entire dialogue should be real. The actress doesn't know that it is a Trick Believability improvisation, and she shouldn't if the actor wants the best results. Her response to his attack feeds his own reality, and before they both know it, they are into the realities of the scene on a totally organic level. From any point in the improvisation they can start the scene. If they carry the improvisation, emotionally, into the lines of the material, the life can be electrifying.

There are some possible consequences to using a Trick Believability approach: the actress might just get so upset that she would leave. It could be taken, after the fact, as though she had been "had," and she might be very angry at being manipulated that way. The director or the other actors might resent your approach and feel that you had taken unprofessional liberties in the name of "Art." So it would be advisable to make sure that you are working with the kind of actors who would welcome such an exciting impetus for creating reality on the stage. Instead of getting angry with you they would be grateful that it worked so well for the material.

Use common sense when doing this technique! If you think you can get away with it, and depending on the nature of the emotional life you are attempting to stimulate, you may never need to tell anyone what you were doing.

If you use Believability as a choice approach, you will discover it to be an extremely proficient and exciting involvement.

6. SELECTIVE EMPHASIS

This is a craft technique that can be used in conjunction with almost all of the other choice approaches. Using it is dependent on isolating a part of something or an element of a whole. It can be done in relation to a real or imaginary object or in relation to a thought process. With Sense Memory it means selectively emphasizing certain questions and responses because you know that will promote your goal. The mechanics of its application vary from one choice approach to another.

Selective Emphasis is the process of isolating a part of any whole and relating only to that *part of the place, person, or object.*

If the actor is working to create an object through the use of Sense Memory, one that does not actually exist on the stage at this time, he could use Selective Emphasis to explore and create the specific parts of the object that will take him in the direction he wishes to go. After establishing the object by asking the necessary amount of sensory questions, he can selectively emphasize his exploration, in order to appeal to the emotions which are right for the material.

SENSORIALLY SELECTIVELY EMPHASIZING

(Having already established the existence of the person.) *What do I see in her eyes? . . . What colors do I see mixing with the whites of her eyes? . . . Where do I see her tears? . . . What is that physical position of her body? . . . What do I hear? . . . What do those sobs sound like? . . . How deeply affected do her sounds indicate she is? . . . What tells me how hurt she is? . . . Where are her tears in relation to her cheeks? . . .*

It is quite obvious that these questions are specifically in one certain area and are structured to affect the person asking them.

The selectively emphasized Sensory Exploration can relate to emotional responses or to particular parts of the senses. The way the process is used in relation to Sense Memory is totally dependent on the desired result.

An example I use in my classes defines Selective Emphasis in a very clear frame:

There is a painting by Goya that depicts an execution by firing squad. The soldiers have their rifles raised in firing position, and the victims are blindfolded and terrified. Strewn on the ground are the dead. Everywhere you look are blood and death and the visual statement of man's inhumanity to man.

If you look at the painting you may be angered, repelled, morbidly curious, or empathetic. Let us imagine, however, that in the upper left corner of this bestial statement there is a shaft of beautiful sunlight falling on a tree just beginning to bud. Birds are flying happily all around the nectar of the blossoms on the tree, which is surrounded by the richest green grass. If the actor chose to look only at that part of the painting, if he selectively emphasized that tree, the sunlight, the birds, and the evidence of life, not death, his response would be quite different from what the whole painting really stimulates. So it could be with any object an actor relates to. If, for some reason, he wanted to change the way he felt in an environment or about an object, he could selectively emphasize a part of it and be affected by that singular element.

USING SELECTIVE EMPHASIS
IN RELATION TO OTHER CHOICE APPROACHES

Available Stimulus. This depends on isolating the part of the object that will affect you. The actor you are working with stimulates certain feelings and responses. You want, however, to feel other things about him, so you use him as available stimulus and selectively emphasize mannerisms he has. He does certain things with his lips that you find distasteful and unattractive, and if you selectively relate mostly to his mouth, you can hope that you will feel the necessary revulsion toward the character.

Evocative Words. Saying the right words—the loaded phrases that will impel you to feel and respond the way the character does—is a selectively emphasized way to that choice approach.

Believability. This is much the same as Evocative Words. The actor creatively leads himself to subjects and events that he knows will affect the other actor and promote the desired emotional relationship.

Imaginary Monologues. Selective Emphasis can be used from the very choice of the person the actor decides to relate to. He can also isolate just certain parts of that person's behavior and experiences he has had with this person, and then selectively emphasize what he talks about to that imaginary person.

Inner Monologues. Whatever the kind of Inner Monologue, the actor can use Selective Emphasis, directing everything he says to himself with the intelligence related to the obligations of the piece.

Affective Memory. This is approached specifically through the use of Sense Memory. If the actor emphasizes the right kinds of questions and isolates the right parts of the experience to relate to, he will definitely have greater success with that choice approach.

In every choice approach that depends on Sense Memory, the Selective Emphasis technique is the same. The questions and the parts of the instrument to which they are directed influence the outcome of the process.

Personal Realities. Using what is real in your life at this very moment can be enhanced by purposely selectively emphasizing parts of the realities.

Today you had an interview for a part in a film. It looks good. Your agent told you that they liked you and are considering you for the job. That is a personal reality, and you feel terrific about it, but the rest of your life is intense and not fulfilling at the moment. By selectively emphasizing the personal reality that occurred earlier in the day, you can pick yourself up, stimulate joy and an excitement that you might need for this scene.

The seven choice approaches that I listed as examples of how to employ Selective Emphasis should give you a very clear picture of how it is used in relation to all the other choice approaches.

THE OBLIGATION: (**Relationship obligation— the characters are brother and sister.**)	To feel close to her, to love her, and to have the need to protect her because of her shyness and social terror.
THE CHOICE:	The actress he is working with.
THE CHOICE APPROACH:	Available Stimulus, using Selective Emphasis: picking out all the features and personality elements of the actress that stimulate the obligated feelings.

7. ENDOWMENTS

This choice approach involves the process of changing an object or a person by *endowing* that object or person with qualities, elements, or features that the object or person does not possess. The Endowment process is done sensorially. Here is yet another choice approach which depends on Sense Memory to be executed.

Starting with an "available" object and slowly adding elements to it or changing its size, dimensions, color, shape, weight, texture, you can end up relating to a totally different stimulus. There are virtually no limitations to what can be accomplished by using this choice approach.

You can create long, flowing blond hair on a person who really has very short dark hair; make a person taller, shorter, thinner, heavier, beautiful, or repulsive. It is possible to endow the other actor with emotions that are not really there; change attitudes, complexions; distort the body of the other actor so that you can feel sympathy or whatever. You can take a healthy, vibrant actor and endow him with the physical manifestations of a terminal disease. It is possible to change a small room into the anteroom of a large castle, affect the color of the walls, sensorially build a fireplace—complete with a roaring fire—in a room that never had one! You can endow a dusty old samovar sitting in the corner with a new life, steaming with freshly brewed tea and gleaming with joy. You can create muscles in your own body that you have only dreamed of having. You can work to endow the other actor with the features of someone you love and thereby get a sense of that person on the stage. You can animate a record player so that the turntable is rotating and music is coming from the speakers. All of a sudden a bearded man is clean-shaven, or just the reverse. It is possible to endow people with clothing or props that do not in reality exist. You can also go in the opposite direction and by the process of Endowment undress a person down to the natural state or naked from the waist up or down. It is possible to make a woman a man, or a man a woman. An old jalopy can turn into a beautiful high-performance automobile with a shiny finish, plush leather upholstery, and the sound that only a Ferrari can make.

When starting the Endowment process, the actor asks the same kind of sensory questions that he might ask if he were creating an object of any kind. The difference is that you are relating to an already existing object with the goal of effecting a change in it.

For the sake of an example, let's say you want to age and physically deteriorate a very healthy actor so that you can experience a relationship change. You want to feel sad for this person who seems to have less time left on this earth than he has already lived. You would start with the actor and begin to endow him with the sensory elements that will change him into a much older and sickly person.

THE ENDOWMENT PROCESS

What do I see in his eyes? . . . How wide is the white circle around the iris of each eye? . . . Where does the cloudy cataract substance start? . . . What is the shape . . . color . . . of that substance? . . . How much of the pupil does it obscure? . . . Where else in the entire eye do I see degeneration? . . . How does it manifest itself in the white portion of the eyeball? . . . (All of these sensory questions are responded to in the sense that is involved.) *The blood vessels, what shape do they take? . . . How many can I see in each eye? . . . What is the color of the skin just beneath the eye? . . . What is the difference in the color of the cheek? . . . How much darker is his skin in the hollow corners of the eyes? . . . What about the eyes tells me that he is ill? . . . How about the texture of the skin on his face? . . . What is the color? . . . Does it vary? . . . If so, where? . . . Is there anything about the color or texture of his skin that confirms his illness? . . . What is that? . . . How many wrinkles do I see on his forehead? . . . What are the shapes? . . . How deep is each one? . . . How long? . . . How far back is his hairline? . . . What is the texture of the remaining hair? . . . What is it about the hair that makes it look lifeless? . . . If I were to touch his cheek, what would the skin feel like?* (This can actually be done if it fits the circumstances, or the sensory question can be answered by Sensory Speculation.) *What is the temperature of the skin? . . . Where in my fingers do I feel that temperature? . . . How does the temperature of his flesh feel different from my own body temperature? . . . What does he smell like? . . . Can I detect the odor of illness? . . . What does that smell like? . . . What are the component odors? . . . How do the ravages of age and disease manifest themselves in his posture? . . . How does his head hang from his neck? . . . How far forward does it lean? . . . The shoulders—what is their position? . . . Do I detect a tremor in his body? . . . How does that manifest itself? . . . in the head? . . . in the shoulders? . . . in the hands? . . . As he tries to speak, what happens in the mouth? . . . How do the lips move? . . . Do I see a tremor there? . . . When I can see into his mouth, what is the first thing I see? . . . What do his gums look like? . . . What is their color? . . . How many teeth does he have left? Where are they? . . . What are the colors of the remaining teeth? . . . As he speaks, what do I hear? . . . What is the' sound of his voice? . . . Where in his throat does it seem to be coming from? . . . How does he form his words? . . .*

Many more sensory questions could be explored in each area, and the technique can go on for as long as it takes to complete the Endowment process. As the "healthy" actor begins to transform into this much older and unwell person, you can start to feel the change in your emotional point of view toward him, and that should be encouraged. In fact, as you begin to succeed and become emotionally affected by the changes you are creating, even the nature of the sensory questions changes.

This entire involvement might have been selected in order to confront a relationship obligation as well as an emotional obligation, so that the actor with one choice and one choice approach deals with two obligations of the material. As is true with any obligation or group of obligations, there are many possibilities of choices and choice approaches. The decision as to which ones to use is dependent on a number of factors: which approach appeals to the actor, which choice seems the most affecting, which choice approach fits into the structure of the material the best, and which seems the least obtrusive.

A master carpenter seems always to know exactly which tool to select for a job, and so it is when an actor reaches the status of master craftsman.

THE OBLIGATION:	To feel sad about another person's state of health and to feel in a different place in life; to sense the contrast between the two of you.
THE CHOICE:	An old and sickly person whom you could care about; the physical manifestations of disease and age.
THE CHOICE APPROACH:	Endowments (starting with the available actor, changing him sensorially).

When you are working for another person in relation to the actor on stage, the process varies somewhat. It is still a Sensory Exploration, but you start with comparisons and contrasts. Using the similarities of the available stimulus allows you to get some thrust forward into the Endowment process through what might already exist. The contrast further takes advantage of the existing realities.

ENDOWING THE OTHER ACTOR WITH THE FEATURES OF SOMEONE ELSE

Quite often an actor finds it convenient to "work for another person" in relation to the other actor in the play—someone who has a similar impact on him as is required by the material. Starting with the real, in-the-flesh actor on the stage, he can systematically endow that actor with the features, mannerisms, and essence of the imaginary person. It is very important to note here that success with this choice approach means that the actor accomplishes a conglomerate stimulus, a combination of the real actor and a full sense of the imaginary person. The real actor is *there*, and that is a very strong stimulus, which cannot be discounted or overlooked. Therefore, the inclusion of the reality, coupled with the sensory creation of the imaginary person, accomplishes the desired relationship for the play. In other words, the person created by the actor and the other real actor become the living embodiment of the imaginary person, who moves around the room, says the words written in the script, responds to the actor, and fully becomes his choice.

USING THE APPROACH

The responsibilities of the following hypothetical piece are that the main character is married to a lovely woman whom he loves deeply and on many levels. They have been together for many years and are now facing a great crisis in their lives. The action of the play surrounds their dealing with the conflicts involved in this crisis.

Before the actor even begins to confront the conflicts of the play, his relationship to the actress playing his wife must be dealt with. First, according to the material, he has been married to her for a number of years. They know each other intimately—habits, thoughts, idiosyncrasies, etc. They have a full and satisfying sexual relationship and are quite affectionate throughout the play. Second, on an emotional level, he is very much in love with her, he respects her intellect, and they have great communication.

Here the actor is confronted with the two elements of a relationship obligation that he must deal with before he can address the conflict in the play.

FIRST OBLIGATION: Establishing the reality of intimacy, of having been with a person for many years, and accomplishing the complexity (for himself and the audience) of all those prior experiences. Responding to the actress with all of the familiarity that comes from shared intimacies.

SECOND OBLIGATION: The emotional responsibilities—how he feels about her. The script says that he is very much in love with her, respects and admires her, and shares all of his feelings with her.

Understanding the relationship obligation, the actor decides to work for his own wife in relation to the actress in the play. In order to create his own wife, who makes him feel very much the way the character does in the piece, he elects to use Endowments as his choice approach.

The Approach (Using Sense Memory): What is the similarity in the shape of the face? (Visually exploring all the curves and angles of the actress' face, attempting to find the parallels.) *The forehead? . . . the cheeks? . . . How is her mouth similar? . . . What are the differences? . . . Mouth? . . . Chin? . . . Cheeks? . . . What do I see in her eyes that is like my wife's? . . . Shape? . . . Color? . . . Size? . . . How about the bone structure around the eyes? . . . What are the similarities in skin color? . . . complexion? . . . What about the hair? . . . the hairline? . . . How does my wife's hairline differ from hers? . . .* (As he makes the comparisons and contrasts, the actor begins to sensorially endow the actress with his wife's features, changing shapes and colors, sensorially molding the angles of the face and drawing a new hairline.) *What does she smell like? . . . What is her unique odor?* (Responding with the olfactory sense and endowing the actress with the component parts of his wife's odors.) *What is the difference in the body shapes? . . . How are her shoulders alike? . . . What is the main difference there? . . . The length of the neck? . . . Can I see the cords and veins in her neck? . . . What is the color of her veins just beneath the surface of the skin? . . . How do the color of her skin and the color of her veins contrast? . . . Her chest? . . . What are the similarities? . . . differences? . . . How does the outline of her breasts affect the blouse she is wearing? . . . What are the shapes of her breasts? . . . What do they look like when they are exposed?* (Visual sensorial re-creation from memory of his wife's breasts. Questions like these establish a prior knowledge which begins to build the unconscious relationship with the actress.) *If I were to touch her face, what would her skin feel like? . . . the texture? . . . the temperature? . . . How would that little mole on her cheek feel on my fingers as I brushed past it? . . . When she starts to speak, what is the first thing I hear? . . . What are the similarities between the two? . . . Voice quality? . . . Sound? How does she say my name? . . . What do her lips do as she forms the word? . . . What do her teeth look like? . . . How wide is that separation in her front teeth? . . . What is it about the sound in her voice that is so uniquely her? . . . As she moves, what is her overall rhythm? . . . How does she move her arms when she moves? . . . her upper body? . . .*

The exploration can go on for several hundred questions or more if necessary. After he has investigated all the similarities and contrasts, the actor begins to endow the actress with the features, mannerisms, rhythms, odors, and sounds of his wife. At some point in the process, he will start to believe that this is indeed his real wife, and the emotional life will begin to flow into the scene. Everything the actress does or says becomes the behavior of his choice. He can endow her with different words, words that mean more to him than the dialogue of the play and that promote for him the feelings and thoughts the character has in those moments of the play. Once he has successfully established the relationship, he can go on to the other obligations of the material.

The Endowment process can be used in relation to almost anything that the actor wants to modify. He can make a papier mâché prop become a priceless objet d'art. A cheap violin can be transformed into a rare Stradivarius. He can even endow a harmless actor with the omnipresence of evil.

8. IMAGINARY MONOLOGUES

This choice approach is activated by talking to an imaginary person as if that person were here now. It should be someone who is meaningful to you and toward whom you have an emotional point of view. You talk to the imaginary person about things (selectively emphasized) that would hopefully make you feel the way you want to feel in the scene. The Imaginary Monologue then relates to picking the right person for the identified obligation and talking to that person about the right things to stimulate the emotional life that you are responsible for.

THE OBLIGATION: To feel unappreciated and hurt that your efforts have gone unnoticed. You admire, respect, and love the other person in the play and feel invisible to him.

THE CHOICE: A person in your life who makes you feel very much the same way—*your father!*

THE CHOICE APPROACH: Imaginary Monologue.

The Imaginary Monologue: It's really hard to talk to you . . . I feel that at any moment you're going to interrupt me and correct my grammar. I have for years been trying to communicate with you, and I haven't been able to, Dad! . . . I don't think that's just my fault . . . I love you—very much—but I can't talk to you . . . I know that I'm not your favorite . . . And please don't tell me that you have no favorite, that you love all your children equally, because your actions prove otherwise! I accept that you love Laurie more than me, but can't you give me some credit for who and what I am? . . . I've busted my ass trying to get your approval! . . . I went to the school you wanted me to go to, I achieved until I couldn't stand the sound of that word anymore, I played sports because that's what you did . . . I wanted you to be proud of me . . . and what did it get me? An occasional nod of approval—begrudgingly . . . I'm a person with feelings—yes, Dad, feelings, those emotional things that you're embarrassed by— and I want to be seen by you, appreciated . . . I want you to put your arms around me and tell me that you love me—that you respect me for the man I have become!

The above Imaginary Monologue can be used as a preparation for getting into the scene or, with the aid of an Inner Monologue, under and in between the dialogue of the scene.

By exploring and experimenting with a variety of people, the actor can usually come up with a perfect parallel for the obligations of the material.

Imaginary Monologue is perhaps one of the most commonly used choice approaches, the reason being that it is simple to do. It is unobtrusive, and we all have volumes of unsaid things we'd like to have told persons living and dead. The actor can creatively manipulate and selectively emphasize the content of the monologue to suit any purpose. Since the impact of the approach depends largely on the things that he says, picking the impacting words is a matter of knowing what will affect him.

If, while you are doing an Imaginary Monologue, you support the process with some sensory supplementation, it will dimensionalize the reality. Seeing the person you are talking to allows for his responses to you and to the things you are saying to him. Using both a sensory choice approach and an Imaginary Monologue together quite frequently stimulates a greater degree of unpredictability in the expression of the Imaginary Monologue.

When you are doing the two choice approaches at the same time, the sensory questions are asked in between the words of the monologue.

Example (the two together):

How far away is he standing? . . . How tall is he? . . . What is the shape of his face? . . . the color of his eyes? . . . How far apart are his eyes? . . . What is the shape of his nose? . . . (All these sensory questions are responded to by the individual senses.)

It's really hard to talk to you . . . (What is his mouth like? . . . How is he looking at me as I talk to him?) I feel that at any moment you're going to interrupt me and correct my grammar. (What is it in his behavior that tells me he might interrupt me? . . . How has he changed his standing position? . . . Where is his weight balanced in this position? . . . What emotion do I see in his eyes? . . . What is the rest of his face doing?) I have been trying to communicate with you, and I haven't been able to, Dad! . . . (What do I see now? . . . Is he responding to what I just said? . . . Where are the lines in his face? . . . Has his attitude changed at all? . . . How does it manifest itself?) I don't think that's just my fault . . . I love you—very much—but I can't talk to you . . . I know that I'm not your favorite. (What is his response to that? . . . Has he moved? . . . What do I see around his eyes? . . . Has the set of his body changed? . . . How?) And please don't tell me that you have no favorite, that you love all your children equally, because your actions prove otherwise! (What do I see happening now? . . . around the mouth? . . . Does he look as though he's going to say something? . . . What do I see?)

The Sense Memory part of the process can begin before the words of the Imaginary Monologue and continue after the monologue is over.

This choice approach can be used to deal with any of the seven major obligations. If, by doing an Imaginary Monologue, you can promote the realities that make up the life or the impulses relating to any of the obligation areas, then the choice approach is a valid one. For instance, if you are attempting to establish a relationship in a scene, talking to a person with whom you have a similar relationship in real life would definitely promote a relationship of that kind with the other actor. If it was an emotional obligation you were trying to fulfill, the nature of the things you talked about would stimulate those impulses. Suppose you identified a character element as part of a character obligation and chose to pique a part of your own personality that was very much like the character in the scene: talking to the "right person" in a specific emotional area that ventilated that "part" of you would confront the character obligation. You might even deal with a time-and-place obligation by simply choosing to talk to another person about "these beautiful surroundings." The success of the approach is dependent on the intelligence and specificity of the choice and the content of the monologue.

Imaginary Monologues allow for a great deal of freedom; you can talk to anyone living or dead, about anything you want to talk about, and allow the monologue to go in any direction. With the aid of Creative Manipulation or Selective Emphasis, you can confront any responsibility related to the material, knowing approximately where your choice will lead.

9. IMAGINARY DIALOGUES

This is simply the act of two people doing Imaginary Monologues together. It is also a very impelling choice approach and, when used in the right framework, works extremely well to promote the requirements of a piece of material. It is best done out loud so that the actors can hear each other. If it is done as an Inner Monologue, it ceases to be an Imaginary Dialogue and becomes two actors doing Imaginary Monologues. The value of the approach is that while both actors are speaking to their respective imaginary people, they are relating these words to each other. If each of them allows himself to accept what the other is saying as coming from the imaginary choice, it can stimulate some very exciting life and quite satisfactorily fulfill the relationship obligation, as well as the emotional life of the scene.

Succeeding with this approach depends on making the right decisions about the respective choices. It is a collaboration between the actors in the scene. If, after identifying the obligations of both characters, each of the actors can pick an imaginary person out of his own life who will fit the circumstances of the material, this will stimulate the realities existing in the relationship and the inner organic emotional life that takes place in the scene.

USING THE APPROACH

As a skeletal framework on which to hang the obligations and the choices, let's refer to an old play by Clifford Odets called *Waiting for Lefty* and, more specifically, to the Joe and Edna sequence. What is happening in the scene surrounds the conflict between a husband and his wife during the height of the Depression. He drives a cab and isn't earning enough to feed his family. She is after him to get together with the other cabbies and form a union to strike for higher percentages and more benefits. He is frightened of getting killed as he knows others have been. She insults him, humiliates him, and even lies to him in order to get him to take action. Throughout the scene, he feels attacked, helpless, and angry, both at her and at the situation. He feels that he has been working as hard as he can and that Edna doesn't accept this fact.

HER OBLIGATIONS:

She is angry and frustrated, worried about her hungry kids. She loves Joe but is frustrated with his lack of action. She has lost some respect for him. She feels somewhat helpless.

HIS OBLIGATIONS:

He is tired. He too is frustrated with the situation. He loves Edna but feels unjustly attacked. He feels anger and helplessness.

There is a transition near the end of the scene where they are both electrified into action and excited about what Joe is going to do. The transition is another part of the emotional obligation.

Here too exist the elements of a relationship obligation. They are married, have two "blondie" kids asleep in the other room, and have known each other intimately for quite some time.

HER CHOICE:

A man with whom she has been involved for seven years, who won't make a commitment to her because he says he can't afford to get married. At the same time he will not do anything to change his financial position.

HIS CHOICE:

His wife, who is constantly nagging him to give up being a "dreamer" and find a profession that will afford them both a better life!

THE CHOICE APPROACH: Imaginary Dialogues.

SHE: (The actress really talking to her boyfriend while she relates to the actor in the scene.) I'm really tired of living in the future. I don't believe you're ever going to make a real commitment to me! . . . You tell me how hard you're trying to better yourself, but I don't see anything changing!

HE: (The actor, really talking to his wife as he relates to the actress in the scene.) You don't ever acknowledge anything that I do accomplish! I work very hard at getting acting work, I call people, I bug my agent, I send out pictures!

SHE: That doesn't seem to be enough, does it? We haven't moved forward in seven years, and I'm telling you, Pete, I'm not up for another seven. I won't hang in there with you!

HE: God damn it, Shirley, don't threaten me. I'm not going to let you push me around! I'm doing everything I can to make it!

SHE: Why shouldn't I push you around? Everybody else does! You've been working for the same company for all of the time we have been together, and how much have you advanced there?

HE: I have worked! You know the kind of business I'm in. My God, I was doing this when you met me. It's no surprise.

SHE: I'm tired of your excuses. Why don't you march into your boss's office tomorrow morning and tell him that if he doesn't give you a substantial raise, you're leaving?

HE: I'll tell you why I won't do anything as crazy as that—because I'll be out in the cold with no income at all!

SHE: You're a coward, do you know that?

HE: Hey, you listen to me—I'll smack you right in the face if you say that to me again!

SHE: Oh, that would be an act of real bravery. I weigh all of one hundred pounds, and you almost double that!

The Imaginary Dialogue almost totally parallels the written scene while at the same time being one hundred percent accurate in relation to what the real actors feel about the people they are talking to through the Imaginary Dialogue.

In addition to relating on a basis of reality, both actors are firing each other's "emotional furnace" through the dialogue. Not only does this improvisation fit the scene; it is totally consistent with their own personal realities. The only adjustment necessary to promote the parallel is selectively emphasizing the personal elements in their private lives so that they will be the focal point of the conflict in the material. At first, the actors might find some disparity in the dialogue, but, as they choose to believe that what is being said is coming from their respective choices, the entire involvement falls into place.

I have seen actors start the Imaginary Dialogue using the name of the other character in the play and end up using their choice's name, becoming completely involved in their own personal conflict. Two actors using this choice approach can carry the stimulated life right into the scene and most often can do the entire scene completely from the realities created by the Imaginary Dialogue.

10. EXTERNALS

This category of choice approaches is probably one of the richest of the group and at the same time one of the more complex. I have often said to the actors in my classes that an entire acting approach could be created with just this one area. It embodies four separate involvements: animals, people, inanimate objects, and insects. The goal of this technique is to *get a physical sense of all of the above through your own instrument.*

By using the technique involved in the exploration of Externals, the actor can get a physical sense of an animal or another person or an insect as well as accomplish the sense of an inanimate object. All this actually means is *experiencing a sense of any one of the above Externals through his own body.*

When this is accomplished and translated into human behavior, the actor is affected on a variety of levels, depending, of course, on the choice (the specific animal or person). His entire physical essence might change, as well as his personality. Often the Externals choice approach is the only way an actor can reach the part of himself that the material calls for. By achieving the sense of some animals, an actor can ventilate a basic primal part of himself that may not have been available through any other means.

There are instances where an actor is emotionally right for a role and just cannot fit into the physical requirements of the part. And I don't mean size or weight; I am referring to the physical attitudes, the way a particular character relates to the world and the objects around him. A very sensitive actor is aware of people's immediate space and will not infringe on it by, say, crowding people standing in line to see a film; whereas a less sensitive person might physically intrude on everyone around without being aware that he is doing that. A person with manners will relate to objects like silverware and clothing quite differently from an individual who is less well-mannered and aware. These elements manifest themselves in the body, the movements, the attitude, and the entire essence of a person. Accomplishing a complete physical sense of an animal or another person not only affects the outside but also stimulates thoughts and impulses. It can totally influence an actor's behavior, so that he is almost unrecognizable in terms of other things you may have seen him do.

A. ANIMALS

Many years ago when I was studying acting, I was working on the part of Eben in a scene from *Desire Under the Elms*. I think I did the scene about thirty times and wore out three different actresses in the process. I was having a lot of trouble with it, particularly with achieving the character elements of Eben. Every week I was there on the stage trying some new choice or technique, and always the critique was the same: "You just don't look like, or behave like, a farmer, someone who is close to the earth. You seem much too sophisticated and sensitive. No one would ever believe that you have dirt under your fingernails, horse manure on your shoes, and the odor of perspiration all over your body. Eben is basic, much closer to the animal than you are, Eric!" Well, it was true. I was born in Chicago, and I am a big-city boy. The closest I ever came to a farm was looking out a train window.

I had a great deal of trouble achieving the basic visceral sense of the character—the animal in him. The way he spoke and moved and related to the other characters in the play was not only uncomfortable to me; it was alien. But I have always been very stubborn, and I wasn't about to walk away from this scene and have it come back and haunt me as an "incomplete" in my life; there are enough things in the world that create the bricks of our walls of insecurity. So I doggedly continued to work on the scene.

It was about that time that I started "working on an animal." I spent a whole year in front of a gibbon's cage at the Los Angeles Zoo. Every Monday, Wednesday, and Friday, I studied and observed that animal for about three hours. Then I would go home and attempt to reproduce what I had observed that day. That period of time was probably one of the most productive and exciting periods in my entire life. My teacher had turned me loose to work on animals with just two technical instructions: "Study the animal's rhythms and limitations." I did this for a while but found that it did not really accomplish an absorption of the animal through my physical instrument, so I discovered and invented other techniques that made the process more practical. As I introduced yet other elements of observation and study, I came closer to assimilating the animal into my being. I went from the gibbon to the gorilla, and soon I found that I could do them all. I brought the sense of the gorilla into the character of Eben, and it made *all the difference!* Everything fell into place. I thought and moved like that character and related to Abbie, the other character, from an entirely different place. I felt close to the earth, and even my thought and speech patterns slowed and faltered. What the gorilla did for my BEING state was *incredible!* My entire essence had changed, and the very same people in the class who had criticized me felt that I came from *that place,* and indeed believed I was a farmer.

Achieving the "spine" of that animal and translating it into human behavior fulfilled not only the physical character elements but the emotional also. These discoveries opened up a whole new world to me! I went from the animal to people, from people to inanimate objects, and then to insects, finding that these new techniques worked as well in all the other areas. The "animal discoveries" gave way to other choice approaches which came later. It opened doors to understanding that the key to inner life often was turned by approaching that life from the outside in. The way to pique unconscious responses seemed to be to follow this path from the primitive parts of ourselves. My entire concept of "keys to the unconscious" started with the exploration of animals.

THE PURPOSE OF THIS CHOICE APPROACH

1. To fulfill character elements
2. To stimulate emotional impulses, points of view, thought processes and behavior that other choices and approaches cannot elicit in us
3. To pique primal and primitive elements in each of us
4. To effect a total change in our physical instrument
5. To effect a change in the way we relate to the world itself
6. To address as many of the seven major obligations as possible

The moment you experience what it feels like to get a sense of an animal, it will make all the words of description seem impotent. The experience takes over the entire body and piques impulses that were not there just a few moments ago. A timid actor can be transformed into a menacing threat in the time it takes to achieve the sense of a particular animal. A two-hundred-fifty-pound bruiser can organically turn into a cowering mass of jelly huddling in the corner of the room. I have often heard actors say, "I just don't think like that or behave that way. Nothing has ever made me respond the way this character does." We are all made up of hundreds of personality elements. We all have just about everything in our beings, so it just becomes a process of finding whatever it is that will pique that special part of us. It has been my experience that Externals are a powerful tool for prying open those personality treasure chests.

THE APPROACH TECHNIQUES

There are a number of techniques for observing and achieving the total sense of an animal. These techniques do have a specific order of approach; however, they can be varied for certain purposes.

Find a place where you can watch a particular animal for a long period of time. It's no good if the animal quickly disappears into the forest after just a few minutes of observation. I don't like zoos, because I feel animals should not be caged; those places do, however, exist, and since we can learn something from them, we should.

Go to the zoo, pick an animal that you are attracted to, and study it in terms of its overall rhythm: the rhythm of movement, active and static rhythms. If it is possible without calling too much attention to yourself, assume the physical position of the animal you have selected. If it is a four-legged animal, get down on all fours. Attempt to assume or feel the rhythm by slowly repeating the movements of the animal. Stay with just the rhythm until you begin to feel it fill your body. Often you can succeed in accomplishing the rhythm of the animal by repeating certain of its movements over and over. When you get home, continue to explore that single element of overall rhythm until you begin to experience it. In a sense, the rhythm leads to the *spine* of the animal.

The next element you might become aware of is the leading center of your animal. The leading center is that part of the animal that seems to cross an imaginary line first. It might be the forehead or the nose, or even the left front paw. Adding the leading center to your exploration helps to further dimensionalize the process of acquiring the sense of the animal. So, at this point, you are working with the rhythm and have observed and added a second element, the leading center. You will find that the two elements fit together much like pieces of a jigsaw puzzle purposely cut to fit perfectly. In fact achieving the center will solidify the rhythm. Again, take your observations and experience with these two elements home, and practice with the two together for as long as it takes to assimilate them into your instrument.

Having accomplished a sense of confidence with these elements, you might feel ready to encounter the third one, which is secondary centers. The secondary center of an animal is that part of its body that closely follows the leading center across that imaginary line. If, for example, your animal's leading center is its forehead, the secondary center might be its shoulders. Most of the time it is quite simple to spot both centers, since in some way they seem to be connected with each other. Watch the animal move; be particularly aware, at this point, of the rhythm, the leading center, and the secondary center. Practice them, move around your living room in the physical position of the animal, and attempt to get a sense of those three elements. You will, of course, encounter your own limitations in being on all fours, since we as humans walk erect. Dragging your feet behind you will seem somewhat awkward; do the best you can in spite of this handicap.

At some point you must also deal with the animal's limitations. These vary from one animal to another. An animal that walks on four legs is limited in the erect position. An animal with no hands uses its mouth in a different way from one with hands or paws. Certain apes and monkeys have a very short and inactive thumb, so they grasp objects with their elongated fingers. Other animals have extremely short necks, so they use more of their whole body when they turn around to look at something. The front paws of a kangaroo, while very powerful, seem limited in reach and usage. Observe your animal's limitations, and incorporate them in your exploration.

Adding a fifth element to your approach technique, you become cognizant of a center of weight, balance, and power—that is, the part of the animal that often propels it to leap, spring, run, and so on. If you look at a lion's hindquarters, you will quickly see that the rear legs seem to be surrounded by larger muscles than the front legs and even seem more powerful to the eyes. Most of the weight of a kangaroo is in the hindquarters; in fact, the animal rests on its tail, which seems to act as a tripod: the kangaroo leaps from there, and most of its bulk, as well as its power, is centered there. The chicken seems to have its balance center in the breast, while the gorilla has most of its power and weight in the chest and the arms, as you will notice if you ever see a gorilla running upright. Once you have established this center of weight, balance, and power, add it to the techniques that you are already investigating. By approaching the animal one element at a time, you are actually building the sense of it in your own body.

At this point you might try the technique of isolations, which has a dual purpose. In the first instance, it educates the parts of your own body to function independently—the head from the shoulders, the shoulders from the chest, the thorax from the hips, the hips from the other parts of the body, and so on. Doing these isolations while working with the animal allows you to move certain parts of your body completely independently of others, and that frees you to get certain overall rhythms, limitations, and centers of weight, balance, and power of the animals you explore. Dancers practice isolations as part of their dance disciplines to free the body to move more variedly. The second reason for using isolations is to break the animal down into component parts and put it together again.

Work with the rhythm of the head and the neck only, until you get that down; then relate only to the shoulders and the rear quarters; then put them all together again. If you accomplish isolations, it will significantly influence your ability to isolate parts of the animal while you are acquiring the specifics of movement and rhythms.

Your next involvement might be the area of corresponding and contrasting rhythms. This directly relates to the parts of the animal that move together and in harmony with each other, and the parts that seem to be in contrasting movement rhythms. A chicken's head moves with one specific rhythm while its feet seem to be keeping time to a different drummer. In other animals there seems to be a contrast between the front and hind legs as they run. The short, stubby legs of the ape family seem to create a contrasting rhythm between the upper body and the lower movement. You might also notice that when a big cat is walking, the left front and rear legs move in corresponding rhythms. The squirrel is another interesting example of a collection of varying rhythms. Whatever the identifiable contrasting and corresponding rhythms are, they will help you to accomplish the complete sense of the animal if you work with them through your own instrument.

As you work to gain a total sense of an animal, all the elements you observe and then apply will begin to pay off as it all seems to fall into place.

The tempo is the speed of the rhythm of the animal and should be explored when you have a full command of the various rhythms. From personal experience, having worked many years on animals, I reserve dealing with the tempo element until I have totally explored at least the overall rhythm. I will sometimes repeat specific movements again and again in order to accomplish a sense of the animal's rhythm. When I feel secure, the tempo becomes part of the involvement. I also like to "sneak up" on the tempo. That is to say, I start speeding up the rhythm by degrees until I have reached the proper tempo, which can be felt.

The time frame for working on any animal is completely up to you, and, of course, it changes from one animal to the next. The system of approaching the technique is fairly specific.

Find a place where you can observe an animal for long periods. Assume the physical position of the animal, and start by observing the overall rhythm, attempting to get a sense of that rhythm in your own body. Take it home, and practice just that much; then go back to your place of study and confront the next element, doing the same thing with it as you did with the first. You systematically put the techniques together and separate them again until you can approach the animal through your instrument with all the different elements you have used thus far.

The next step deals with mannerisms. There are species mannerisms, which all animals in that one species have in common, and individual mannerisms, which are peculiar to one particular animal as an individual. Animals, like people, are different, and they too have completely different personalities. Certain small monkeys move their eyes back and forth with lightning speed; this is a mannerism shared by that whole species of monkey. A gibbon uses his hands to scratch himself in a particular manner which is indigenous to the species. However, a specific gibbon might beg for peanuts in a very individual way, unlike other gibbons. He might move around in circles and thrust his hand through the bars of his cage, while the gibbon right alongside him will sit there calmly with his hand outstretched and still.

Most gorillas beat their chests as a show of aggression or power; that too is a species mannerism. You will find that, if you look for them, there are a great number of mannerisms in both categories that you must include in your process of achieving a sense of the animal. Putting all of these areas together makes for a complete experience. When you are approaching mannerisms, the species mannerisms are, of course, the more important of the two, at least to begin with, since getting a sense of those will help you to establish the animal through yourself. Individual mannerisms will help you to create a specific member of the ape family, for example.

APPROACH-TECHNIQUE CHECKLIST

Observing the animal for:

1. Overall rhythm: Watch the animal, picking out the rhythm and practicing the movements of the rhythm at home. Bring this back to the zoo. Repeat as often as necessary.

2. Leading center: Identify the center and apply it to yourself, practicing the use of the animal's center in relation to your own instrument. Back to the animal and away again to practice some more.

3. Secondary center: Find the center and, doing the same as with the leading center, start to put the various areas of exploration together.

4. Limitations: Study the animal for the specific limitations, and add them to your involvement, one at a time. Practice at home; then check yourself out when you are with the animal once more.

5. Centers of weight, balance, and power: Further identify these specific parts of the animal, and, once again, adapt them to your body and assume the specific centers in your own movements. Usually, the weight centers of an animal are also the power centers, but that is not a hard and fast rule. Separate the centers; then put them back together.

6. Isolations: Practice the body isolations to free the body so that it can experience independent movement. Also, isolate the various parts of the animal for study and exploration. Practice with various parts of the animal privately, and again watch the animal. Put it all together, and break it down again.

7. Corresponding and contrasting rhythms: Identify the different rhythms and work with each one separately. Then try them together. Keep repeating the process until you can get your body to function in corresponding and contrasting rhythms like the animal you are working for.

8. Species and individual mannerisms: Do the same thing in this area. Once you have defined a specific mannerism, repeat it until it becomes a part of your sense of the animal. When the elements of the approach become a part of the whole experience, each element finds its own level of subtlety.

TRANSLATING THE ANIMAL
INTO HUMAN BEHAVIOR

Once the actor has accomplished "getting a sense" of a particular animal, he must find the way to translate it into human behavior, so that he can use it in a scene or a play. If you are working for an animal that walks on four legs, of course you must be able to retain a sense of it on two legs, standing erect as a man or a woman.

Essentially the translation should be done slowly and in degrees: at first from an on-all-fours position to a crouching position, making sure that you retain the rhythms, centers, tempo, and mannerisms of the animal while you are slowly making the translation to human behavior. When you have reached a full standing position, you might move around the area, still very broadly, like the animal you have worked with. You must retain the elements of the animal throughout the transition process. If you lose the animal at any point in the translation, don't panic; simply get down on the ground again and reinvest in the process of getting a sense of it again. As is true with everything we do, as you master the approach you will be able to translate more quickly and with greater confidence.

After walking your animal around the room for a while, begin to make the rhythms, tempo, and mannerisms more subtle. Retain the centers, but make all of the elements less defined. The degree to which you might want to refine the animal depends on the role, the character you are dealing with. In some instances, you will want to retain obvious animal characteristics because the person in the play is that way. At other times, you may want to refine the characteristics so that there aren't any outward manifestations of the animal at all. Your goal is to accomplish an inner sense of the animal complete with the emotional impulses stimulated by retaining that inner essence. As you make the animal behavior more and more human, you will get a feeling of how the various elements need to be toned down or elevated. When it feels right, you can retain that level of translation and carry it into the scene. The first few times you experience using an animal in this manner, you will be shocked at how the words come out. Accomplishing successfully the sense of an animal has an overwhelming effect on you physically, emotionally, intellectually, and vocally. While you are learning the translation process, feel free to go back to the "total animal" anytime you feel you need to, and isolate certain areas for translation, just as you isolated them when you were working to create the animal.

USING AN ANIMAL AS A CHOICE AND
EXTERNALS AS A CHOICE APPROACH

This choice approach can be used to deal with almost all of the obligation areas. The actual choice (the animal) and the way you apply the choice approach will confront historic obligations as well as character obligations. However the sense of the animal affects the actor and whatever impulses and emotional life it produces can be related and adjusted to the requirements of any piece of material.

From the time I started exploring animals in my own personal career, I have had the opportunity to use them at least a dozen times. Once when I was playing a hired foreign killer in a *Suspense Theatre,* I used a panther for the character I played. In the film, he is spoken about as being someone who is stealthy, quiet, and moves like a cat, so I used a big cat! It not only fulfilled the physical requirements of the piece but stimulated emotional aspects as well. The entire essence of my character became ominous and lethal. When I was doing *End as a Man,* I worked for an eagle in relation to the character, with equal success and pleasure. As a German officer in *Hogan's Heroes,* I got a sense of a peacock, and that too had good results. There are a number of other experiences with animals that I remember with a feeling of fun and accomplishment.

In each of the instances in which I chose to use an animal as a choice, there was a specific obligation I was dealing with. As the German officer, I wanted to feel the impulse to strut, to be full of myself. I chose the eagle to stimulate an "eagle eye" kind of perception and erratic movements, with the underlying sense of being deadly if provoked. Each of the animals produced a thought process, impulses, and feelings that dimensionalized the character in some way.

For the character of Eben in the scene from *Desire Under the Elms,* working for a gorilla transformed a city boy with very little animal relation to the earth into a hulking farm boy with basic impulses and expressions. I became a carnal being whose consciousness perimeters were eating, sleeping, working, having sex, and keeping what belonged to him.

There are very obvious instances where using an animal is actually necessary to approaching the role—as in *Greystroke: The Legend of Tarzan,* where the character was almost as much an ape as a man. The gorillas were mostly actors doing animals and, I must say, doing them extremely well.

There have been plays and movies over the years where someone is actually turned into an animal or thinks he is. Many scripts describe a character as being "animal-like." There are hundreds of examples of plays and films where the character in the piece could have been approached with an animal. That is not to say that almost any role can use an animal at the spine or foundation of its creation. However, there are certain characters that truly lend themselves to the Externals choice approach.

CHARACTERS IN PLAYS AND FILMS FOR WHOM AN ANIMAL COULD BE USED

Stanley Kowalski in *A Streetcar Named Desire,* physically, could easily be structured using some member of the ape family.

The King in *The Lion in Winter* has the essence of a giant proud bird of some kind.

For Patton in *Patton* an obvious choice, but a good one, would be an American bald eagle—intense, proud, aloof, and deadly.

The Mexican bandit in *The Treasure of Sierra Madre* had a slothlike quality to his movements and intellect. It is important to note that in this instance the character could remind you of a particular animal in quality, but because of other behavioral and emotional traits another animal might fulfill him much better.

Zorba in *Zorba the Greek* might be approached by using a bear—the kind of bear that could be trained to perform.

The female character in *The Postman Always Rings Twice* has a sensual feline quality. A natural choice might be one of the smaller wild cats, like a lynx.

Cat People makes it necessary to create a sense of the black cat that both characters turn into.

In *One Flew Over the Cuckoo's Nest* there are a host of characters that could be approached through the use of a variety of animals, from a ferret to a squirrel.

In *High Noon* Gary Cooper might have worked for a stalked leopard and then a stalking leopard.

In the film *Iceman,* the character of the Neanderthal is another obvious example of the need for animal characterization.

The list of plays and films where animals could be successfully applied could fill its own book, but let it suffice to say that the use of Externals related to material is a huge attribute to the actor!

THE SOUNDS OF AN ANIMAL

Almost every animal has its own voice. It makes some kinds of sounds, and these sounds emanating from it change with its changes in moods and behavior. It is an important involvement for the actor to explore the sounds of the particular animal that he is working on, for several reasons. While it is rare that he will have to carry those exact sounds into the play, achieving them will help him to solidify the sense of the animal he is exploring.

Reproducing the sounds of certain animals also reaches down deep into our own primitive roots and excites the animal that lives in all of us. You can deal with the sounds at the same time you're exploring the other elements of the animal; or you can deal directly with the physical elements before you confront the exploration of the animal's voice. Do whichever works best for you.

The first thing to be aware of when exploring this area is: Where do the sounds come from in the animal—where in its body do they seem to start? Other questions to ask are: Do any movements accompany the production of those sounds? What are the component parts of the sounds you hear? What precipitates the expression of the sound? What is the pitch, the depth, the duration of each sound? How does the sound vary or change? Is it always the same? What are the different sounds that the animal makes? What does each sound seem to express? What is the animal saying? How do the similar sounds of each species vary from animal to animal?

As you observe each animal, you will be able to ask more questions in relation to the individual animal. Asking questions like these will help you to structure your exploration so that you can reproduce the sounds of the animal you are working on.

When a lion roars, he raises his head and opens his mouth, and a deep rumbling sound issues from deep in his chest. With the gorilla, the sounds seem to come from different places in the body, sometimes high in the chest and sculptured by the lips, at other times shrilly from the throat. We have all seen birds whistling while their throats vibrated as though a motor were running in there. The meow of a cat emanates from a totally different part of the animal from its hisses of fear or anger; the mouth of the cat assumes different shapes for the placement of the two sounds.

When you attempt to reproduce a specific sound, and after you have observed the animal for a period, start by creating the other elements of the animal first: rhythm, centers, tempo, limitations, etc. Assume the position of the animal as it makes the sound, and re-create that sound, bringing it out from the same part of the body as the animal does. Repeat it many times until you feel that the placement is correct. Experiment with it by moving it around in your own body. Bring it from low in the chest to a high position and then into the throat. Change the position of your lips, and find out what all of these adjustments do to the sounds you make. When you achieve a similar sound, you will immediately know it, and your experimentation with its production will be the lesson in how to repeat it again and again. Varying the notes and the pitch is very much like singing. After you do it for a while, you will become facile in the reproduction of animal sounds. Quite often, the voice of an animal can be directly translated into the voice of the character and can provide an extremely interesting character facet.

DEALING WITH VARIOUS OBLIGATIONS USING THE EXTERNALS APPROACH

Whatever the impulses, thoughts, behavior, and physical attitudes stimulated by the accomplishment of an animal, the results can be applied to the fulfillment of many of the major obligations.

THE OBLIGATION: (Emotional, Character)	Aggressive, combative, hostile, a bully, constantly aggressing on others offensively; but, like the bully, actually a coward.
THE CHOICE:	A mandrill.
THE CHOICE APPROACH:	Externals (using the process to create a sense of the animal).

The above obligation describes the personality of a mandrill quite well. Exploring the animal could definitely stimulate the required life of the character; however, in some cases an animal that parallels a character exactly might affect the actor quite differently. In such a case, the actor might have to make certain adjustments in the animal or work for an entirely different animal.

THE OBLIGATION: (Time and Place)	A feeling of protective ownership of place, an almost avaricious "It's mine, and you'd better not try to take it from me" quality.
THE CHOICE:	A Doberman.
THE CHOICE APPROACH:	Externals.

The obligation here relates to the behavior of a character who, in this hypothetical example, responds the way he or she does because of his or her relationship to the place. It is the character's involvement and concern with the environment that stimulates the obligated emotional life. There are, of course, alternative choices and choice approaches for this and any other obligation.

THE OBLIGATION: (Character)	The person is a meticulous and precise organizer of things, who moves frenetically and with a wary and suspicious demeanor.
THE CHOICE:	A raccoon.

THE CHOICE APPROACH: Externals.

The choice of a raccoon might stimulate not only the physical require-ments of the character but also the emotional. If the choice proves un-worthy of the responsibility, the actor might try a variety of other crea-tures, such as a squirrel, a possum, a mink, a ferret, a rat, and so on until he achieves success. With a slight risk of confusion, it is possible to com-bine animals. I have had success using the top part of one animal and the lower half of another.

THE OBLIGATION: (Historic, Character)	The formal demeanor and attitude of a sixteenth-century adviser to the King of France.
THE CHOICE:	A peacock.
THE CHOICE APPROACH:	Externals.

Working for this bird would certainly produce obvious character ele-ments, but with a certain emphasis it could also promote the conscious-ness and attitude of a time in history.

Almost any choice can be creatively manipulated and selectively em-phasized so that it will promote the fulfillment of an obligation.

Before leaving the area of animals, I would like to mention that I also include reptiles in this category. Snakes and other reptilians are very good choices, and I have seen their use produce very exciting results. The approach to creating a sense of a reptile is essentially the same as with any other animal; the adjustments exist in the areas of limitations and tempo.

A word about using animals in rehearsals: If you are in a private re-hearsal with just another person, in a scene for a class or in an audition, it would be all right to crawl around on the floor in the original position of the animal; but if you are in a public rehearsal with a director and other actors or on a soundstage with fifty others, I would advise you to bring to the rehearsal only the translated form of the animal you are working on. If, on the other hand, you are working with people who work your way, any-thing goes! It is important to remember that the work or process of a mas-ter craftsman is undetectable except to the eyes of an expert!

B. PEOPLE

Another part of the Externals choice approach is the accomplishment of another person in relation to your own instrument—getting the sense, es-sence, and physical mannerisms of an entirely different human being.

The approach technique is quite similar to the one used for animals, except that there isn't any need for translation from the animal to human behavior.

Working to attain the sense of another person starts with observation, breaking down the elements in exactly the same way as you did with the animal. First, the overall rhythm: observe and then attempt to get a physical sense of it; move it around until you feel the overall rhythm of that person. Next, identify the leading center. With humans it seems easier to spot. Starting at the top of the head and working down to the soles of the feet, determine which exact point on a person's body seems to lead him across an imaginary line. You might also imagine that, right at that point, there was a string attached to his body which pulled him from there across that imaginary line. Once you have established the leading center, identify the secondary center, which again seems to be connected to the leading center and closely follows it.

Separate these elements and then put them together, constantly exploring their effect on one another. The centers supplement the rhythm, and the rhythm supports the centers. When you are ready, move into the area of limitations, which differs slightly from that of the animal insomuch as the human limitations are indigenous to all of us. We are going to deal with self-imposed limitations, personal-characteristic limitations, and handicaps.

Let's say that a person has very tight shoulders and consequently moves his neck and shoulders very rigidly. That would be considered a personal-characteristic limitation, and you would have to include it in the structure of your process of creating a sense of that person. If he had a limp, that would fall into the category of handicaps, temporary or permanent. A self-imposed posture or a mannered way of moving would be related to self-imposed limitations. All of these areas of limitation would be part of the structured approach technique.

Relating to the centers of weight, balance, and power is significantly modified when you are working to get a sense of another person. You would just deal directly with the weight of the person if it was significantly different from your own. As for balance and power, that would not be applicable unless you were dealing with a sumo wrestler.

Using isolations is always a good technique for getting the most out of your own body, but in the case of working for another person, it would be a good device for separating the body into component parts and then putting them back together. In the case of animals, isolations are a much more important element because of the great variety of physical structural differences between animals and humans: using isolations actually helps the actor to learn to move the various parts of his body with the very different structure and rhythms of the animal.

Corresponding and contrasting rhythms for people are very individual and not related to the species. The corresponding and contrasting rhythms of the body are a result of individual characteristics and developed mannerisms. They should not, however, be discounted or overlooked because they are a very important part of establishing the sense of a particular person. We have all noticed people walking down the street as if they were keeping time to their own internal marching band: the head is bobbing with a certain beat while the body is playing the melody, and the feet seemingly move as if they want nothing to do with any of it. This is a descriptive example of a variety of corresponding and contrasting rhythms.

When you arrive at the species mannerisms, you're a shoo-in: you were born with those! So, moving right along into the individual mannerisms, we are confronted by a bottomless well. There is no limit to the kinds and numbers of individual mannerisms humans can have, from rolling the eyes to smacking the lips and an encyclopediaful of twitches. The actor working for the sense of another person must include all of these mannerisms if he hopes to achieve an authentic and complete sense of that person.

The purpose of working to get a sense of another human being is the same as that of working for an animal: to fulfill a variety of obligations. It is just another set of tools, another category of choices available to the actor.

Sometimes the advantage of selecting a human choice as opposed to an animal is having the great variety of identifiable personality elements. Once the actor specifically identifies all of the facets of the character he is approaching, he can possibly find a living parallel to that character. If, for example, you were confronted with a character very much more flamboyant than you are, infinitely more expressive and also gregarious, meeting such a challenge might mean using a half-dozen different choices, if indeed they would work in the first place. Then why not try working for a person who is really like that?

Exact parallels are not the only reason you choose to work for another person; sometimes the person you select to get a sense of has no resemblance to the character at all. You, however, identify an internal emotional quality which you think might supply the inner organic fabric and emotional structure of the character. The outward physical and behavioral manifestations of a person mirror what that person is like inside. So, if you were to accomplish an *external sense* of that person, wouldn't it be possible for you to also stimulate his or her inner life inside you? That is one of the reasons for using this choice area to begin with.

After successfully achieving the sense of another person through your instrument, you would carry the resulting impulses and behavior into the scene. The lines would come from the inner life and the outer life of what you have created. If it were necessary to use any supplemental choices, those would be approached through the created sense of that person. What might affect *you* as *you* might not have an equal impact on the choice you have created, so some adjustment in the nature of the choice would be in order.

DEALING WITH OBLIGATIONS
USING ANOTHER PERSON AS A CHOICE

THE OBLIGATION: A man playing a woman—really obligated to look, act, and move like a woman, hopefully even to have the thoughts and impulses of a woman.

THE CHOICE: A particular woman who has the qualities or essence of that character.

THE CHOICE APPROACH: Externals (working for the sense of another person—a woman!).

A perfect example of the above is the film *Tootsie*. The star, Dustin Hoffman, said that he was using his own mother for the role. This, of course, is a rare example of the use of this technique. I did choose it purposely, to dramatically illustrate how using another person would address a specific obligation.

C. INANIMATE OBJECTS

This is a less scientific approach, more dependent on the imagination. Working to create a sense of an inanimate object in relation to your body starts with selecting the object, which can be almost anything from a thimble to a Greyhound bus. You might, at this point, ask, Why work for an inanimate object at all? It's not a bad question! Why? I could be funny and say, "Because it's there!" but I won't. The real answer to that question is that accomplishing a sense of something inanimate can stimulate some very exciting emotional life on the stage—not to mention its incredible effect on the physical instrument. Successfully using this area often impels the actor to thoughts, impulses, and emotional responses that deal with a variety of obligations. It is also a marvelous choice area for creating personality character elements.

After selecting a particular object to explore, you attempt, through your own body, to assume the physical attitude and position of the object. If you are using an overstuffed chair, for example, you get into a sitting position, with outstretched arms, and attempt to resemble that chair through the position and use of your body—somewhat like imitating the chair. At this point, you try to get a sense of the weight and mass of the object, which is done by sensorially imagining that in your body. After accomplishing that, you approach the static rhythm of the object. Since the object doesn't move, is stationary, there aren't any active rhythms, so you try to get a sense of its static rhythm. That is not as strange as one might think. If you allow yourself to be imaginatively drawn into the essence of an object, you will be very surprised to discover that you feel things from it; and when you assume whatever static rhythms you sense from it and translate them into your physical behavior, things start to happen! Once you have:

1. assumed the physical position of the object
2. sensorially created a physical sense of the weight and mass—i.e., the specific distribution of the weight and the bulk in relation to your body
3. created a physical sense of the static rhythms

allow yourself to feel and animate the impulses stimulated by the process you have just been involved in. No one knows whether an inanimate object indeed feels anything or has any kind of consciousness. That doesn't matter, though, because it is the actor's relationship to an object that determines the use of it as a choice. You look at a piano and you ask, "What must it feel like to be a piano?" and you have some kind of response—a feeling, an imaginative sense of what being a piano might feel like. At the very point where you have established a sense of that piano through the use of the approach process and your own body, *you translate the position and the static rhythm into active human behavior, slowly, moving away from the static position into an upright active position.* When all of that has been accomplished, you start the scene, retaining a sense of the piano and attempting to carry the life over into the relationship and words of the material.

Playwrights often describe characters by using inanimate objects. He is as solid as a *rock*. He is as hard as *cold steel*. She behaves like a *bulldozer*. Her skin is like *porcelain,* her countenance like a *marble statue*. She is like a *bomb,* ready to explode. You have read hundreds of such character descriptions as well as heard such things in the dialogue of dramatic material. Essentially, the writer has given a personality to an inanimate object for the purpose of dramatizing behavior. *Objects do have a kind of personality. Why do some people go wild over one kind of car and not another?*

A very good way for the actor to approach this area of Externals is to follow his feelings about a particular object and then investigate it to see where it will take him. If you choose an inanimate object, hoping that it will confront a specific obligation element, trust your feelings about it and experiment with it. If it doesn't do for you what you thought it might, choose something else.

DEALING WITH OBLIGATIONS
USING INANIMATES AS A CHOICE

THE OBLIGATION: A sad, despondent person lying around, apathetic about everything.

THE CHOICE: A faded and wrinkled blanket drooping over a banister.

THE CHOICE APPROACH: Externals (inanimates).

The choices an actor makes in any area, particularly this one, needn't be logical or parallel the description. *The point is to be affected* in a particular way, and any object that will stimulate the desired responses is the right one!

D. INSECTS

This final category in the Externals choice approach area might not even exist if it weren't for Bruce Mars, one of my students many years ago. I had just begun experimenting with the use of insects as a choice, feeling impatient with the whole thing because it was so difficult to find one to observe. They were so small and moved so quickly, it was almost impossible to deal with any of the approach techniques while observing them.

One evening in class, Bruce jumped up on the stage and announced that he was going to "try" for an insect. No one else had ever brought that exercise into class, so there was real interest in what we were about to see. He looked around for a moment or two and then assumed a very strange prone position on the floor of the stage. Both his elbows jutted high over the level of his head, while his hands remained palms down on the stage. His hindquarters assumed a position I didn't think was possible for the human body. His head pulled into his body and, at the same time, somewhat elevated, creating a curve in the neck I had never seen anyone have before. His eyes grew intense and almost seemed as if they had separated and moved farther apart. For a very long time he lay there transfixed on a single point of focus, moving very slightly with the most incredible insectlike movements. It was an *electrifying* experience, fascinating and frightening at the same time. After about eight or nine minutes, he slowly returned to his human form and pulled up a chair, ready to discuss the exercise. No one said a word. I just sat there and stared at him, unable to summon up anything to say. I wasn't quite sure what it was that we had all just experienced, but whatever it was, it had to have been the most incredible theater I had ever seen!

When I finally found my voice, I said, "OK, what would you like to tell us?"—which is exactly what I always say at the end of an exercise or scene. Bruce began by telling us that he had been having a ball working on this and that it was only the beginning of his exploration. He said he had been rummaging around the field next to his house in Laurel Canyon looking for a belt buckle he had lost, when he found a praying mantis, which he trapped in the palm of his hand and then put into a bottle, sticking an upright piece of tree branch in with it so that the mantis would feel right at home. Then he ran around town trying to find out what the diet for a praying mantis was. "You would be surprised," he said, "at how ignorant people are about praying mantises." He went on to tell us that he had been watching it for a couple of weeks, trying to approach it the way we do animals. He said it was difficult but not impossible. Having achieved a magnificent sense of that insect, he was anxious to attempt a translation to human behavior and try it in a scene.

After that, I spent a fair amount of time capturing a variety of insects and attempting to study them. At one point in this exploration, my wife wondered whether I was still an actor or whether I had become whatever you call those scientists who study insects.

It is easier with larger insects than with smaller ones: you can define more in relation to their movements. I found that you can identify an overall rhythm and a tempo. In some insects, there is a leading center with limitations related to head, thorax, and abdominal movements; and with some there are corresponding and contrasting rhythms. These elements seemed enough to get a handle on the insect. I was not about to try to establish individual mannerisms or make a cockroach a pet; it was enough that a grasshopper was a grasshopper, and once you had seen one cockroach you had seen them all!

Essentially the approach process is very similar to that of working with animals, except that the human limitations are greater. Insects have a lot of legs and antennae! The speed at which some insects move is also very difficult to reproduce. However, I found that using the approach process varied from one insect to another. Sometimes I could identify the rhythm and the centers, and at other times it was just a matter of getting a sense of the overall insect through the use of whatever approach elements applied. Occasionally, acquiring a single authentic mannerism of an insect gave me the entire feeling of that bug. It is a process of experimentation.

Start by assuming the position of the insect, and, following the approach blueprint, work with the rhythms, tempo, and centers (if you can find them). Put the parts together, and separate them again until, with the help of isolations, it all falls into place. Repeat specific movements and particular involvements of the insect you are working with, because it is this kind of repetition that promotes the sense through your body. The translation, again, is very much the same. Slowly move into an erect position, retaining the rhythms, centers, and tempo as well as the limitations. Make any adjustments that you find necessary. Progressively make more subtle the obvious insect characteristics, converting them into human terms while retaining the sense and essence of the insect. Allow the feelings, impulses, and physical behavior to "inhabit" the character in the scene, and irreverently go wherever it leads you.

One might think that an additional category such as insects is somewhat overkill, but that's not the case! You may not have the need to use this part of the Externals choice approach area very often, but, when you need it, it can really fill an important gap! It may relate to an unusual character element that other choices you tried failed to produce; it might involve a particular emotional fabric that an insect characterization could totally accomplish. It is yet another set of tools to use when the opportunity arises.

USING INSECTS TO DEAL WITH OBLIGATIONS

THE OBLIGATION: (Character)	An ominous and stoic individual with a foreboding, lethal essence.
THE CHOICE:	A black widow spider.
THE CHOICE APPROACH:	Externals (insects).

The entire category of Externals is wonderfully rich with possibilities. It is an adventurous journey into endless discovery and will stimulate and excite you as well as help you do your art and your job.

11. OBJECTS THAT COME INTO CONTACT WITH THE BODY

This choice approach relates to clothing and other objects that we wear or hold or use. We all know that what we wear has a definite effect on how we feel and how we relate to the world. Our ego states are significantly influenced by our clothing, jewelry, and so on. Strong emotions can be stimulated by creating a sense of an object you are holding or one that is somehow attached to your body. A person's sexuality can be elevated simply by creating a very tight and clinging garment that accentuates certain parts of the anatomy. A tuxedo can totally change one's physical behavior, while at the same time stimulating an emotional formality. Wearing a riding habit can affect the way a person walks, talks, and even thinks. A hat has a strong effect. A pair of western-style boots can change a person's walk and attitude. The changes can range from broad, obvious changes to very subtle adjustments of behavior.

The objects can be almost anything we physically relate to: any article of clothing, a cane, a hat, an umbrella or parasol, boots of all kinds, a monocle, sunglasses, a long cigarette holder, a swagger stick, a gun in a holster strapped to the waist, a bow tie, a cape, pajamas, shorts, silk undergarments, a negligee, high heels, a bikini bathing suit, an expensive evening gown, an original dress creation, a diamond bracelet, a broadsword, a baseball hat, and so on indefinitely.

At a weekend workshop I was conducting not too long ago, I demonstrated the effect of a pair of boots as opposed to a pair of loafers I was wearing. Shortly after I put the boots on and started walking around the stage, my feelings and behavior began to visibly change. The entire rhythm of my body was affected. I began to feel internal changes, and at first I wasn't even sure what the specific emotional difference was. I began to be more in touch with my body. I became aware of a subtle swagger and of being somewhat more ego-centered. I felt bigger, taller, and sexier. All of these responses came from putting on a pair of Western boots. If I wanted to feel those particular things in a scene, all I would have to do would be to sensorially create the sense of wearing a pair of Western boots. Even if the costuming for the play was quite different, I could, through the use of Sense Memory, create those boots.

Objects that Come into Contact with the Body is a choice approach that depends on Sense Memory as a craft technique to activate the reality. If it isn't possible to actually wear the garment or hold the article in the scene, you must sensorially create it so that it becomes a reality to you.

At the same weekend workshop, I shared the experience of strapping a pistol in a fast-draw holster to my side. In my early years as an actor, Westerns were very big in films and on television, so I thought it might be wise to learn how to ride a horse and quick-draw with a gun. I took lessons in both skills, but in my entire career as an actor I did *one* Western: I rode slowly into town on the back of a horse, and my gun never left the holster. However, it was a great deal of fun learning the skills. I have a very strong emotional relationship to guns and, more specifically, to wearing one. I belted the holster to my waist, inserted the "empty" single-action Colt forty-four special into the holster, and began to walk around the stage, relating to all the actors in the room watching this strange spectacle. My entire behavior organically underwent startling changes. I felt stronger, taller, and, in a strange way, calmer. I felt a sense of power that was overwhelming! I experienced the sensation of complete impregnability—"No one messes with *me!*" It changed the way I walked, talked, and felt.

I have used that object many times as a choice, and it always affects me in a similar way. Suppose that I was playing a character in a three-piece suit, a Madison Avenue advertising executive who feels confident and strong and takes command of every situation with a conviction of his complete superiority over all those around him. That is a clear definition of character and emotional obligation. I could work for the gun and the holster; the audience sees the three-piece suit, and I have sensorially created the gun and the holster belted to my waist.

Whatever the object or clothing, the actor has the ability, with the aid of Sense Memory, to create any object in the world that he needs in order to accomplish the feelings and behavior he is responsible for.

THE APPROACH TECHNIQUE

(Using the gun and holster in the above example, through a sensory process, as the choice.)

What do I feel around my waist? (Respond sensorially in that part of the body.) *Around the sides of the waist? . . . in the back at waist level? . . . As I breathe, what do I feel? . . . Where exactly do I feel that pressure? . . . the resistance?* (When attempting to use this object as a choice, the actor should work with and without the real object. In order to create it on a stage when it really doesn't exist, he must sense-memorize it by working with the real object.)

Where do I feel the weight? . . . How far down from the waist on the right side do I feel it? . . . As I look down, what does the belt buckle look like from this angle? . . . What color is it? . . . What is the color of the belt itself? . . . its texture? . . . If I touch it, what does it feel like? . . . Where in each finger do I make contact with it? . . . What does the texture feel like to each finger? . . . Is there a temperature? . . . What is it? . . . How does the temperature differ from my own? . . . Can I smell the object? . . . What does it smell like? . . . Does the object have more than one odor? . . . What other odors do I detect? . . . Where in my nose do I smell those odors? . . . How does the object feel on my thigh? . . . Where exactly do I feel it on that thigh? . . . What does it feel like . . . when I stand still? . . . If I move that leg, what happens? . . . Now how does it feel? . . . As I move that leg slowly, can I hear anything? . . . What is the first sound I hear? . . . Where is that sound coming from? . . . With which ear do I hear the most? . . . As I move a little more, what does the weight do? . . . What do I feel around my waist now? . . . What is the change? . . .

All of the sensory questions must be responded to directly in the part of each sense that they are aimed at. The actor must take the necessary time to allow the sense involved to respond fully if he wants to succeed in getting a real sense of the object.

As I drop my right hand downward, what is the first thing I feel? . . . What part of my hand is touching the object? . . . What does it feel like? . . . What is its temperature? . . . its texture? . . . As I put my hand around the object, where in the palm of my hand do I feel it? . . . What does it feel like? . . . What is the shape of the object as it fills my hand? . . . Which part of my entire hand feels the most? . . . If I begin to squeeze the object, where do I feel the ·resistance of it in my hand? . . . What does it feel like? . . . As I lift the object, how much energy must I apply before I feel it move upward? . . . What muscles in the arms are involved? . . . How much must I tense that one muscle in order to lift the object into movement? . . . As the object moves upward, what do I hear? . . . What exactly does that sound like? . . . Is it more than one sound? . . . How many sounds do I hear? . . . As the object moves upward, what is the change in the position of my right arm? . . . How much farther up is the right elbow? . . . What about the weight of the object? . . . Where do I feel that? . . . How many places in my arm? . . . in my hand? . . . in my fingers? . . .

The sensory process must continue until the actor has totally investigated the object and can re-create it when in reality it is not there. The sense-memorizing involvement must be complete. If the actor, in his exploration, takes too many things for granted, there will be gaps in his sensory memory when he is attempting to work without the object.

Any object an actor decides to use as a choice, whether it is a piece of clothing or an object he holds in his hands, is approached the same way, through the use of Sense Memory. If, on the other hand, the actor is using an object that comes into contact with the body and he can actually wear the real article of clothing in the play, then the approach process becomes Available Stimulus. It is still the same choice approach area; the only difference is the craft technique.

DEALING WITH OBLIGATIONS USING OBJECTS THAT COME INTO CONTACT WITH THE BODY

THE OBLIGATION: (Emotional)	An intense feeling of helplessness and fear, accompanied by a feeling of restriction.
THE CHOICE:	A pair of handcuffs binding your hands to your belt.
THE CHOICE APPROACH:	Objects that Come into Contact with the Body (using Sense Memory to create the object).

12. AFFECTIVE MEMORY

This is quite possibly the most bandied-about approach and the least understood of all of them. I have personally heard hundreds of actors in a large variety of environments say that they were "doing an Affective Memory thing" or that they used Affective Memory to accomplish the scene we had all just witnessed. It was very obvious that they were not involved in any such process and didn't even understand the technique in the first place.

The misunderstandings of this particular technique consist in thinking that it means remembering or affecting memory or recalling a specific event. The origin of this approach is Stanislavsky: he called his interpretation of it "Emotional Recall" or "Memory of Emotion." Later, Lee Strasberg modified the technique and called it Affective Memory. It is one of the few approaches that I had when I first started to teach acting.

Affective Memory is the process of re-creating an entire experience from your life, including everything that led up to the very moment of that experience. You could start the Affective Memory process early in the morning of the day when the event occurred.

The entire process is done through the use of Sense Memory. In order to be able to execute an Affective Memory approach successfully, you must have a fairly advanced understanding and mastery of the Sense Memory approach and process!

Let us say that the actress wants to re-create an experience that had a great impact on her life. It happened four years ago: it was her wedding day, and the groom never showed up for the wedding. The trauma, the embarrassment, and the shock of that experience are what she wants to relive for the play she is in.

Where would she begin the exploration process? She might start to approach the event by creating that morning, getting up on the day of the wedding with the anticipation of the great event. She could sensorially re-create the bedroom, the very way it was that morning: the wallpaper, the sunlight in the room, the furniture, the sounds in and outside the room, the odors, getting dressed, what other people were there, how they were dressed, the sound of their voices, what they said—all of the intricate elements of the objects in the place. Then, proceeding to the chapel or wherever the wedding was to take place, she continues creating the place: all the people, the decor, the excitement, the sounds, the wedding gown— all the elements leading up to the time when the clock ticks on and it becomes evident that there is no groom and that he is not coming! If the reason the actress chose to use this Affective Memory experience was to fulfill a similar obligation in the material, then it would very likely be the right decision about a choice approach.

Usually an actor decides on Affective Memory because he wants to have a much more complete experience than another choice approach might produce or because it is the only way he can reach a particular emotional life. If there is a simpler way to reach your goal, you should definitely take that road! Affective Memory is a very involved and complex undertaking. It is for the master of Sense Memory to confront.

The first time an actor (a qualified craftsman) explores a specific experience with Affective Memory, it may take him two or three hours to reach the actual moment or moments of the experience. Each successive time he approaches the technique, it will take less and less time, until, having found the "triggers" of the experience, he can accomplish the whole impact of the Affective Memory in minutes on the stage.

The key to successfully accomplishing an Affective Memory exploration is the in-depth and meticulous use of Sense Memory, creating all the environmental realities and stimuli through a conscious process. You must pique a total unconscious reexperiencing of the original event. (Affective Memory is not just remembering an experience.)

This is accomplished by asking sensorial questions about there and then on a here-and-now basis. It is not "What were the colors of the walls?" It is "What *are* the colors of the walls? . . . What *is* hanging on that wall? . . . What color *is* the hanging object? . . . How *am* I dressed? . . . What *is* the texture of my blouse?"

All of the questions are investigated in the present! You are indeed dealing with something that may have happened many years in the past, but what you are after is the reexperience in the present. In order to trap the unconscious into releasing all that stored-up response, you must not approach it retrospectively.

When an Affective Memory process works, there is nothing like the experience. You are back there, seeing, tasting, smelling, and feeling all those things just as they happened then.

The reason for using Affective Memory is to have a total experience, a relationship to an environment and a time filled with people and objects that stimulate a varied group of impulses and emotional points of view. It is a very good approach when an actor wishes to fulfill several obligations such as creating the time and place, along with the relationships that may parallel the play, and the emotional life of the character. Affective Memory often leads to a very complete experience on the stage.

This approach is also well suited to restimulating an emotional life and piquing personality elements beyond which you might have already grown or evolved.

Here is an example: Up until the time you were twenty-eight years old, you were very insecure. You had no facility with women and found it very difficult to be comfortable in public circumstances. As the years passed, and with the help of some therapy and other successes, you conquered almost all of your insecurities, particularly with the opposite sex. You are now playing a role that totally describes you in the years before you reached thirty. If only you could get back to the organic fabric of those realities!

Affective Memory would be the ideal choice approach because, if you succeeded in releasing those unconscious impulses, you would actually be victimized by the shyness and fears of not being enough. You might even be terrified of women again. Bringing that kind of experimental reality to the stage is what acting is all about.

Sometimes Affective Memory is the only way to reach certain emotions and to break through a defense system that you set up to protect yourself. Up to a certain age, people often give themselves permission to be vulnerable. After that point, they feel peer pressure to give that vulnerability up *or else!* So it goes with a lot of other very important human responses. This exercise helps you to reach a deeper and more organic level of life.

Considering the time involvement in doing Affective Memory and the great variety of objects that the actor explores, the depth of the experience surpasses a less complex investigation.

It is sometimes an antidote for an actor who is too general with a single sensory choice. It encourages a more specific exploration and involvement with stimuli that could really absorb the actor in a significant experience. Affective Memory serves as a connection with the unconscious. If he is successful, the actor will definitely build a bridge from the conscious into the unconscious.

The biggest part of any actor's talent lives in the unconscious, and when the actor steps over that magic line, he steps into never-never-land experience. That's just what I have always called that incredibly special feeling of being taken over by the unconscious. That is when the actor "catches fire," an experience that he and the audience never forget! Sometimes an actor will use an applicable Affective Memory experience in hopes that it will push him over that line into the *Ultimate Consciousness.*

Again the how is through the sensory process. Starting well in advance of the moment of the experience you are after, you slowly create the objects and elements that take you to the time and place of the actual event. You kind of sneak up on the unconscious in order to trap it in that net of realities where it has no other alternative but to cooperate. The sensorial questions are the same as in any Sense Memory exercise. They are related to one object at a time and encourage the employment of all five senses. *Remember to ask the sensory questions on a here-and-now basis! Do not be retrospective with them!* Surround yourself with the environment of the experience and establish a sense of *being there* again, but *now.*

THE OBLIGATION: (Time and Place, Relationship, Emotional, Character)	The circumstance is that of receiving the Medal of Honor from the President of the United States, with an incredible feeling of pride! The exchange between the character and his mother and father, who are present, is one of complete love and approval. The character stands fully as an example of a Marine.
THE CHOICE:	The graduation ceremonies at college, when you were awarded honors and a scholarship for being number one in your class. The president of the university made a special speech about you and gave you the award himself. Your mother and father were there, and you experienced their elation. It was the summit of your life.
THE CHOICE APPROACH:	Affective Memory.

In this example there is a strong parallel to the filmic obligations, but we all have hundreds of such parallels in our lives. When they are not so closely aligned with the material circumstances, a minor adjustment might make them perfect.

13. INNER MONOLOGUES: A CHOICE APPROACH AND A CRAFT TECHNIQUE

This choice approach can be used in relation to many of the others. When it is used that way it becomes a craft technique. Doing Inner Monologues is simply "talking to yourself" about whatever will promote the emotional life you are after. During the rehearsal process, the actor can make his Inner Monologue audible, going back and forth between the lines of the play and the Inner Monologue. Sometimes this is a good rehearsal exercise for exploring that approach technique, since it prevents the actor from becoming cerebral with the monologue.

Doing any Inner Monologue is a process of creating an internal verbal flow—sometimes just a stream of consciousness, at other times with a structured and selectively emphasized subject or theme. Whatever the content of the Inner Monologue, the approach process is the same. Be aware that there is a difference between "thinking" and "talking to yourself" internally. While you do not actually form the words with your lips or use the voice box, you do create a structured verbal process, internally, which is made up of a specific verbal monologue with a beginning, a middle, and an end. If the actor does not discipline himself to structure an Inner Monologue, he will just be thinking it. When that happens, the thought process wanders, and the actor is distracted from the point; he loses the thrust of the Inner Monologue. If you practice this choice approach by doing it audibly, you can avoid the "thinking process."

MOMENT-TO-MOMENT INNER MONOLOGUE

Using the technique in this way makes it a choice approach. There are a number of reasons for doing a Moment-to-Moment Inner Monologue. The main purpose is to stay in the reality of the moment. Even experienced craftsmen can fall into the traps of leadership and promoting emotions that fulfill concepts. Quite often, an actor becomes so involved in getting where he wants to go that he will lose touch with his internal, impulsive reality. At moments like these, using a Moment-to-Moment Inner Monologue is an incredible antidote.

It is done by including between the words of the play what is going on inside, allowing what you feel to affect the words and the real emotional life expressed through them.

Example (using a nursery rhyme for the words of a play):

Mary had a little... (*I feel uncomfortable... looking around the room...*) lamb, its fleece was white... (*I feel a little disjointed. I hear my own voice... I hate that...*) as snow, and everywhere that Mary... (*I like this place... I like the other actors... They seem sensitive...*) went, the lamb was sure to go... (*I feel better... Saying these words reminds me of being a child in school...*) It followed her to school... (*All of a sudden I feel very vulnerable... I don't know why, and I don't care, either...*)

As the actor pursues this technique, he should encourage all the impulses to be expressed through the dialogue of the play.

Another very good reason for using Moment-to-Moment Inner Monologues is to take advantage of an available reality. If, for example, the actor feels things similar to what the character he is playing does, then ventilating his own moment-to-moment feelings and impulses through the lines will certainly promote the reality of the scene. When that happens, there is no alternative but to take advantage of the inner life, since nothing is stronger than reality.

CHARACTER INNER MONOLOGUE

This too is a choice approach, since it does not employ any of the other approaches. A Character Inner Monologue depends on structuring internally a monologue that promotes the thinking of the character in the play. It's like creating the inner life of the character behind the lines. It is very important to note here that you do not try to think the thoughts of the character but to parallel his thought process using your own realities. Many actors fall into the trap of trying to become the character, to be someone else. That isn't possible, and it isn't necessary either. Once you identify how the character functions, his emotional points of view, his prejudices, and essentially the way he thinks, you can find parallels from your own life that can be used to construct an Inner Monologue which feeds the realities of the piece.

Let us imagine that the character is a "chickenshit colonel," a by-the-book career Army officer. He does not bend, and he accepts no excuses. If I were going to approach this part, I would have no literal parallels. I served in the Army, but I certainly did not get into it as a career. I did my job and went back to civilian life, so I certainly cannot relate to the character's commitment to the military. I can, however, find a parallel in my work. I do not compromise with my work! I don't want to hear any stories from people doing presentational acting or coming to me with lame excuses about not having the time to work for creative craft choices. Do the work and fail, but don't give me excuses about not fulfilling your responsibilities as an actor!

What I have just expressed is a total parallel to the way the colonel thinks and feels; it is every bit as unbending as he is. What I substituted was my own belief structure, my own realities, from which I could create an Inner Monologue much like the thought process of the character in the play.

The actor creates an Inner Monologue that is sustained under the lines of each scene. He picks the subject of the Inner Monologue and finds a personal parallel of his own which will "fuel" the scene with the desired emotional life. The words and relationships of the scene are influenced by the emotions stimulated by the Character Inner Monologue. Finding the right words is a matter of experimentation. However, the actor is free to vary the Inner Monologue somewhat from performance to performance.

An Inner Monologue can be used with almost any of the other choice approaches. Again, when you do that, it becomes a craft technique in tandem with another choice approach.

INNER IMAGINARY MONOLOGUE

We have already been through Imaginary Monologues as a choice approach. Using the Inner Monologue technique allows the actor to do an Imaginary Monologue silently to himself. Whatever the obligation may be, the actor may decide that an Imaginary Monologue is the right choice approach to use for the scene, and he would have to create that monologue on an internal level.

THE SCENE:

The climax of the play. Our main character is finally speaking up for herself after being abused and taken advantage of for three acts. She tells her husband off and leaves.

SHE: My bags are packed and standing over by the door. I'm leaving, and I'm not coming back; but before I go there are a few things that I want to tell you. You are the most self-centered, self-involved human being on this earth! How I tolerated you for so long is a statement either of my tenacity or of my stupidity! You have no feelings for anyone but yourself, and you treat the servants like animals! You don't understand the meaning of love, and I'm convinced that you have never experienced it!

Throughout this entire written monologue, the actress could be doing an Inner Imaginary Monologue to someone in her life about whom she feels that way. Her choice would be the specific person she selected to talk to, her choice approach would be Imaginary Monologues, and the approach process would be an Inner Monologue used as a craft technique.

USING INNER MONOLOGUES IN RELATION TO OTHER CHOICE APPROACHES

The Inner Monologue technique can be used with:

Evocative Words	Personal Realities	Selective Emphasis
Believability	Sub-personalities	Sensory Speculation
Prior Knowledge	Available Stimulus	Creative Imagery

In every case, the Inner Monologue technique would have to be adjusted to the specific choice approach. With Evocative Words, the Inner Monologue would consist of words or short phrases related to the subject matter the actor chose to stimulate the desired life. It would be exactly the same as if he were doing the process out loud, except that he would do it as an Inner Monologue.

The Evocative-Words Inner Monologue: It's beautiful here . . . sunlight . . . blue skies . . . smells . . . wonderful . . . The warmth is enveloping! . . . There she is . . . love her . . . blond hair . . . brown skin . . . eyes . . . beautiful . . . want to hold her . . . her smell . . . The sand is white . . . The ocean . . . hear it . . .

The above Inner Monologue is executed under and in between the lines of the written scene.

Whatever the choice approach, the Inner Monologue can be tailored to its specific requirements.

THE OBLIGATION: (Character)	A bigoted and angry man, filled with prejudice and judgment of others, spewing his hate at everyone.
THE CHOICE:	The selectively emphasized prejudices of the actor; the areas of anger, hate, and judgment.
THE CHOICE APPROACH:	Inner Monologue. (It could be a Character Inner Monologue.)

14. SUBSTITUTING OTHER WORDS FOR THE LINES

This is a very simple process that the actor can use when necessary. This choice approach is done by using an Inner Monologue as a craft technique also. The actor simply substitutes his own words for the words of the scene. He selects words that come from a personal, real place, and, under the words of the scene, he says his own more impacting words.

Let's take a classic example to demonstrate the choice approach—*The Lady's Not for Burning,* by Christopher Frye. "You fog-blathering, chin-chuntering, chap-flapping, liturgical, turgical . . . " (Substitutions—Inner Monologue: *You are an idiot . . . a stupid . . . unconscious idiot . . . numb and unaware.)* "base old man. What about my murders?" *(You act as if you were already senile. Answer my questions, dummy.)*

The content of the Inner Monologue could come from what you really feel in relation to the other actor, or it can relate to another person. Whatever the substitution may be, it should come from a meaningful place and be about something that affects you.

THE OBLIGATION:	A "give me liberty or give me death" kind of soliloquy; a patriotic and passionate statement about freedom and individual rights.
THE CHOICE:	The actor's passions about freedom; the love he has for America and his hatred for Communism and tyranny.
THE CHOICE APPROACH:	Substituting Other Words for the Lines (using an Inner Monologue craft technique).

15. ESSENCES AND ABSTRACTS

This is a highly imaginative choice approach, one that can also be a great deal of fun. It consists of "getting the sense of" the hood ornament of a 1937 Pontiac, a freshly opened can of coffee, a locomotive leaving Penn Station in New York, a cocked revolver, a moving metronome, a freshly opened bottle of effervescing champagne, a piece of chewed bubble gum melting on a hot sidewalk, scrambling eggs, popping bacon frying in a pan, a standing ashtray of the 1930s, and so on. Any animate or inanimate object can be used in this area. You attempt to get the sense of an object through your own body. It is a "physicalization" — getting the physical sense of an object through the use of Sense Memory and the imagination.

You start the process by assuming the physical position or attitude of the object that you are working with. If, for example, you were trying to get the sense of the hood ornament on a new Rolls-Royce, you might bend forward, sticking your arms rearward like the wings of that ornament, and ask sensory questions about the mass, weight, position, and texture of the object, relating the sensory responses to your own body. This choice approach is highly dependent on the actor's imagination and his ability to translate that imagination into a physical state that promotes thoughts, feelings, attitudes, and emotional life. Once he successfully achieves the sense of an object, he must then translate it into human behavior. It is much like the process related to animals—retaining the essences and feelings produced by the object.

This choice approach can be very effective in any of the obligation areas. It can produce character elements as well as address relationship responsibilities.

Joan, an actress in my class, once played a middle-aged dowager who was an alcoholic and always covered up her drunken behavior by being bubbly and effervescent. Joan worked for an Essence-and-Abstract choice approach of a freshly opened bottle of bubbling champagne. When I saw the film, I could see how that choice backed up her entire characterization, giving it depth and reality and, with a single stroke, fulfilling a dozen character elements.

It is impossible to know how the hood ornament of an automobile or any other such object feels. So what is important is how getting a physical sense of it makes *you* feel, what it does for you, and what it stimulates in your work.

THE OBLIGATION: An awkward and whimsical character who is very easygoing and resilient, who

	laughs easily and can take a joke even when it is on him.
THE CHOICE: **(Inanimate object)**	A Bobo—one of those plastic clowns weighted with sand on the bottom so that it bounces up after it is knocked down.
THE CHOICE APPROACH:	Essences and Abstracts (creating a sense of that object's size, weight, position, attitude, and movement, and then translating that into human behavior).

Retaining the abstract essence of scrambling eggs in a frying pan is a matter of creating that essence through your imagination and Sense Memory and maintaining that movement and rhythm in the human translation. This particular choice approach can produce some startling results.

16. ILLNESSES AND RESTRICTIONS

This is another choice-approach area dependent on Sense Memory as an approach technique. It encompasses all sorts of physical maladies and restrictions: headache, toothache, backache, stiffness anywhere in the body, dizziness, faintness, a body brace, leg casts, a body cast, being in a confined area, being tied up or restricted in any way, pains anywhere in the body, and so on.

You are playing a very irritable character who is short-fused and seemingly disturbed by everything: noises, people moving around, and so on. You might work for a bad headache, which in reality would produce this kind of sensitivity to noise and would stimulate irritability. The audience doesn't know that you are working to create a headache; they just experience the results, which manifest themselves as particular character elements. The process of creating the headache is pure Sense Memory—asking sensorial questions and responding directly in the specified area. An actor working to create a body brace that went all the way up the body to the chin would certainly experience quite an impact on his freedom of movement. This kind of choice would have an enormous effect on his emotional state. It would not only create a specific physical statement, but also influence the way he felt and related to the other people in the play.

Any restriction would affect the way the actor feels. If he was prone to claustrophobia, he might work to create a very confined area. Sensorially restricting oneself in movement and space can stimulate panic, fear, anger, frustration, and so on. Creating a sense of being bound and gagged can stimulate a complete feeling of helplessness, not to mention terror. If an actor had to play a paraplegic confined to a wheelchair, he might work sensorially to encase himself from the waist down in heavy plaster. In any scene where the actor needed to experience discomfort or pain, the logical choice approach would be Illnesses and Restrictions.

Many actors disregard the necessity for creating *real pain* when it is an obligation of the piece. They feel that if you communicate that you are in pain, that is sufficient. They don't consider, however, that when a person is *really* in pain he behaves quite differently. Even his voice has the presence of that pain. The base reality is responsible for all the behavior that results from the stimulus; the impetus in this case might be pain, and the actor *must* create that in order to have a basis for inner organic reality in the scene.

Illnesses and Restrictions can stimulate a variety of very meaningful life.

WORKING TO CREATE A HEADACHE

You approach this through the use of Sense Memory:

What do I feel in my forehead? (Answer in that part of the forehead at which you aimed the question.) *How high above my eyebrows do I feel anything? . . . What do I feel? . . . Where do I feel the most? . . . How far does that feeling reach?* (Relate to the pain.) *The right side of my forehead? . . . The left side? . . .* (All these sensory questions are responded to in that exact area of the head.) *How high up the head can I feel that?* (Relate to the pain.) *Where do I feel it the most? . . . How about around the sides of my head? . . . At the back of my head, what is the difference? . . . As I slowly move my head from side to side, what do I experience? . . . When I close my eyes, what happens to the feeling? . . . Where does the pain seem to come from? . . . How does it change as it moves away from that point? . . . As I move my body, what happens in my head? . . . When I stop the movement, does the feeling change? . . . How do the sounds in this room affect the feeling in my head? . . . What sounds particularly affect the pain? . . . As I bend my head forward, what happens? . . . Backward, what happens? . . . Where do I feel those changes? . . . What is pain? . . . What does it specifically feel like? . . . How does that part where the pain is differ from where there isn't any pain?*

The sensory questions can continue for as long as is necessary to create the headache. Remember, all sensory questions are answered in the *sense,* not intellectually.

Working for a restriction of any kind is approached the same way, through the Sense Memory process. If you were creating a neck brace, the questions would relate to the presence of the brace around your neck: *Where in the back of my neck do I feel the object? . . . What does it feel like? . . . What part of my neck is it touching? . . . What is the texture of the object at that point? . . . What is its temperature? . . . What do I feel in my chin? . . . What does that feel like? . . . How much can I move my chin? . . . What do I feel as I open my mouth?* (And so on, until you felt as though you were wearing a neck brace.)

Illnesses and Restrictions is a wonderful choice approach, particularly if used in a circumstance that lends itself to this choice-approach area.

THE OBLIGATION: (Emotional)	A growing panic, almost unbearable to tolerate.
THE CHOICE:	A vessel filling up with water.
THE CHOICE APPROACH:	Illnesses and Restrictions (creating a state of being bound and restricted in a vessel filling up with water reaching just below the chin and rising).

17. PRIOR KNOWLEDGE

This choice approach is one of the cluster of approaches that make up Available Stimulus. It is, however, a separate approach with its own specific elements and emphasis.

Prior Knowledge is what you already know about the place and the people in the play or film—their lives, relationships, background, and so on. In short, it is all the information you have about anyone or anything that you might be able to use to fulfill your responsibilities to the piece. It might be something that you have read, heard, or witnessed. No one need know that you have this knowledge; it is for your own use.

To use this approach, you either "talk to yourself" about what you know, or you do an Inner Monologue related to the specific information.

Let us imagine that you are doing a scene with an actor you know a lot about. Your knowledge of him comes from things you have observed, information gathered over a long period of time, experiences other people have had and told you about, and your own experiences with him. The obligation of the scene is a feeling of disgust and revulsion for the other character in the piece. Although you do not feel that way about the actor you are working with, there are things you know that do make you feel that way about him. If you were to selectively emphasize that Prior Knowledge, you could easily stimulate the obligated emotional life.

During the rehearsal process, you would do an Inner Monologue, relating all the things about the other actor that might make you feel disgust and revulsion. You would use this technique while doing the scene—under and in between the lines. The other actor should not be aware of what you are doing, nor does anyone need to know what your acting process is.

The Inner Monologue dealing with Prior Knowledge might sound something like the monologue below (this monologue is going on internally, either while you are rehearsing the scene or when you are in performance):

You are really something . . . You hurt people! . . . I know at least five women you have screwed over! . . . You are selfish . . . You have no conscience! . . . You cheat people . . . borrow money that you never return . . . and you lie! . . . You enjoy pitting people against each other so that you can have the pleasure of watching the conflict . . . I have heard you say that you used to kill animals . . . Even in this play you have been selfish and unconcerned with the needs of the other actors . . . I won't let you use me, so you have gone around and told everyone that I am uncooperative . . . You pick out the weaker, more sensitive people to abuse, and you get your kick out of that! . . . You are a despicable human being!

The Inner Monologue can continue for as long as is necessary to stimulate the desired life. Once you have succeeded in that, you can stop doing it until you need to "reinvest" in it. Once a choice starts to work, it is advisable to go with the impulses that have been stimulated by it until you dry up, at which time you go back to the choice.

There are times when your prior knowledge functions and stimulates impulses just by your relating to the objects or person. You might be in a place you know things about—a place that has a history, a background that you grew up hearing about—and being in this place makes you feel a certain way which happens to be right for the material you are doing. In a situation like that, all you have to do is relate to the place. In the case of a person, the same thing might hold true. Just looking at the person, talking to her, is enough to spark the component parts of your prior knowledge related to her.

There are other times when the pertinent and impacting knowledge is surrounded by layers of other personality elements that obscure the nucleus of meaningful stimuli. At such times you must dig into the person for the elements that you need, selectively emphasizing those elements and weaving them into a structured Inner Monologue that will affect you the way you want to be affected.

Prior knowledge can consist of anything. You don't even have to know how you know what you know; just that you know is enough.

THE OBLIGATION: (Relationship, Emotional)	Admiration and respect for the other character. A sense of awe. Wanting to be like the other character.
THE CHOICE:	The actor you are working with.

THE CHOICE APPROACH: Prior Knowledge. (In this particular instance, you might use a combination of Available Stimulus and Inner Monologue.)

The approach process can be anything that will activate the choice approach and make it work. If, in the above example, just relating to the other actor is enough, then that is all that is necessary. If it proves not to be sufficient, you can structure the information into an Inner Monologue.

18. SENSORY SPECULATION

As its title suggests, this too is a sensorially activated choice approach. It is quite simple to do, since it is a basic Sense Memory technique.

This choice approach is valuable for a variety of reasons: It is an excellent device for stimulating impulses and responses to objects that you cannot actually come into contact with. It is used to explore an object that you have not had any experience with, a person to whom you have not been close, whom you have not touched or smelled, and so on. An object might be across the stage from you, but it is one toward which you need an emotional point of view.

Example:

In this hypothetical scene, the camera discovers the actor sitting at a table in a restaurant across from a very attractive woman. He is studying her, and, as we see, he becomes more and more interested in her and curious about her. At a certain point in the scene he gets up, crosses to her, and introduces himself. The actor's obligation is to be interested, attracted, and very curious about the woman. Using Sensory Speculation, he can sensorially investigate the actress, speculatively, by asking sensory questions.

I wonder what it would feel like to touch the skin on her face . . . Where on my fingertips would I feel that? . . . What would it feel like? . . . What would the texture of her skin feel like in each of my fingers? . . . If I traced the shape of her nose, how would that feel to my index finger? . . . What would she smell like up close? . . . Her hair? . . . If I put my lips next to hers, what would that feel like? . . . Where on my lips would hers touch? . . . My lower lip? . . . My upper lip?

All the sensory questions would be responded to in the same way as in a conventional Sense Memory exercise, the only difference being that you have never really experienced this object nor investigated it before. Therefore, all the sensory responses would be speculative.

What the actor accomplishes by using this choice approach is to use his sensory apparatus to stimulate the emotional life that he is obligated to by the material. Sensory Speculation in this case would take the actor far beyond just exploring the actress through a "wonderment approach." It would excite and pique sensory responses which would lead to the stimulation of feelings and needs, impelling him to action. If the obligation was, for instance, attraction to the woman at the table, there would be a physical response resulting from the sensory involvement.

Using this approach, you can "speculate" sensorially about anything. You could create terror, speculating about how exactly it would feel if the person coming toward you were to plunge a sword directly into your stomach; or about the rush you might experience taking your first step out the door of an airplane fifteen thousand feet above the ground; or what it might feel like in your hands and fingers if you were strangling a person you hate to death—the actual sensory experience of feeling the windpipe shatter under your grip. Gruesome, you think? Well, you might someday have to play a part where you *must feel* those kinds of urges and needs! How many times do actors "die" in films and on the stage? Since none of us has ever really died, Sensory Speculation can really help in creating a reasonable facsimile.

Sensory Endowments are also speculative. When you want to change a person's attitude or behavior, you "endow" him with sensory elements of the behavior you want him to be experiencing. If you have never seen him express that particular kind of life, then it would call for Sensory Speculation.

THE OBLIGATION:	An overwhelming sexual attraction to a woman the actor meets in an elevator.
THE CHOICE:	The actress playing the woman in the elevator.
THE CHOICE APPROACH:	Sensory Speculation (speculatively exploring all the elements and features of the actress that are designed to stimulate incredible attraction and desire).

19. PERSONAL REALITIES

This is another of the Available Stimulus choice approaches. A Personal Reality is something that the actor believes—a belief structure, a prejudice, feelings he has about anything, a sense of life—in short, anything that really exists and can be related to which might confront and fulfill an obligation of a piece of material.

One of my actors in New York was recently doing a scene from *Lenny*, and when I asked him what he worked for as Lenny doing one of his routines, he said, "The character is telling jokes. I love telling jokes; it's one of my things."

What he was doing was using a Personal Reality as impetus for the scene. He could just accept the fact that he likes telling jokes and jump into the scene with the belief that the circumstance would provide a Personal Reality. He could simply (out loud) remind himself of how much he loves storytelling. He could do a more elaborate Inner Monologue dealing with "talking about" telling jokes. He could get a little more complex in his effort to take advantage of the Personal Reality by working sensorially to create an experience where he actually was telling funny stories and loving it.

A Personal Reality can be anything that is happening on or off the stage between you and the other actor. It can be an offstage love affair that is brought into the play or an ongoing conflict that started during the first week of rehearsals. It can be something which occurred at lunch today that makes you feel just the way the character in the play does.

An acting company that has members who have been together for a long time and have done many plays together is usually very rich in Prior Knowledge and Available Realities.

Anything that happens to us on the stage, while in performance, and happens to promote the play is Personal Realities, which is usable as a choice approach.

THE OBLIGATION:	An adversary relationship to the other character, with whom your character is always in conflict about theories and process.
THE CHOICE:	The other actor.
THE CHOICE APPROACH:	Personal Realities. (You and the other actor work quite differently. You disagree violently with his acting approach, and the two of you are always arguing about it.)

20. CREATIVE MANIPULATION

This is a craft technique. It is the process of directing yourself into the area that you want to be in. It consists of manipulating an Inner Monologue so that you say things to yourself in order to affect yourself in a certain way or, in a Sense Memory exercise, asking the kinds of questions that you know will appeal to your senses as well as to your emotions.

This craft technique is very important to the actor because it helps him to get right to the target of a choice. Knowing himself is very important to the actor, and once he does know himself, he can select choices that will take him in the direction in which he wants to go. With Creative Manipulation, he can use a choice to its fullest while cutting down on the time it takes to explore it.

This craft technique can be used in relation to most of the other choice approaches. In Believability, the actor must do a certain amount of Creative Manipulation in order to build the untrue elements of the Believability. Imaginary Monologues are constantly being manipulated into areas of the greatest impact.

IMAGINARY MONOLOGUE
USING CREATIVE MANIPULATION

You hurt me! . . . I always try to do what's best for you, and you always throw it in my face . . . You're insensitive to my feelings . . . You know that I worry about you, and you stay out all night without even a telephone call! . . . You yell at me . . . and you are very unkind most of the time . . . and if I didn't love you so much, I would leave!

The entire thrust of this Imaginary Monologue is how hurt the person is. Everything the actor chose to say was creatively manipulated to promote the hurt and to feel sorry for himself. He did not mention any of the good things in the relationship or the love he experiences from the other person—just the hurts. This was done purposely to stimulate the desired emotional life for the scene.

Using the technique in relation to Evocative Words is the same: the actor just selects the words and phrases that have the most impact and meaning and those that will fit into the fabric of the material.

There is an important warning here, though. Creative Manipulation is not leadership; it is not result involvement. The word "creative" says it all! The difference between Creative Manipulation and leadership is that leadership involves itself with the resulting behavior, while Creative Manipulation confines itself to the choice and the choice approach. It involves itself with the impetus, not the response.

21. SUB-PERSONALITIES

This is another complex and very rich area. It covers a vast amount of material and techniques and is a tremendous tool for the actor. The concept originated with Carl G. Jung, who dealt with the theoretical development of sub-personality archetypes and believed that a person is a complex collection of many parts, with many facets to what we call the personality. These facets seem to have their own life and power, the power to take over a person and totally control his life. Without getting into an in-depth history of the origin of this technique, I would like to say that I discovered it from a psychologist with whom I was in therapy, Dr. Hal Stone. He and his wife, Sidra, introduced a technique called Voice Dialogue, a way of "talking" to various personalities and calling them forth if they are reluctant to speak. I was there only a couple of times before I discovered the incredible possibilities that this technique afforded the actor. I immediately set to work modifying the process for use in acting. After quite a lot of experimentation I found ways of using sub-personalities as a tool for the actor to employ in the fulfillment of material. In this book I am going to limit the exploration of sub-personalities to a choice approach and leave the other areas of this technique for another book. Though the origin of the technique is psychotherapy, as it is used in my work it is *acting!*

The concept is that we are made up of many sub-personalities or, as I sometimes think of it, sub-persons. There are, of course, the "archetypes," the basic sub-personalities that are universal: the child archetypes, the critic, Aphrodite, the satanic part, the pusher, the judge, the protector, the killer, the warrior, and so on. There are quite a number of them. Then there are the ones we individually have in our lives, whoever they are: my coward, the one who always makes excuses; the lazy one; the liar; the clown; etc. We may have these in common with many other people on this earth, but they are not the standard archetypes.

The therapeutic theory is that when a sub-personality seizes power over our lives and takes control, we lose balance and become a victim of the one in power. Without consciousness, we submit to that control, not even knowing that the reason we are failing in life is that the one in power wants that. Also, the reason we can't seem to take responsibility for our lives is that the irresponsible child is running the show. Whatever the reality might be, that is the theory, and out of that theory comes a magnificent choice approach.

In order to comprehend my concept related to acting, you must understand that the various parts of us behave in a variety of different ways and that it is important for the actor who intends to use this approach to become familiar with his sub-personalities. If he knows who they are and how they operate, and he further understands the technique of calling them forth, he has a powerful tool for the fulfillment of the major obligations of dramatic material.

The first step in getting to know your sub-personalities is to acknowledge that they exist. Begin to notice your mood swings and the changes in your personality throughout the day. Also, become aware of the stimuli that create those mood changes and behavioral differences. As you become familiar with the various parts of yourself, you will begin to see the patterns of behavior. The frightened child is afraid and behaves in a certain way, while the warrior acts quite differently and wants to do combat. You will notice the kinds of impetus, people, and circumstances which call forth the various parts. Become very aware of the stimuli, since you will need certain choices to bring the various sub-personalities to the surface.

In the therapy framework, they are brought out through the technique of Voice Dialogue, where a "facilitator" talks to them and asks them to come to the forefront and speak. During the facilitation process, the person being facilitated actually moves his body a couple of feet to accommodate the "new personality." In this manner the various sub-personalities are separated from one another. I have used the Voice Dialogue technique with actors for the purpose of reaching a particular sub-personality, but I find an inherent danger in this approach. Of course, it depends on the talent and insight of the facilitator, but it is too easy for the actor to *assume* behavior rather than really get into an organic oneness with a particular part of himself. This, of course, leads to imposition and representation of life rather than the authentic experience of reality. I have experimented with other, more successful approach techniques for reaching and ventilating a specific sub-personality, which I will get into shortly.

First, I would like to take the time to explain the logic of this choice approach. If the characters in a play are people like us, who behave in a certain way and relate to each other and the world in a specific manner, then they too must be subject to having sub-personalities in control of their lives. They must be in "relationship dances" just as we are. If that is true, then if we, as actors, identify the specific personality that a character in a play goes in and out of, is it not logical that if we elicit a similar sub-personality of our own, we can do the entire scene or, in fact, possibly the entire play with a single choice and a single choice approach? Not only would we shorten the creative process, but we would bring to the stage an incredible dimensional reality coming from a "qualified" part of ourselves that has a unique intelligence for the content of this material, which other parts of us neither understand nor, in fact, relate to. So you see what an incredible, enormous tool this choice approach can be to the actor. It does, in fact, bring him completely together with the character. They become one in the experience of a similar facet of personality. So, if an actor has difficulty identifying with a specific character, it might well be that he or she is approaching the play from a sub-personality that neither relates to nor understands the sub-personality of the character in the play. "The part is out of my range," "I don't identify with the character": We have all either said those things or heard others say them. It may be the truth, and then again it may be a sub-personality conflict.

There are many sub-personalities. In fact, you go on discovering new ones endlessly. There is the victim, a very notorious sub-personality, who loves to indulge in being victimized. When that one is in the driver's seat of our life, we suffer a lot and really enjoy the suffering. We have all seen characters in plays who are victims throughout the entire piece. If the actor had to confront such a character, who better could understand and fulfill the obligations than his own victim?

The free spirit is another famous sub-person. This is the part of us that is impulsive, fun-loving, energetic, often artistic and creative, and can get us into trouble by doing irresponsible and bizarre things that the other, responsible parts would not allow. The free spirit does what it feels like doing. It can be a lot of fun to let it take over for a short period of time, but not control our entire lives. We have all seen people like this and characters in films and plays who seem to be impelled by that free-spirit energy. If the actor had to confront such a character responsibility, he would find it so much easier and infinitely more fulfilling to approach the character through that sub-personality.

There are the father, the mother, the harlot, all of the child archetypes, like the magical child (very important to the actor, this one is the part of us that loves to fantasize, pretend, act, and so on), the vulnerable child, the frightened child, the mischievous child, etc. We all have the beach bum, the part of us that wants only to "kick back" and lie around on the beach, do nothing, and loaf. There are the depressed sub-persons, who, when they take over, can take us on quite a depressive journey. Another sub-personality is the Martin Luther sub-personality, the part of us that is the moralist, the pious believer in God, with not an inch of room for anything less than total devotion to God and good. A perfect theatrical example of a character totally controlled by that sub-personality is the Preacher in *Rain,* who spends the entire length of the play preaching and moralizing to Sadie Thompson and then succumbs to another of his own sub-personalities, the lustful part of his satanic energy. When you break characters down in these terms, it seems to make the whole job of interpreting characterization so simple and understandable.

The Apollonian sub-personality is the part of the person that is logical, sequential, and ordered—the thinker, the intellectual, the "left brain" part of us—while the Dionysian sub-personality, related to the opposite pole, is the energy that is hedonistic, indulgent, pleasure-seeking, and bacchanalian. These are all archetypes. Aphrodite, the feminine sexual sub-personality, and the male counterpart, the Don Juan sub-personality, and the extremes of nymphomaniac and satyr—all of these energies, sub-personalities, have a thrust of their own. They exist exclusively to be what they are. That is their only purpose for being, and they simply do what they do best. The Aphrodite sub-personality exists only for sexuality; her function is totally sexual.

The earth energies encompass the cold principle, which is an archetypal category under which the satanic or demonic sub-personality embodies the killer, the anger, the power, the ruthless, the sexual, the sensual, the selfish, the cold and unfeeling parts, the parts that are totally capable of cutting off all feelings. Out of these archetypes come the Hitlers, Attila the Hun, the mass murderers of history, Robespierre, and all the modern-day theatrical characters who are archetypal villains. In fact, there are many characters in dramatic literature who are not villains but nonetheless are controlled or influenced by the demonic energy. If an actor identifies behavioral character elements that fit the pattern, he should attempt to call forth his own demonic sub-personality.

MAJOR SUB-PERSONALITY ARCHETYPES

The following list will give you some idea of the areas of personality and behavior available to you as possible choices for the fulfillment of material obligations.

The critic, the pusher, and the perfectionist. These three operate as a triumvirate; they work together to push the person to accomplish, and they criticize him for not being perfect. Do you know anyone like that in your own life experience?

The good father and the bad father. The good father is the part of us that is the giving, nurturing, and helpful provider, the one who takes care of things. The bad father is the counterpart that punishes us and withdraws the good things from us for not listening to the good father.

The nurturing mother and the critical mother. Similar to the good and bad fathers.

The wise person or wisdom voice. This sub-personality is a kind of guide for us; it helps us to see the truth, to distinguish between reality and illusion, to make wise decisions.

Aphrodite. The feminine sexual energy.

Don Juan. The masculine sexual energy.

The pleaser. This one wants to be approved of, will do anything to please others. "Love me, like me, see how good I am!"

The child archetypes. These include the vulnerable child, the frightened child, the magical child, the mischievous child, the rebellious child, the lonely child.

The obedient son/daughter.

The judge. This sub-personality sits in judgment over other people's actions. The positive side of this one is the discerner, the part that perceives things and makes positive critical judgments helpful to us.

The guru or messiah. This sub-personality wants to save the world. He must lead everyone out of the darkness into the light, and he gathers followers, people who are willing to sit at the feet of the Savior.

The controller and the master controller. The controller is the part that allows things to happen or not to happen. The master controller is in control of the person and calls the shots.

The hero. This is the part that forges into new territory, the explorer, the adventurer, the heroic part that is the champion of all good causes.

The spiritual or mystical. The opposite of the earth energies (the satanic). This area of sub-personality is the higher power of God and the spirit; it relates to what is good in man, the ethereal involvement.

The satanic or demonic. This embodies all of those earth energies already discussed. It is a powerful energy. The dictator is a part of that group.

There are variations of sub-personalities; as you explore your own, you will become more familiar with the offshoots and varieties of sub-persons. Use the above list as a blueprint for categorically identifying and ventilating the various sub-personalities inhabiting your being.

DISOWNING SUB-PERSONALITIES

I think it is necessary to say a few words about disowning our parts. All of us have areas of behavior that are difficult to reach or even impossible to contact. That is why certain characters seem so unapproachable. For one reason or another, as we grow up we suppress, deny, or in some way disown some of our sub-personalities. We build defense systems to protect ourselves from a punitive father, so we hide the satanic energies until they are not available to us. In order to get approval from parents and peer groups we develop our pleaser, who jumps into the driver's seat and takes control of our lives at the cost of many other powerful energies. We suppress our anger, our hero sub-personality, our sexual energies, because the protective energies deny them. Whatever the reason for which this disowning takes place, we are *poorer* because of the unavailability of these important sub-personalities. We all know people who seem always to be the same. They have very little variety of expression, or they are always "nice," or they are the most hostile, volatile people we know.

The reason for these kinds of behavior is that there is an imbalance in the person. He is being controlled by a specific sub-personality that is blocking the other parts from coming out. If the sub-personality that is in control has been there for a long time and has grown very powerful, there is a denial and even a disowning of conflicting or contrasting sub-personalities.

We need all of our parts! A complete person is a person with all the parts in balance. They are all needed for dimension and balance by our *consciousness,* a consciousness that does not allow any of them to take over or to control our lives. An actor must be in touch with all of himself and be able to call upon any sub-personality at any time to come and do the work of the character in the play. The antidote to a disowned sub-personality is, first, becoming aware and conscious of the denial and then, attempting to "talk" to the disowned part and encouraging it to express itself. This is done through Voice Dialogue and by working for choices that will appeal to that part of you. Repeat the process of contacting that sub-personality as many times as necessary to gain its confidence and encourage it to speak and come forth. As a sub-personality gains confidence through expression, it gains strength. As it becomes stronger, it comes forth more easily. At the same time, you become more conscious of the entire reality and process and begin to pave the way for disowned parts to be embraced and become a part of the whole you.

USING SUB-PERSONALITIES AS A CHOICE APPROACH

The use of a sub-personality to fulfill any of the obligations of material is dependent on encouraging the specific "sub" to come out in full force and essentially take over. In effect, you, the actor, become that sub-person, thinking, feeling, and behaving as that part of you does. If it happens to be the free spirit that you call upon, then you would be impelled by all the personality traits of the free spirit. You would behave impulsively without much responsibility, giving in to all your whims, having fun, and seeking fun. There are a lot of such characters in plays and films.

Using a particular sub-personality is not always done to parallel the character's personality; sometimes it is done to elicit certain emotional responses or to pique emotions that elude other choices and approaches.

There are several ways to call up a sub-personality, and the first is Voice Dialogue—talking to the part of you that you want to come forth. This is a two-person involvement. It takes a facilitator and the person being facilitated. The facilitator asks to talk to a particular part of the person being facilitated. The person then tries to "feel" that part inside himself. He then moves over a foot or so and encourages that part to speak to the facilitator.

FACILITATOR: Could I speak to the angry part of you? . . .

PERSON:	(Attemtping to get in touch with that part, those feelings.) All right. (Moving over a couple of feet.)
FACILITATOR:	Hi, how are you?
PERSON:	(The angry part seems to be inhabiting him.) Why do you want to know, and why should I tell you? Who the hell are you, anyway?
FACILITATOR:	I would like to know you; you seem interesting. How do you function in the life of [name of person being facilitated]?
PERSON:	How do I function? What the hell does that mean? "Function"—that's a laugh! Goody-Goody never lets me come out!
FACILITATOR:	You sound very angry.
PERSON:	That's an understatement. I'm livid! I'm so angry!
FACILITATOR:	What are you so angry about?
PERSON:	You really want to know? (The facilitator nods affirmatively.) I'm mad at all the others who sit on me. I'm tired of all the crap being dumped on him. I'd like to start dumping it back on all the people in his life!
FACILITATOR:	So why don't you?
PERSON:	Goody-Goody won't let me out!
FACILITATOR:	Who is Goody-Goody?
PERSON:	The one who wants everybody to love him and think he's a nice guy. It makes me sick! I'd like to kick them all in the balls!
FACILITATOR:	So it's the pleaser who keeps you shut up?
PERSON:	I don't know what you would call him—he's a fool!
FACILITATOR:	Is he the only thing that you're angry at?
PERSON:	Hell, no, I'm angry at everything! I'm angry at the stupids of the world, the idiots! I'm mad at the freedom all the others have to express themselves. It's always been that way. Ever since he was a kid, I've been cooped up inside.
FACILITATOR:	Did you ever come out and express yourself?

PERSON: Yeah. When he was real young, I remember rais-
ing hell a couple of times. Then they all jumped
on me and stayed there!

This dialogue can go on for ten or fifteen minutes if necessary. The
facilitator can ask to speak to other sub-personalities, going back and forth
to as many as he feels is expedient and in the interest of the person being
facilitated. The facilitator should *never* make any judgments or allow his
own prejudices to influence the objectivity with which he relates to the
various sub-personalities! There is a natural tendency to like some subs
and have a feeling of conflict with others. This should not enter into the
facilitation! If it does, the sub-personality will stop relating, and the effec-
tiveness of the facilitator will come to an end. The facilitator should
always return the person to an objective place—the ego state or a state of
consciousness. Never leave the person being facilitated in a sub-
personality!

Actors can learn to do this facilitation process to each other in the interest of getting in touch with certain sub-personalities. With practice and
repetition, they can get quite capable of contacting large numbers of sub-
personalities.

The purpose, of course, is to get in touch with a specific part of yourself
that will fulfill the requirements of the scene, and to let the sub-personality
do the behaving in the piece. You want to allow all the feelings and impulses of the sub-personality that has been facilitated to take over and
express themselves throughout the entire scene.

When the actor doesn't have another person to facilitate him, he can
attempt to call on the sub-personality he wishes to contact and ask it to
come out and take the driver's seat. This works sometimes, and at other
times it does not. The best way to approach it is from a very objective and
conscious place. If you attempt to elicit the response of a particular sub-
personality from another sub-personality that is in any way in conflict
with the one you want to reach, you probably will not be successful.

Eliciting a sub-personality is done simply by asking that particular part
of yourself to speak.

ACTOR: I would like to hear from my pusher. . . Are you around?
(The actor should move over a foot or two to accommodate
the pusher in case he wants to make himself present.)

PUSHER: Yes, I'm here. Why are you standing around playing games?
Why aren't you working? You have lines to memorize, a rehearsal to get to. Why is it that you always have to be pushed
into doing what you have to do? Come on, get responsible
and study the script!

Well, it is quite evident that the pusher is alive and in good form. He responded to the call immediately. Other sub-personalities might take more coaxing, more manipulation; but if you continue to try to reach them, they will usually respond.

Once you feel that the sub-personality is in position, that is to say in control, you are ready to begin the rehearsal or the performance.

Another way to reach sub-personalities is by working to create an atmosphere or circumstance that usually piques their response in life. If you understand the mechanics of how, and under what specific conditions, a sub-personality ventilates itself, all you have to do is duplicate those conditions.

If you see a person being mistreated by another and that piques a certain part of you, then all you would have to do to reach that part of yourself at will would be to create a similar stimulus. If the magical child comes out at the zoo or the circus or as a result of a particular piece of music, you can create the stimulus that coaxes that sub-personality to the surface. If you are attempting to deal with the pious obligations of an evangelist, spouting fire and brimstone at all the sinners in the world, you might want the help of your own moralist, the Martin Luther part of you. All you have to do is ask yourself when that part presents itself. Is it when you see the hookers walking down Sunset Boulevard? Or when you see youngsters smoking grass and popping pills? Whatever would do it for you, work to create the circumstance that will bring that sub-personality to the surface.

A bonus of the approach is that, when you are in a sub-personality, the choices you make for the rest of the play will be made by that part of you that *knows what affects it!* If the character in the play is functioning in terms of some predominant sub-personality, then all of the circumstances contained in the play, and all of the impetus that affects the character, are affecting the sub-personality from which he is functioning. Therefore, if the actor achieves a parallel personality, that part of him will make qualified choices of stimuli for the rest of the obligations in the play.

Even if the actor chose not to use the sub-personality in the final decision, possibly because he decided it was too limiting, using it to make some of the pertinent choices for the play would have been a real advantage.

When attempting to pique a specific sub-personality, the actor might work for any number of different choices and with a variety of choice approaches. He could use Sense Memory, Imaginary Monologues, Believability, Inner Monologues, and so on. Using Sub-personalities as a choice approach is dependent on reaching the desired sub-personality and bringing it to the forefront position where the personality who is talking and behaving is found. When that is accomplished, the actor is in the enviable position of experiencing some very exciting and irreverent organic life.

THE APPROACH TECHNIQUES FOR REACHING AND PIQUING SUB-PERSONALITIES

Voice Dialogue: A two-people process of facilitating communication with the various parts.

Personal Voice Dialogue: The process of the actor talking to the desired sub-personality and encouraging it to respond and speak.

Working to Create Stimuli, Circumstances, and Conditions That Reach a Specific Sub-personality: By knowing what piques certain parts of himself, the actor can reproduce that stimulus or relate to an available stimulus, hoping that it will call forth the desired part.

It can be something as simple as an article of clothing or an object that bears personal meaning to a particular part of the actor. Have you ever seen what happens to a man when you put a rifle into his hands? If he is out in the field, he wants to start shooting everything that moves. Which sub-personality do you suppose is brought out by that rifle? In any case, you get the idea.

THE OBLIGATION:	A violent killer who kills without feeling or conscience. He is angry and violent, frequently erupting into destructive outbursts.
THE CHOICE:	The demonic-archetype sub-personality, emphasizing the killer and angry-power energies.
THE CHOICE APPROACH:	Sub-personalities.

Sub-personalities can be used in all of the seven major obligation areas. It is just a matter of defining specifically the desired emphasis and then choosing the right sub-personality to use. With practice, you will find this area rich beyond description. Be courageous in your exploration of this choice approach!

22. CREATIVE VISUALIZATION

This is the twenty-second and last of the choice approaches, at least for the time being. It is an imaginative adventure. I sometimes refer to it as Creative Imagery. Either name describes it well.

All the choice approaches have individual application. Some of them fit certain responsibilities uniquely, while others have more universality. Creative Visualization is marvelous for taking you somewhere. It can transport you away from the stage and take you to the Himalayas.

The reason an actor might find this choice approach valuable is that it can be a foundation for a time-and-place relationship and can as well stimulate varieties of emotional life.

It is done simply by closing your eyes and visualizing a place, guiding yourself into an environment. It could be a place where you have been before or one where you have never been. You can visualize a place with all of its colors, objects, sounds, and smells and, at the same time, call on all of your senses to support the visualization. If, in this place that you are creatively visualizing, an important event took place, you can visualize and sensorially support all the elements of that experience. As you do the process, it may become a matter of directing yourself through the visualization the way someone moves through a dream, going from one event to another.

It is important that the actor avoid staying in his head. He can do that by using his entire sensory apparatus. As he is affected by his visualization, he should get a sense of being in that place—which stimulates an unconscious relationship to it and to the events that took place there. As the unconscious begins to function, thoughts and impulses emerge, and the actor starts to experience many of the things that he felt in that place at that time. At this point, he may want to open his eyes and begin to relate to the scene he is involved with, talking to the other actor and saying the lines from whatever emotional space he is in. The carryover is usually substantial. Even though the actor opens his eyes and is again in the stage environment, the Creative Visualization will pique impulses and unconscious connections that carry into the scene. If he supplements the choice approach by working for additional choices related to the environment, he will establish the place he has creatively visualized.

This choice approach should not be compared or confused with Affective Memory. It is an entirely different process and experience.

Once the actor identifies the obligation and knows where he wants to be and what he wants to feel, he can select a place, an experience, or an environment designed (hopefully) to stimulate the relationship to place and emotional life that fits the obligation. He may take himself to a lonely mountaintop away from civilization, with a heavenly view of the world beneath, feeling as though he is part of the earth and the sky and creating a oneness with all of life and nature. He may spend quite some time building this Creative Visualization, and when he leaves the mountain and returns to the theater, he may bring back with him the feeling of peace and spirituality that creates a glow around him. He may visualize the most beautiful forest, not of this earth, and fill it with life that excites his imagination. He may guide himself to the barbed-wire fence that surrounded Auschwitz and lead himself through the labyrinth of that nightmare.

There are no limitations to the use of Creative Visualization: you can be anywhere, experience anything, and carry the experience back onto the stage with you. If you succeed in making the connection with the unconscious, the life it produces is terribly exciting for both you and the audience.

In addition to its value as a choice approach, the process is very relaxing and can be a very fulfilling adventure. When we were children we did this for play, not work. Wouldn't it be wonderful if we, as actors, could get back to that place of play?

While I would suggest that you start experimenting with Creative Visualization by closing your eyes, you might later try the approach with your eyes open. Once you become facile with this process, you can creatively visualize with the "inner eye." Always remember that all life is a *sensory experience,* and so should acting be. *Support all visualization by using all five senses.*

THE OBLIGATION:	Being a spiritual person, mellow and loving, with a great connection to God and all living things; living in a place like the legendary Shangri-La.
THE CHOICE:	The top of a volcanic crater in Hawaii.
THE CHOICE APPROACH:	Creative Visualization. (I have spent a little time in Hawaii, and the feelings that were stimulated in me match exactly the responsibility of the obligation.)

Creative Visualization is a technique that can be used to fulfill all or any of the seven major obligations. The emphasis of the choice approach depends on the specific contents of the visualization.

THE ELEVENTH LEVEL OF CONSCIOUSNESS

This is one of my concepts, and it is not at all scientific. It does, however, relate to a real phenomenon. I can't say how many times I have been asked the same question by actors: "If you are experiencing a total reality on the stage, how is it that you don't really kill the actress at the end of the second act?"

The answer is that *there is a part of you that knows you are acting.* That part of you lives on the "Eleventh Level" of your consciousness.

Why the eleventh level and not the seventh? Because I felt that if you could be involved on the first ten levels of consciousness in the reality of the play, that was a deep enough involvement not to be interfered with by the eleventh. Of course, it is just an arbitrary choice of mine to choose the number eleven.

I had been working with the craft for some time when I began to relate to this concept. Sometimes as an actor, I would get involved more deeply than at other times. When the level of consciousness was too close to a third or fourth level, I was aware of being on the stage of acting, commenting on my work and falling short of an involved organic experience. With more work and increased proficiency with the craft, I found that my acting consciousness level drew farther and farther back in terms of my awareness of being on the stage. However, at the same time, this Eleventh Level carried me to the places on the stage where I needed to be; it remembered my lines and cues, and served me well without interfering with my involvement and the reality of the play.

It is like having a dream. You are asleep and dreaming. You are totally involved in this dream, but there exists a part in you that knows you are dreaming. The Eleventh Level of Consciousness is something like that, only not quite so remote.

How do you create an Eleventh Level of Consciousness? Well, not by pushing a button, that's for sure! It is a phenomenon that evolves with the work. The more you know how to apply the process, the greater the involvement in the realities produced by that process. In other words, the more you believe in the here-and-now reality, the farther back you push your consciousness that you are acting. So, as you evolve into a craftsman, a by-product of your growth is the Eleventh Level of Consciousness.

Sometimes people ask, "What if one doesn't have or develop that level of consciousness?" To that I say that person has no business being on the stage. He is dangerous and shouldn't be involved with acting!

When the unconscious takes you over on the stage, the results are usually electrifying. It is this experience that we work toward each time we act. The Eleventh Level of Consciousness does not interrupt or interfere with that connection to the unconscious; it just seems to take three steps back.

Next time you step onto a stage, take an inventory of your consciousness level and become aware of how it moves around as you become more involved and affected.

Chapter 5

THE CIRCLE
OF THE WORK

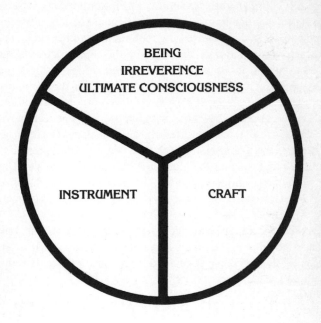

Everything in life depends on some kind of balance. We hear that from doctors treating us for a "chemical imbalance"; we refer to people who seem to have difficulty functioning in life as "out of balance"; spiritual leaders speak of balance of mind, body, and spirit; and so on into all phases of life. Acting too has a necessary balance, and a primary balance is that between the instrument and the craft.

When the actor addresses the necessity of eliminating instrumental obstacles (stripping away social protective membranes), he achieves a state of BEING. Once he has reached that BEING state, he is ready to use the craft, which is designed to affect the BEING state and modify it into the area of the required BEING states obligated by the material. This is the balance of instrumental availability for craftual impact.

In the training period, the actor must divide his time between instrumental emphasis and the learning of the craft. At first, more time is spent dealing with the instrument, but as the actor becomes more emotionally available and accessible, the time spent in the two areas should become equal. At this point, the work becomes a kind of circle, joining at all points, with no separation between the actor and the approach. When he integrates the work into his life, it becomes a way of living as well as a way of work.

The illustrated circle on the previous page is a graphic attempt to show the goal of this entire approach to acting. The lower portion of the body of the circle represents the pragmatic involvements: The left side relates to the instrument and to the exercises and techniques that help liberate it; the right portion relates to the craft, dealing with the application of techniques that stimulate life on the stage. The pie-shaped wedge at the top of the circle represents the philosophy and resulting goals of the entire process. *The actor reaches a state of BEING through irreverence, which leads to Ultimate Consciousness!* That is the state of complete connection with the unconscious flow of life. Since most of the actor's talent lives in the unconscious, reaching the unconscious frees that talent to be expressed on the stage, putting the actor into the highest state of creativity. The Ultimate Consciousness is the ultimate goal of the performing artist. Once it is reached in a performance, the actor needs to do nothing but get out of its way and go wherever it leads.

It is this place we all aspire to, because from this state we can make our performance indelible in the minds of an audience, forever. It is what all the work on all the preceding pages is designed to produce. It is the goal and the purpose of acting.

THE VIRTUE AND NECESSITY OF SELFISHNESS

The irreverent actor is a selfish animal who must work for his own benefit. If, through the irreverent exploration of choices and choice approaches he arrives at reality on the stage or in front of the camera, both he and the audience benefit from the results. He must be selfish enough to demand the right to do his work, to work the way he wants to without succumbing to the concepts of others. He must be able to use the rehearsal for what it was designed for, and to make his own statement in every character he plays.

THE MAVERICK, THE REBEL, THE IRREVERENT

Throughout history, the individual thinker or the innovator has had to climb over enormous obstacles and resistance in order to make his statement or contribution. In every field you will find horror stories about interference with anyone who wanted to do anything which departed from the conventional or the norm. Wilhelm Reich was imprisoned because of his "insane ideas and practices"; Freud fought his own colleagues to bring his theories out into the world. The stories are endless, but how many innovators fell in this combat, never to have made their contribution? As a society, we have matured to some degree. Our psychological awareness has elevated somewhat, and so has the level of our consciousness. However, there is still great resistance to new forms and new approaches to art, medicine, philosophy, and so on. Acting remained essentially the same for a hundred years. Then, when new thoughts and ideas were introduced by Stanislavsky with his system, they were, on a large scale, rejected. To this day, the Method, as an approach to acting, isn't used except by a small fraction of the actors in the world—mostly in the United States. Most acting has become a refined level of representation. The major change from the old, very representational acting of the silent movies to today's work has been the result of social movement toward demanding more truth and reality, and of our growing psychological awareness. The modern actor has risen to that challenge, not by creating reality on the stage but by refining the old acting approaches into a more facile kind of representational reality. It is still representational, but now the actor makes it look more like reality.

Every once in a while, someone comes along and makes a different kind of statement which is usually, at first, rejected, scoffed at, or even ridiculed. There are, however, individuals who survive the resistance and do make a mark. They succeed, and the world takes a second look at their statement. Because so many others are responding to that statement, these individuals are heralded as geniuses and innovators, and then there are two hundred and fifty thousand actors imitating their style. The world is filled with "success worshippers" who cannot see the forest for the trees. They think that imitating success will bring it to them, and in this imitating process they actually stifle the very part of themselves that might have had impact. *The metamorphosis from rebellious to unique is recognition!* All it takes is for one successful person to hear what you are saying and then stand up for it, and the battle is over. The greatest laundry in the world is success; it removes all stains and odors.

The actor must ask himself every day, Who am *I?* What do *I* feel? How do *I* see that? What do *I* want to say? He must have the courage to tell his truth every time he opens his mouth. He may be called a rebel, a maverick, or even worse. But if we are to glean the joys of life and do what we want with our lives, we must be irreverent to the conformity and safety that other, less courageous artists choose.

IRREVERENCE IS THE ROAD TO PERSONAL AND INDIVIDUAL STATEMENT!

ic demonstrating the Choice Approach, Objects That Come Into Contact With The Body.